PARANOID

Paranoid

Black Days with Sabbath & Other Rock Icons

Mick Wall

MAINSTREAM
PUBLISHING

EDINBURGH AND LONDON

First published in Great Britain in 1999 by
MAINSTREAM PUBLISHING COMPANY (EDINBURGH) LTD
7 Albany Street
Edinburgh EH1 3UG

ISBN 1 85158 993 7

Reprinted 2001

A CIP catalogue record for this book is available from the
British Library

Typeset in 11 on 14pt Berkeley
Printed and bound in Great Britain by
Creative Print and Design Wales

Contents

Dedicated to no one

1

Lucifer Rising

I took the needle and stuck it right in my arm. You never hit a vein straight off usually, but this time it went in no trouble. The luck was with me and I watched fascinated as the dark-red plume of blood spiralled up the chamber of the syringe. I had seen it a thousand times before but I never tired of succumbing to that wondrous vision, that delicate blossom of hate and joy.

By then, all the day-to-day shit of being a junkie – getting hold of the money for the gear, finding a clean works, or some that hadn't been used too often, even tying up and probing for a vein, digging amongst the sores and track marks for that one tiny blue tube that would still yield the opening I craved – was such a huge fucking hassle that the only security I had come to know was in that one final, glorious moment before I gently pushed the plunger back down and sent the newly polluted blood rushing back into my veins. Nothing and no one could stand between me and my hit then, and I became engulfed by a suppurating warmth, arrogant suddenly about who I was and what I was about to do. Free.

'Look at this,' I said, pleased. 'Fuckin' straight in!'

But Mandy wasn't listening. He'd gone first and was already out of the game. He looked like one of those toy dogs you see in the rear windows of cars, head wagging like a finger, the tip of his tongue poking out. He looked like he wanted to look.

We called our works 'guns'. I slowly squeezed the trigger on mine and waited for the bullet to hit. 'Go on, you slag!' I hissed, watching the red disappear down the plug-hole of my arm.

I could smell it going in, taste it. It was like salt and steel and lit matches, and when it hit, nothing else mattered. The world, briefly, became conquerable. I was the world! My warmth, my darkness enveloping everything like black snow, smothering every crass voice, every unnecessary obstacle, in a thick blanket of low-volume, grouched-out hiss . . .

Did I ever stop to question what I was actually doing to myself? No more than when I was straight. Does a fish dream of the sea as it swims along the ocean floor? It was the same with smack. Better. It was the hook, not the bait, that this water-breather was after.

It didn't matter that when the day next broke to find me, I would be shuddering on the bed, saucer-eyed, the toxins gushing out of me like a burst pipe in winter. As long as I had enough gear on hand to rectify the situation immediately, I quite liked waking up sick each morning. It made that first hit of the day even more marvellous and purposeful.

'Get your day off to the right start,' Mandy would smirk, as we sat there cooking up 'breakfast' together like some wizened old marrieds crooning over their eggs. 'Full of all the nutrition your body needs to keep you going till lunchtime,' he would chuckle malevolently, a blurred junkie smile flickering across his pinched, porcelain-white features.

Mandy was the smack shaman. I used to think we were equals on that score, but no way. No fucking way, boyo. He really knew how to shake the stick.

Straight from the beery valleys of the Rhondda to the bloodied crook of London's elbow, Mandy was one of several provincial punk-fanzine types who had migrated to the Big City in the late-1970s and later got lucky with jobs on the established music press. But whatever 'new-wave attitude' Mandy had brought with him down the M4 had swiftly been subsumed by the sudden realisation that the London music scene had existed perfectly well up until then without his 'insights' and would no doubt continue to do so long after he'd grown up and got a proper job. Like in PR or something . . .

But Mandy and I were of the glassy-eyed generation that grew up believing rock music had something important to say and that, by extension, anyone working towards that goal – from the guy holding the towels at the side of the stage to the bigwig with the desk and cigar who signed the cheques – must be possessed of the same 'creative spirit'. Or some such. We were genuinely shocked to discover that the music business was, in fact, populated by artless twats with some of the worst record collections you'd ever seen. The people who never lost themselves to music or bothered to decipher the lyrics.

And it wasn't just the suits. As Mandy used to say: 'Meet one rock star and you've met them all.' They weren't quite all the same, but what they had to say hardly differed: love me unequivocally, buy my records indiscriminately, and, above all, keep listening to *me* talk about *me* . . . Whatever side of the music/business axis you spun from, the message was clear: art for art's sake, hit records for fuck's sake. There was never any anarchy in the UK. The song really did remain the same.

Once he'd grasped this, though, Mandy had been quick to make for the door. He kept the easy job, but his real interests now lay elsewhere. Which, in a roundabout way, is how he ended up sharing a place and a time with me. My details were somewhat different but my reaction had been just the same. We would put on our own 'live performances', we decided. Real 'adult-oriented' stuff. The venue: any room with a door that locked from the inside.

'Look at this! Look at this!' he would cry, holding up a mirror with several different-coloured lines of powder on it. 'The brown is smack, the slightly sort of off-white one is smack, the really white one is coke and the pasty-looking white one on the end is speed. And I am going to *snort the fuckin' lot, boy!'*

And he would. One after the other, non-stop, like a wolf devouring its moonlit supper. Then he would look at me. 'Want some? Or is that a black man's large penis I see up your arse?'

He hardly needed to ask. Looking at Mandy, listening to him, sometimes it was like watching my own reflection – not of how I was but of how I wished to be. All the daring and defiance that rock now failed to inspire me with were there in Mandy's manic, yellow-toothed grimace every time he went into another one of his over-the-top junkie-as-pied-piper routines. I admired what seemed to be his rampant disregard for the received wisdom of the age. I adored his spitefulness. You could learn things around a guy like this that not even Keith Richards could teach you. Here was someone who was *not* a rock star and *couldn't afford it* but was *going to do it anyway!* Just for the merry fucking hell of it. I liked that.

Being with Mandy was like being in touch with the good part of myself again. There was one crucial difference between us, though: Mandy was a lifer. He really meant it, and after all these years and days and lifetimes that have passed since then, it is an odd thing to know that Mandy has never once moved from that room I used to share with him; the junk-dungeon by the side of the road marked: World's End.

Nearly twenty years later, the image of Mandy still sitting in some dusty room aiming thunderbolts into his arm continues to haunt me. While I was in LA, riding around in a limo and peeking up Stevie Nicks's dress as I followed her up a ladder to her own 'private space'; while I was in London, presenting my own TV show and faking it for the money; while I was watching my mother die of cancer at forty-eight as my old man did wheelies in her wheelchair, clutching his bottle of Strongbow; while I was learning Tai Chi, writing mediocre 'rock biographies' and devoting years of my life to entirely the wrong woman; while I was having a nervous breakdown and losing all my hair, then moving out to the country-side and thinking about what it was going to be like to be fucked and in your forties; while I was busy biting my toenails and stroking the dog and admiring the shape of the sun as it slipped away on red September evenings, it has always been a strangely humbling thing to recall now and then that, wherever I was and whatever I was doing, Mandy had never once got up and even opened the door of that fucking room.

He's still there now, like the guy at the end of *2001*, his past, present and future all there in the room with him. He has gone so far beyond that there is now simply no way back for him. But isn't it the same for most of us once we reach a certain stage in life? When who's right and who's wrong is no longer the point; when it's just a question of what *is*. Just because you don't take heroin it doesn't mean you're not fucked up, that you're not addicted. For some, it's sex, for others it's money, art, religion, music, politics, sport, fashion . . . At root, though, the problem is always the same, whatever method we choose to express it: not how to get off the gear, but how to stay on it. It could have been anything, but for Mandy, and for a while, me, too, it was smack. 'God's own medicine', wise old man Burroughs called it, and we knew why.

Like Mandy, I loved heroin. As drugs go, it was the best. Booze, coke, dope, even acid, they were social drugs, party tricks, something you shared with a crowded room. The difference between tripping on acid and tripping on smack was like the difference between the latest Hollywood blockbuster and a small art-house movie from Europe. One was about fuck-wow special effects and peer-approved happy endings; the other was about something much more freakish and unresolved. Smack was for connoisseurs of the anti-social, the solo artists and mavericks who stood for nothing except a vampire's desire to be what we were without persecution; to fix and spill blood without prejudice. It wasn't just escape we were after. As serious smackheads, we didn't use gear just to get out of it, we used it to get *into* it. Smack was not a 'recreational' drug: it was a vocation.

Or so it seemed, anyway, in the days before we had reached that more advanced stage as junkies where all such pretensions are hurled out the window as a much more brutal and compelling reality begins to assert itself: when smack ceases to be a personal statement and becomes purely a matter of day-to-day survival.

It was this last, terminal stage we were then just entering the cusp of in that hot, muzzy summer of '81. We still had friends, but none left that didn't do gear, too. None we bothered to stay in touch with, anyway. And we had stopped offering our gear around when people came by, like you would wine or coke or whatever, and started selling. Just bits and pieces, barely enough to keep up our own habits, but we were very serious about it. Every last grain was accounted for.

The end was nigh but we were still caught up in the dream of the dream and we liked to think of smack in the same way we thought of modern jazz. Wilfully perverse, unashamedly self-absorbed, insistently élitist – jazz was the perfect junk soundtrack. Like punk and speed, reggae and dope, Hendrix and acid – or, these days, dance and E – jazz and smack simply belonged together. You could have one without the other and come away with some clues, but you would never know the real story until you had both. Preferably simultaneously. The jazz players had their horns and we had our guns, and it soon became the only music – the only life – Mandy or I could tolerate for long periods without wanting to throw up.

Like smack, jazz defied its audience to pass judgement on it. It questioned your assumptions, scrambled your faculties and turned self-doubt into a contagion. It gave you the beautiful truth about no happy endings. On the nod and deep into Miles or Chet or the 'Trane or whoever, there came a moment where nothing else made sense and it wasn't just the substance – the music, the opiate – you were grooving on, it was what it meant to have it within you. To know something about life that those who had never tried it that way seemed unable or unwilling to comprehend. That there is no safety in numbers. That the crowd is always wrong. That all the jobs and cars and happy families in the world won't stop the crowd going to their graves still as in fear of the dark as the day they emerged screaming from the womb.

As Mandy never used to tire of reminding people: 'It's not just heroin that kills people.' A large enough dose of television was enough to finish off most of us by the time we'd reached puberty. And, in the early days, before the need for smack had been reduced to one of mere requirement, every fix we took was like a big, beautiful fuck-off to the world.

The secret of life was death. Everybody knew it but acted as if they didn't. Sitting there on the floor together, post-hit, two toxic Buddhas setting the world to rights, sometimes it felt like we were the only ones left who accepted it. 'Life? So what?' we said. 'Death? So what?' People were basically stupid; they believed everything they read in the newspapers and saw on TV. They believed they were the only thinking beings in the universe and that one fix and you'd be hooked for life. They believed in their bibles and their queens. Worse, they wanted you to believe in it, too. Even when you resisted, it changed nothing. The world still went backwards as well as forwards. One day the Bomb would drop – the Great Fix in the Sky – and that wouldn't change anything, either.

There was no hope. I was twenty-three, Mandy was a little older, and we had grown up in a world where the really big deals had already been done. VD was treatable, drugs were acceptable, girls took the Pill, men walked the moon, presidents had been proved corrupt and rock 'n' roll had already had its day. If there were any taboos left, we were always going to be the first in line to try and break them. But outside of plain old-fashioned villainy, which didn't really appeal – we wanted vice, not victims – by the start of the '80s, there wasn't much left.

God was dead and the Devil had been reduced to walk-on parts in rock songs and B-movies. Smack, too, was hardly news, but its power and appeal remained intriguingly undiminished. It was a drug with a reputation like no other – *so good it snuffs you out, baby* – which meant we were bound to try it sooner or later.

One of the most popular lines you would hear trotted out at any social gathering back then was: 'I'll take anything – coke, dope, speed, acid, downers, whatever you've got – but I would never touch smack.' Smack was for losers, people who couldn't help themselves. But they had said that about every drug, at one time or another. What made smack so different? What made it so special? Why was it held in such awe?

More to the point, if smack was such bad news, why had there been so many notable exceptions to the rule – modern-day messiahs like Charlie Parker, Miles Davis, John Lennon, William Burroughs or Andy Warhol? All one-offs, admittedly, that it would be ridiculous to try and emulate or even think of oneself in the same terms. Nevertheless, these were the masters whose teachings Mandy and I devoutly followed, the guys who took Orwell's theory that 2+2=5 and erected a whole new metaphysical vocabulary around it, which, when decoded and understood, helped explain everything you needed to know about life in the 'real' world of the late-twentieth century.

And like Johnny Rotten with his safety-pins, if smack was what the New Gods were wearing as their badge of rebellion, it was only a matter of time before disciples like me and Mandy would want to pin one just like it on our own chests. With neither the money nor the charisma to compete, we still fancied ourselves part of the same narcotic anti-scene, of which a full-flowering smack habit was merely the lingua franca.

We had made up our minds, we wanted the real nitty-gritty. So first we would just snort it, then we got into smoking it off the foil – chasing the dragon – and then we got into fixing. We'd been wanting to for ages but didn't know how to go about it. Most of our circle were still either snorting or smoking. Smoking was the closest you could get to fixing without actually taking a shot. Like fixing, you had to have all the paraphernalia – the tinfoil, the matches, the little rolled-up bit of cardboard shaped like a funnel. You placed the gear on the foil, lit a match under it and did your best to suck up as much of the resulting treacly black smoke as you could. A good funnel with a wide rim and a nice tight mouth-hole was essential for maximum smoking pleasure. You didn't want to miss a thing. But we still knew it was a step away from the real thing; and then the inevitable happened and we met an old-time junkie called 'Uncle' Russ, who was prepared to show us, he said, 'how the old school does things'.

Russ had once been a clown in a circus, which is where the 'Uncle' part came from. Then he was the singer in his own punk band, Uncle Russ & The Puss Suckers, who had once released a single that got a good review in the *NME*. He'd since done time for petty theft and now he was back on the gear again, selling whatever he could just to keep up his own habit.

Russ had been fixing for most of his life and reluctantly agreed to acquaint us with the basics. He gave us the old bullshit at first, pretending to try and talk us out of it. We had promised him half a gram for his trouble and he was never going to turn that down; but it wasn't every day someone offered him something just for his knowledge, and Russ was going to make the most of it.

'It's a long road you'll be walking down, boys,' he said with a sad shake of his bald head. 'Are you sure you know what you're doing?'

'Come on, Uncle,' said Mandy. 'We know what we're doing. We just want someone to show us how to do it properly.'

'I don't know, boys. It's a long road you'll be walking down. It's not for everybody.'

'Listen, Uncle,' I said. 'If you don't show us, someone else will.'

'Someone who will fuck it up.'

'Maybe. But that's why we've come to you.'

'I don't know, boys. It's a long road . . .'

Mandy slid the little white half-gram envelope across the table. 'Come on, Uncle. We know what we're doing.'

It was mad. I always squirmed when the doctor had to give me an injection. Now I was going to start injecting myself. Why?

Because I wanted to, would be the simple answer. But it was something more than pure pleasure-seeking. I just *had* to. Mandy was quite prepared to go on up the mountain without me, but he knew I would never let that happen. I couldn't bear to see him run off with the keys to the secret garden and leave me behind to wonder why I hadn't been brave or curious enough to follow him. *I just had to.* We were heading for the mainline, and watching Uncle cook up the gear in the spoon, the excitement was immense, the anticipation almost unbearable. I got a hard-on just cradling the newly bought works.

Tying up my arm, though, I felt like I was being blindfolded before being taken out to face the firing squad. There wasn't even time for a last cigarette. I felt Uncle's soft fingers caressing the inside of my forearm, teasing the virgin veins up like fat, wriggling worms. Then, with one practised junkie movement, he slid the needle full into my arm and loosened the belt I'd tied-up with. I hardly felt a thing.

Then he drew the plunger of the syringe up and I watched enthralled as it began to fill with surprisingly dark blood. Once the syringe had turned completely red, he pressed the plunger slowly back down and I felt the full force of my first rush. You could have pushed me under a train at that moment and it wouldn't have interfered at all. I was rushing so hard I thought my lid was going to flap open.

It was magnificent. It was like going to America for the first time: everything you ever heard or read or thought about, and more. No way I was going back to snorting or smoking now. This was big-boy stuff and we were as smug as college graduates being given their scrolls.

It had taken about eighteen months for us to get from first snort to first fix, but once we became reasonably adept, we couldn't wait to brandish our works in front of all those 'part-timers' we knew who were still just snorting or smoking their gear. Smack could breed a peculiar kind of envy and they looked on us with new eyes – a mixture of fear and respect – while we taunted them for being wasteful. It took so much less to get a really good hit from a fix, we told them, than it did setting fire to a foil and letting half of it burn off into unsmoked oblivion. It was hard to disagree and soon some of them had started fixing, too.

We wouldn't have said yet that smack was the most important thing in our lives, but it was certainly one of them. It became a new way to relate. Like our love of jazz, we weren't just listening in, we were constantly talking about it or reading about it, constantly making jokes about it, or just looking out for signs of it seeping occasionally through the pores of the supposedly squeaky-clean mainstream. Watching *Top of the Pops* and playing Spot The Junkie.

'Look at the eyes on that fucker! They're pinned!' Mandy would crow triumphantly. 'Don't tell me that fucker didn't just have a large belt of the brown before he went on!'

And, like money, we were constantly concerned about whether we would have enough to see us through the week, the month, the year. Nobody ever had enough. And the more you had, the more it seemed you needed. To begin with, we would try and help each other out. Smack dealers are notoriously unreliable and there would be times, inevitably, when one of us would be badly let down, out of gear and sweating. Then one of the others would always lend us the gear to get us back on our feet until we could get something else sorted.

But that sort of occurrence had become increasingly rare as our habits got a proper grip and the concept of 'friends' ground gradually into nothingness. The only relationships that survived were the important smack ones. The ones which passed on info about where the best late-night chemists were to buy syringes over the counter, or who was currently selling the best gear.

There was a singer, Nick, who used to come round sometimes. He didn't fix but his girlfriend, Sally, did. The trouble was her arms were so chubby she always had trouble hitting a vein cleanly, so I had taken to helping her out on occasion. Once, Nick walked in the room as Sal and I were kneeling on the floor together. I was trying to put the spike in for her but it had taken five or six goes and now the pain was making her cry out loud. Her face had become a black-and-white mask of sweat and tear-streaked mascara. I wanted to stop but Sal had worked herself up into such a state that I knew she would not be able to rest until she got some kind of hit. All the misfires had put her into a needle-frenzy.

'Fuck's sake!' she howled, her face demented, as the needle again failed to find its target.

'All right, Sal. Take it easy. We'll get there . . .'

'Fuck's sake! Just stick it in! Please . . .'

Nick stood in the doorway, watching. We did our best to ignore him and carried on trying. Eventually we got there. I managed to hit a vein in the back of her hand, which always hurts, but Sal screamed so loud I thought I'd killed her. But, no, with the smack now coursing through her, she was very much alive.

She threw her bloodied arms around my neck and pressed her hot, teary face against mine. Her eyes were like smudged, red points.

'Oh, thank you! Thank you!' she sobbed. 'Oh, that was so nice! Thank you!'

I didn't know how to react. I wasn't sure how this scene was playing with Nick. But he just came over and put his arms around us both. 'Yes, thank you,' he said, sounding genuinely touched. 'That was the most beautiful thing I've ever seen anybody do for someone.'

Fixing could be more intimate than fucking. For many smack-couples we knew, it had actually replaced it. Mandy and I weren't gay, so we had nothing to replace. But the psychic bond that junk forged between us brought us closer together, physically and mentally, than anyone I had ever shared a bed with.

We both still had nice, soft jobs then. Mandy was on the staff at *Sounds* and I was working in the press office at Virgin Records. Being 'in the biz' meant flexi-hours and expense-accounts and all the excuses you needed for bumming off for a few hours or even a few days at a time. As long as we maintained the pretence of at least being interested in the job, things would be cool. For a while, anyway.

There were even occasional girlfriends, in the very early days. But sex could hardly hold your interest in the same way smack did and soon the only girls left around were the ones who felt the same way.

'You're not interested in me, all you're interested in is getting off your face and lying around listening to jazz,' I remember one of the girls I should have married telling me once. 'And I hate jazz, it's so boring! And I hate drugs, they're boring, too! In fact, I hate you, you're boring! You never used to be, but you are! You're really, really boring now! You never want to go out, you never want to go to gigs or anything, never want to see a film or just go for a drink. I mean, look at you! Look at your face now! You're just not interested . . .'

We lived in a third-floor flat in Primrose Hill – posh London – which we rented from a middle-aged couple, the Abbots, who also worked in the media. Proper stuff like the broadsheets and the Beeb. They lived downstairs with their children – one of whom, a boy of about nine named Jason, had some sort of mental disorder which meant he couldn't be sent to a normal school and had to be taught at home by special tutors. Something to do with his ailment meant that he spent most of the day shouting and swearing at the top of his voice, dishing out severe verbal and often physical abuse to anyone who came near him. The tutors were only there for a few hours each day and were somehow able to put up with it. But there had been an endless stream of live-in nannies who had come and gone during the few months Mandy and I had lived there. The fresh-faced foreign-student types couldn't handle it at all. Lying on the bed some mornings in the afterglow of that first hit, smoking the best cigarette of the day, you could hear it going off around the breakfast table downstairs.

'*Bastard fuck!*' Jason would scream. '*Bastard fucking fuck!*'

There would follow the sound of muffled admonishment as Jason's battle-fatigued parents tried to placate their troubled child. It wasn't his fault, they kept reminding you.

'*You cunt! Get away from me, you cunt!*'

After the last student nanny had broken down sobbing on her first morning, the family took to employing a dour-faced old widow who looked like she could give as good as she got, but even she had trouble dealing with the little bastard. One morning, he ran up the two flights of stairs to my room, followed swiftly by the new nanny.

'Hello. What can I do for you?' I asked as pleasantly as I could while hurriedly shoving the detritus of the morning's fix under the bed.

'*Bastard!*' he screamed. '*Fuck off!*'

The nanny arrived, still breathless from the stairs. 'I'm terribly sorry, I do apologise for Jason's intrusion,' she said in Mary Poppins English. 'Now, come on, young man, I want you downstairs now!'

'*Fuck off, cunting cow!*' he screamed and made to try and clamber under my bed.

Shit! I had to move like lightning but I grabbed him by the feet and, trying to make like we were just playing a little wrestling game, managed to yank the little bastard back out again. Too late. He was clutching a large, blackened dessert spoon. The same one I'd used to cook up a fix less than half an hour before.

'Thank you,' I said, snatching the spoon from him as nonchalantly as blind panic would allow. 'I've been looking for that.'

'*Bastard bloody cunt!*'

He swung his little foot and kicked me in the groin. Hard. I sank to my knees and the spoon clattered to the floor. The pain was fulsome and low. Jason laughed hysterically, then picked up the spoon and ran off with it, straight past the nanny and back down the stairs.

'I'm terribly sorry,' she said again. 'Are you all right?'

No, I wasn't all right. I had to think quickly but my head was still thick with the fog from the fix and my balls felt like they'd just disappeared up my arse. I was still on my knees. The little fucker had pole-axed me.

'I'm fine,' I said, trying to stand. 'I don't know what he found under the bed, but it looked very . . . old and . . . dirty. I'd get it off him and throw it in the bin, if I were you.'

'Don't worry about the spoon,' she said, 'I'll get it back off him for you later.'

I looked at her. The pain doubled. Was the game up then? I didn't know but when I told Mandy what happened later he groaned like a sick dog that had just been kicked in the balls, too.

'That's it, then. At best, they'll kick us out. At worst, they'll call the cops. We better get this place cleaned up . . .'

The Abbots might not have been familiar with the accoutrements of drug culture, but a burned and blackened dessert spoon – what else could it mean? We spent the next few days tiptoeing around, trying to avoid any of the family on the stairs and waiting for the knock on the door. It never came. Maybe the Abbots didn't see the spoon. Maybe the little bastard had buried it in the garden like a bone. Or maybe they just hadn't found it – yet. Maybe he'd stashed it under his own bed, where it still lay, waiting to be discovered like an unexploded bomb. Waiting to go off . . .

We didn't know and with every new fix that went by, we cared a little less. Before the nannies and the tutors, there had also been an endless stream of tenants, none of whom lasted long once Jason had made himself known to them. But, the spoon episode aside, he had never really bothered us. It amused us that this little death-dwarf gave everybody such a hard time. In the days before decent daytime television, the sound of him giving it to them good downstairs gave us something to laugh at as we loaded up our guns. And it meant we could play our records as loud and as late into the night as we wanted. No one would have dared tell us to turn it down after putting up with the *Exorcist*-like soundtrack Jason provided everybody with most days.

'You're the first tenants we've ever had that have been prepared to put up with his tantrums,' the mercifully unworldly Mrs Abbot later told me. We knew then that as long as we kept handing over the rent on time every month and kept the nocturnal comings and goings reasonably discreet, we wouldn't have anything to worry about from downstairs. Jason, in his own strange way, had seen to that. Fucking little fuck. I wonder who he kicks in the balls now?

*

'Can you hear something?' asked Mandy, rousing himself from his stupor. 'Fuckin' . . . bells, is it?'

I thought I answered but I wasn't sure. Sometimes with Mandy there was almost a telepathy that went on. A cobweb of junk that hung between us that allowed us to have conversations with our eyes closed and our mouths drooling, passing messages back and forth with just the disapproving flutter of a cigarette, or the slow, satisfied scratching of a groin. Long before computers allowed people to communicate on the superhighway, junkies were surfing their own internal net. Our only gripe was that we wanted to stay permanently connected and we despised the ignorance and hypocrisy of those who tried to deny us that privilege.

'I can definitely hear bells,' said Mandy, head bowed, talking to the floor, 'and they are doing . . . my . . . fuckin' . . . head in. Listen. Can you hear it?'

I hadn't noticed before but he was right. It was the middle of summer and, being on the third floor, the only way we could stay cool was by keeping all the windows in the place wide open, to try and create a breeze. But on a day like this – one of those slow, achingly blue-sky days you get sometimes in England – there was not a breath in the air and all that came through the windows was the distant, muffled sound of . . . not just of bells, but of something else, too. People's voices. The unsettling hum of a crowd, but coming from somewhere far off.

I got up and went to the window and looked out on the unnaturally empty street. It took me a few moments to work it out, but you could really hear it now, the rest of the world was so quiet. The wedding was taking place at St Paul's Cathedral, which was a few miles away, but London would be at a standstill that day, I realised. Hardly any traffic on the roads, everybody given the day off, all supposed to be at home watching on the telly. Good God, what a nightmare.

'Put the TV on,' I said.

'Why? There's only that shite on,' Mandy said, his Rhondda brogue even more braying and cynical than usual. 'I don't wanna watch that fuckin' shite! Fantasy fuckin' island, that's what that fuckin' shite is!'

'Go on, just turn it on,' I said. 'I wanna see something.'

Reluctantly, he reached over and pinged on the set. The scene was identical on every channel: the wedding of the shy, beautiful princess to the debonair, bonny prince.

'Ah, fuck off! I'm not watching that fuckin' shite!'

'No, listen . . .'

I knelt by the TV and gradually turned the volume down until it merged with the sounds drifting in through our windows.

'Ah, no!' he cried. 'That's fuckin' made my day, that has! Is there no escaping this fuckin' shite!'

We sat there for a while staring at the set with the volume turned low, just the distant but still disturbing sound of mass-jubilation drifting in uninvited through the windows.

'I hope the first baby's black,' Mandy scowled.

'Even if it was, we'd never know it,' I said. 'They'd just replace it with a white one.'

'Correct,' he said, picking up the thread and switching to old-colonel English. 'One bred from the official Royal Spermbank, of course, and administered to no less than three Lady Diana look-alikes at the same time that we arrange for the impregnation of the real Diana. In case of just such an emergency, old boy. Can't be too careful, you know . . .'

'Wouldn't want any . . . slip-ups.'

'Good grief, no! You have to be forward-thinking. The masses will be dining off this tasty little morsel for years to come. We here at The Service will see to it, old boy . . .'

It was an old telly-watching routine of ours and we soon grew bored. Then Mandy had an inspiration.

'Shit! I just remembered! Guess what I got yesterday . . .' He rummaged in his bag and came out with a video cassette which he held aloft like a trophy. 'Guess what this is.'

It was a pirated copy of Kenneth Anger's *Lucifer Rising*, the supposedly occult movie from the '60s that was originally to have starred Mick Jagger – so legend has it – before he chickened out at the last minute.

Like a lot of junkies, Mandy and I had become childishly enthralled by the works of Aleister Crowley. We liked his little slogan: 'Do what thou wilt shall be the whole of the law'. It forgave and explained everything. Meanwhile, Kenneth Anger had styled himself as the Master's latter-day disciple, and *Lucifer Rising* was supposed to contain 'real-life' magic rituals, including the baddie of them all – ritual human sacrifice. As a result, the movie had never been shown publicly. Getting our hands on something like this represented a major coup.

'You mean you had it in your bag since last night?' I asked, astonished.

'Yeah. I watched a bit of it but you'd already crashed out so I thought I'd leave it till today, so we could watch it together.'

This called for another celebratory hit, so before we put the vid on we cooked up another couple of real honkers. On a normal work day, you would ration out your fixes like meals: breakfast, lunch, dinner and supper. But on a day off like today, that sequence would be doubled, maybe trebled, depending on how much gear there was to hand. Today was a good day and we had enough – about a quarter-ounce between us – not to worry unduly. We got it together, no hurry at all.

On the telly, the prince and princess were being driven away from the church in a grand horse-drawn carriage. The thousands of gullibles who lined the streets were cheering and waving cheap little Union Jack flags on sticks. The princess waved back out of the side of the carriage. She looked terrified, stunned. But still smiling, smiling, her arm waving like a prop. She looked like a stand-in actress desperately praying she didn't fluff her lines.

Meanwhile, he sat back trying to look regal. Not unhappy, his eyes said, quite comfortable with this new role, quite pleased with the way the long-term plan was unfolding. Yes, some personal sacrifices would have to made, but at least *the job* was now secure. Or would be once the notional princess had produced the necessary progeny.

The effort they were both making to look good together – to seem real – was so blatant you would have to have been deaf, dumb, blind and stupid not to notice it. Yet still the crowd cheered and cheered. It was worse than *Top of the Pops*. Everything was so choreographed; even sitting at home you could feel the whoosh of the cameras swooping past you, knocking so-called innocent by-standers out of their way as they hunted in packs for the best close-up. The best shot. It was sickening.

'The Prince and Princess of Wales,' Mandy sneered. 'Well, I'm Welsh and I'm telling you he's not my fuckin' prince! My fuckin' prince is *the Dark Lord* and he will *beat the shit* out of your fuckin' prince *any day of the fuckin' week, boy!*'

Neither of us really believed in Crowley's horned Devil, but we believed in the marriage of the fairytale princess even less. The masses might get their kicks out of that sort of low-grade stuff but we preferred our gear uncut.

Mandy pulled the needle out of his arm and squirted a fusillade of blood at the screen. The happy couple began to drip red but still they continued to smile, smile, wave and smile. They were unstoppable.

We put the video on . . .

2

Black Days with Sabbath

The limousine sat grumbling impatiently outside the locked backstage gates at Madison Square Garden. One of the smoked-glass
windows at the back slid open.

'What the fuck's going on?' Paul, the tour manager, yelled at a
passing flunky with a laminated pass and a face like yesterday's love
song.

'Gee, I guess the gates are locked, huh, dude?'

'I can fucking see that! Go and find someone to fucking unlock
'em! And hurry! I've got the fucking band here!'

Suitably alarmed, the flunky hustled off to find somebody. It
might have been comical except that the atmosphere in the back of
the limo was already deathly. We waited for what seemed like a
long time. Nobody spoke. Then a couple of kids in Blue Oyster
Cult T-shirts came sloping down the street. One of them had a
brown paper bag with a bottle in it and they were passing it back
and forth. Seeing the limo, they couldn't help but stare. Then one
saw the window at the back open and dropped the bag and ran.

The kid moved fast and managed to shove his head and one
hand through the open window on Tony's side of the car before any
of us knew what was happening. The kid didn't even seem to look,
he just knew.

'*Tony fuckin' Iommi!*' he screamed. '*Tony fuckin' Iommi! Black
fuckin' Sabbath! Man! I fuckin' love you, man!*'

'Ta very much, mate,' said Tony with a straight face. Somewhere
else in the limo, someone laughed, then stopped. Tony kept looking straight ahead.

'*Tony fuckin' Iommi!*' the kid screamed again. '*Hey, Tony! You remember me, man? You remember me? Hey, Tony! War Pigs, man! Fuckin' War Pigs, man!*'

'Yeah, all right, mate,' said Paul, reaching over and very firmly pushing the kid's head back out the window. 'We remember you all right . . .'

Just then a loud buzzer sounded somewhere and the backstage gates began at last to swing open.

'Thank fuck for that,' said Paul. 'Right, mate, you're outta here ...'

He gave the kid's head a last good shove and almost all but his face returned to the darkness outside the limo. His mouth was the last to go.

'*Hey, Tony, don't do this, man! Hey, I'm your brother! You remember me, man . . . I'm your fuckin' brother!*'

Tony glanced over at last. He was then in his early thirties and still retained much of his English Brummy accent. The kid was maybe nineteen and sounded like he came from the Bronx. Tony said nothing. His hand was already on the button and as the smoky window began to slide back up again, suddenly all you could see were the kid's lips, still moving.

'*But I'm your fuckin' brother, man! Your fuckin' brother, man! I'm your fuckin' brother!*'

Finally, the window slid shut with a comforting thunk and the limo moved forward, the gates swinging closed again behind us.

'Fuckin' nutters,' muttered Tony. 'We always get the fuckin' nutters . . .'

*

I had never been to New York before, except in my dreams, but so far it had lived up to all my expectations. Everything was twenty-four-hour – the television, the shops, the bars, the people – which was always going to please someone coming from a London where TV still wound down at midnight, pubs closed even earlier and people believed in the steady job.

It was like Johnny sang, 'It made you a moron . . .' Living like that, being treated like one, an imbecile too untrustworthy to drink past ten-thirty at night and too dull to want all the shops not to close on a Sunday. It may not be much like that now, but this was 1980 and, compared to New York, London was inhabited by a population of sleep freaks, unable or unwilling to cope with anything that went on past bedtime. Take away their tea-break and they felt violated. You messed with routine at your peril.

Instead, the place to be back then was NYC. Lennon was still living at the dreary-looking Dakota building and planning his dreary comeback; Reagan was about to be voted in as a better-looking, upwardly mobile Frankenstein for the '80s; Burroughs was buried away in his windowless bunker downtown; Bowie was starring off-Broadway in *The Elephant Man*; and Warhol and Bianca and all the other fashionable art-disco divas had turned Manhattan into their own private coke-and-sex salon.

That in itself didn't make it any better than London, just less dull. New York was the bullshit capital of the world – so good they fucked you twice – but at least it was *happening* bullshit. There was something in the air – an exhilaratingly American mix of almost spiritual impatience, childish self-absorption, and a peasant's respect for money – that made New York's bullshit better than anywhere else's. It came gift-wrapped in hundred-dollar bills, with its own special little message from the sender: kiss this.

It wasn't even a matter of whether you liked or disliked it, it was almost the other way around. New York, more than any place in the world, really didn't give a damn what anyone thought about it. You don't like it? So fuck off back to whatever safe little rat-hole you came from! What's your fucking problem anyway, man? You fucking scared or something, man?

As far as I was concerned, there weren't any problems. Not right then. The only thing I was scared of was running out of coke and dope, and, as I was relieved to discover, there was never much chance of that happening in New York. Not while you still had some money in your pocket, anyway.

Back home, I was already into chasing the dragon but it was still early days and I wasn't actually physically addicted yet. So travelling around, pretending to be cool, I could still hack that. I didn't have to have the heavy gear every day yet. But I did have to have something, and as I sat on the plane going over, spacing out on the downers and Bloody Marys I had already kicked-off the flight with, I wondered how easy it would be to actually score once I got there.

I knew New York was loaded with dope, but, like I say, I had never been there before and didn't really know what to expect, except for what I'd seen on TV and in films, and I wasn't sure I believed half of that, either. Surely muscle-bound Hispanics in sweaty white vests and funky black fedoras didn't actually come right up to you on the street and offer you the gear just like that, did they?

Then, as the grubby yellow taxi which took us from JFK pulled up outside the hotel, and I stepped out onto the New York sidewalk for the first time, I got my first taste of fantasy land.

I was the PR for Black Sabbath and had brought two journalists from *Sounds* and *Melody Maker* with me, and we were booked in with the band at the Waldorf Astoria. One of the most famously expensive hotels in Manhattan – Liz Taylor in her own private suite, Jack Jones crooning in the bar – the entrance was swamped with uniformed flunkies crawling all over the big shots like ants on a turd, all mile-high smiles and stiff little bows as they goosed the tuxedos and suits for tips.

Out of this unpromising setting, an unlikely yet strangely familiar figure stepped forward. He looked like something out of a *Furry Freak Bros* comic – blue aviator shades, big walrus moustache, too much hair done up in a long, greasy pony-tail. He was wearing a blue pinstripe suit with a green-and-yellow Grateful Dead T-shirt on underneath, with the words 'JESUS SHAVES!' scrawled across the front. Funny, ha, yeah . . .

His face was suddenly very close to mine. He leaned in and, in a voice like Bugs Bunny, said: 'Hey, man, what's up? Just checking in, man?'

'That's right,' I nodded.

'Hey, you're English, right? You with the band, man?'

'Which band?'

'Sabbath, man! *The* band! You with Sabbath, man?'

'That's right.'

'Far out! That's crazy shit, man!' He leaned in a little further. 'So whaddaya say, you need a little coke, man? A little dope, maybe? Huh? A little weed to chill you out before the show, man?'

Well, yeah, but I had only just landed and this was surely too good to be true. What if he was some sort of undercover cop? Or a hotel dick placed at the door to sift out the fucking weirdos? What if he had a gun?

'I don't know, man,' I said, picking up my bag and making to walk off.

'Hey, you just got here,' he said, matching my stride. 'That's okay, man, that's cool. How about a phone number, man? In case you change your mind? You can gimme me a call, man, whenever you like . . .'

'All right . . .'

He fished out a card and handed it to me. It was crinkled and old and had a number and the words 'Jerome Coern – Personal Services' on it, with a little happy face stencilled in where the full-stop should have been.

'Whatever you want, man – coke, dope, speed, downers, weed, bombers, smack, Quaaludes – just gimme a call. And say hi to Ozzy for me, man! Tell him I said he's the man!'

'Thanks, man. I'll do that.'

The only problem was that by then, of course, Ozzy Osbourne was no longer the singer in Black Sabbath. He had been fired eighteen months before, when Tony, the guitarist who had always led the band, decided he'd finally had enough of Ozzy's 'antics' and persuaded the others to go ahead at last and ditch him.

'I cried for two days afterwards,' Terry 'Geezer' Butler, the bassist, told me years later. But Tony had had a plan and waiting in the wings to take over was former Rainbow vocalist Ronnie James Dio. Together with original drummer Bill Ward, the 'new' Sabbath had actually come up with their most successful album for some years, *Heaven and Hell*, which had been released that summer.

Now they were back on tour and selling out places like Madison Square Garden again, and with his cute like 'devil' hand-signals and his lion's-mane of a voice, prancing around as if he owned the joint both on stage and off, Dio had apparently achieved what had previously been thought impossible: he'd become a plausible replacement for Ozzy – at least to those Sabbath fans who still bought albums and tickets. But to your average beat on the street, who still thought of 'Paranoid' and V-signs when you mentioned the name, Black Sabbath would always be the band with Ozzy Osbourne in it. They could gnash their teeth and continue to deny it, even to themselves, until the rest of us had grown long, white beards, which is what eventually happened over the next fifteen years, but that's the way it would stay. Rightly or not, to the world at large, Ozzy Osbourne *is* Black Sabbath. And there's nothing even he can do about that now . . .

At heart, I didn't feel much different by then. Ronnie was a fine rock singer and *Heaven and Hell* was a good enough album, but I regretted not having been around to work with the band in their heyday, when Ozzy was still in it. For me, that would have been the real deal. But then, I was the kid buying albums like *Sabbath Bloody Sabbath* in 1973 and sticking blurred-hair shots of Ozzy on my bedroom wall. There would have been that rare connection that sometimes happens in the music business where you get to work with an artist you were actually once a genuine fan of. I didn't know then that that could also be one of the worst, most self-destructive relationships of all to get sucked into. I still thought it might be a buzz.

But Ozzy was gone and so was much of the buzz, even among the band themselves, it seemed. Bill Ward had also been dumped – or had walked out, depending on who you talked to – by the time the US tour had started in September, to be replaced by the much more 'reliable' New Yorker, Vinnie Appice. Although some of the fans may have been disappointed, backstage I wasn't the only one who quietly breathed a sigh of relief at the news. No more being hunted down after a gig and being hustled into the dressing-room where Bill would be waiting for me. Whatever happened to Bill during the course of a gig, from breaking a drumstick to missing a cue or merely standing up and waving at someone in the audience, he wanted it all put down on a press release, he said, and sent out urgently to the local papers in whatever town we were in. He would sit there, a sweat-drenched mass of blubbery white flesh, completely cuckoo-faced, and make me write it all down and then read it back to him.

'Good fella,' he would smile when we were done. 'Now make sure that cunt goes out on the wire tonight, y'understand? Tonight!'

Then, as I finally made it out of the dressing-room again, and back down the corridor to the safety of the backstage bar, I would rip the sheet into tiny little bits and throw it like mad confetti at the nearest roadie.

But Bill's coke- and alcohol-fuelled rages and his manic 'mood swings' had put me on edge from the first time we met. That had been in Paris, at the start of the year, where I had gone to meet them all and discuss plans for the forthcoming album and tour.

I had been working for about a year at an independent PR company in London and as I was the only one in the office who actually knew anything about Sabbath, the task had fallen to me to deal with them personally. It felt strange. I thought they would have sent in a bigger fish than me for a job like that. I didn't know then that companies often make the easy decision before the right one. I was just a small-time stringer for *Sounds*, who had worked for a few months answering the phones at Mark P's post-*Sniffin' Glue* indie label, Step Forward Records, before being fired for 'prolonged absenteeism' and 'a general lack of interest' by one of those sad cunts who still believed in 'the cause'.

I had only lucked into the PR gig when Nina, one of the partners in the firm, took a fancy to me after a drunken outing one night to see one of her bands play. As chance would have it, she lived not far from my parents' house in Ealing, where I was staying at the time, and so she offered to drive me home. On the way, she suggested stopping off at her gaff. She had a tape she wanted me to have, she said. Or something.

She led the way. Big place. Gold discs on the walls. Thick white carpet. It turned out she was also the wife of the manager of one of the biggest rock bands in the world. Money would never be a problem again. But the old man spent so much time away on the road, making all that moolah, well, a girl got lonely. Only this was no girl any more. This was one of those powerful thirtysomething women you only got in the '70s, before *Dallas* turned them all into pouting, miniskirted, man-dependents again.

Nina had survived being a teenager in the free-love '60s, and had grown up and gone far in the over-indulged music business of the '70s, to the point where she was now running her own successful PR company and was married to a millionaire. She had all the trappings, for sure, but she had earned them by doing it her way. You could see it in the way she drove her car too fast or just flung open a door. It wasn't theatrical, she had just won the right. Yes, she had compromised where she'd had to, on survival-of-the-fittest principles, like any man with brains would. But her sense of direction had never wavered; she was a rock 'n' roll chick from the Old School. She had wanted it all and wanted it now, long before it became a cliché.

Now she had got it. She was an earth mother bitch queen who had already been to all the parties and eaten all the cake, and you were a silly little dick-shake just starting out with no idea how any of it worked yet.

So, anyway, out came the brandy with the coffee and then out came the coke. She kept it in a little pink compact case, with a gold razorblade with one edge blunted so you could press your forefinger against it and use the other edge to cut with. She chopped four fat white lines out on the vanity mirror of the compact and snorted two of them, one for each nostril, using the empty shell of an old Bic biro. Her eyes glittered; she tried on a smile, it fitted, then she stood up and handed the little compact and the Bic to me.

This was some time before I got involved with smack, and though I had smoked my fair share of joints by then and displayed the usual over-enthusiastic response to amphetamines, I had never done coke before. Not that I let on. I just snorted it and hoped it wouldn't act like speed on me, which always did my head in much worse than I wanted. This seemed different, though. Smoother, cleaner, more subtle than speed, but in its own way more powerful, too. And much more expensive. I was impressed.

'Now,' she said, looking me straight in the eyes, 'am I going to drive you home to mummy, or are you going to take me upstairs and fuck the arse off me?'

I sat there brushing coke crumbs from my nose and wondering if I'd heard right. Was she kidding? I looked at her. No, she wasn't.

'I've got to go for a piss,' I said.

I needed a moment to think, but it was the wrong move. The toilet was upstairs and after I'd forced a piss out and thrown cold water on my face, I came out knowing exactly where she was.

'I'm in here!' she called from the bedroom.

I walked over and stuck my head around the door, but it was too late. She was already in bed, her clothes all stacked neatly on a chair in the corner.

'Come on in,' she said, 'make yourself comfortable.'

I began to unbutton my shirt and she leapt up from the bed and threw herself at me, ripping the shirt off like a rag and yanking at the belt of my jeans. Inside, I tried to stay cool. Just another rock 'n' roll rite of passage, I told myself. Fucking the rich-bitch wife of a fortune. I tried to go with it and filled my mind with all manner of unhinged coke fantasies, but it just wasn't happening. Nina was no teenage flower-child any more, and the face, even with all the make-up still on, was no longer a young and pretty one but prematurely old, grandmotherish almost. The body, though, *that* she had kept. They say you can keep the body or the face as you grow older, but you can't keep both. Look at Mick Jagger.

Nina was the same. Slender, boyish hips, tiny waist and firm, good-sized tits, and although she was no longer the right age, she let her hair grow right down to her waist. A mature man might have looked on her as a rare beauty. I was not a mature man.

'Relax,' she said, putting her smile back on. 'Leave it to me . . .'

She pulled my jeans down to my knees, yanked my cock out from where it was sleeping in my underpants, and shoved the two inches of limp dick into her mouth. She started licking and sucking and slurping but the two inches stayed limp. They may even have gone down to one. She grabbed my arse and dug her nails in so hard I screamed. She stopped.

'What's the matter, sweetie?'

'I don't know . . . nothing . . .'

She helped me get the rest of my clobber off. Then she chopped out another couple of fat ones on the little compact. We snorted them and tried again but the coke only seemed to make it worse. I discovered that money was not a major turn-on in its own right and, to me, my earth queen bitch mother looked like a tripped-out version of one of my mum's mates from across the road. Even with the coke and the brandy, I could no more easily have fucked her than I could have wanked to a picture of the Queen. But Nina was not one to be easily thwarted. She chopped out line after line, she danced for me, pretending to be a stripper, then she let me spank her, pretending she was a naughty schoolgirl and I was the wicked headmaster. But still I could not get an erection.

It felt like the door had been barricaded and we would never get out. We became gloomy. Then Nina had an idea. She reached into the drawer of her bedside table and pulled out a white twelve-inch vibrator. I took it from her and turned it on. *Zzzrrrhhhh!!* It was loud. I didn't care. I went to work . . . *ZZZrrrhhhh!!*

I don't know which if us was more pleased but when she finally, finally, *finally* came and I was allowed at last to turn the Tall Boy off and get dressed and go home, I don't think either of us was too unhappy. We never mentioned it again, of course, but she still used to phone me from time to time, giving me cash to write little press hand-outs for her, or sometimes inviting me to gigs.

Then one day Nina called and asked if I could use a little extra dough. Someone in the office had left suddenly and they needed someone to fill in for a few weeks. The pay was fifty pounds a week, cash in hand. It sounded good. I said yes.

The few weeks had turned into a few months and not long after that Nina left to have a baby. Somehow, in her absence, I had been shoe-horned into becoming a junior partner. I hadn't asked to be, I just found myself there. But my fifty a week suddenly got an extra zero added to it and soon I had a flat in Hampstead with a garden so large the local residents asked if they could hold their annual summer fair there. I even helped with the sack races. I was a great guy, popular with the adults and the kids. I had my hands on the wheel and knew just where I was going . . .

Yeah, right. They gave me a company car – a sporty-looking red Renault – but I had never had driving lessons, and though they offered to pay for some, I couldn't be fucking arsed. I never came home anything but completely out of my head, either on booze or coke, or most often both – there was no way I would ever have driven the thing anywhere.

Instead, I had an open account with half a dozen different London mini-cab firms. My bills were paid automatically by the company, my phone was free, I had my own office and two people working for me. Every Friday afternoon I would draw my wages in cash and every Monday morning a little 'bonus' would be put straight into a savings account for me.

It felt big-time. It wasn't, but I had gone from Nowhere to Somewhere, and that was good enough for now. I wasn't even sure how I'd done it, but it seemed foolish to dwell too long on that. Just go with the flow, baby! Chop 'em out, Charlie! I was the Jean Genie, letting myself go . . .

To begin with, before we shovelled it all up our noses, it had been a reasonably affluent little company. At different times, we had done PR for a lot of different groups – REO Speedwagon, The Damned, Visage, Dire Straits, The Emotions, The Tubes, lots more not so famous, others I can't even remember now. Musically, they may not have had much in common – even philosophically, allegedly, in some cases – but the magazines and newspapers never changed and I never met a band that didn't want the same thing as all the other bands: the front cover. Most of them spent more time thinking about five-star reviews than they did writing five-star songs. It was pathetic.

And then came Black Sabbath and my little trip to Paris, where they were mixing the *Heaven and Hell* album, and though they weren't much different on the surface, it was plain there was something else going on, too, in the background, that you could only guess at. Something troubling them that stopped them being as easily pleased as most bands I'd worked with until then.

With the exception of Ronnie, who scrutinised every little thing you said like a mad scientist mooning over his microscope, you never felt sure if the rest of them were even listening when you spoke to them. You just formed part of the general flunky landscape, a sight they had apparently lost all interest in long ago. And they exhibited none of the expected band 'camaraderie' I had been used to relying on to get me through the sticky patches with most of the other groups I worked with. Not much was done by way of a laugh; everything was hard fucking work. Like pushing a boulder of solid shit up a hill with the tip of an angel's wing.

They didn't seem to be in tune with anyone or anything outside their own little band cosmology. They didn't understand PR, or they did and just couldn't be arsed. Years of being slagged off or ignored by the critics at home in Britain coupled with years of being feted almost everywhere else, including America where every album they had released up until then had been a hit, had left them impervious to the demands of PR. It was just one of those things you needed on the road, like clean towels. As long as there were enough to go round, the band didn't care who brought them in and laid them out.

All that is, except for Ronnie, who cared about everything so much he didn't leave room for anyone else to. But then he was still the new kid in class, and perhaps the most insecure about his place. Ronnie wanted everything to be so right there could be no wrong. Already nearing forty and surely far too old for such things, you just knew he would pore over every word of every review we got for him with a magnifying glass. At our first meeting, in the coffee shop at the Georges Cinq, where they were staying, he came on strong immediately, wanting to know exactly how many front covers we were going to get for him. Meanwhile, Tony and Geezer just sat there waiting for it to end so they could get back to being bored somewhere else. Bill didn't even show up. He was sick, they said.

But Ronnie wanting the red carpet while Tony and Geezer just wanted a quiet life was all fairly standard stuff. The singer always expects extra. I just kept nodding, kept humming, kept singing that same old happy *yeah-yeah-yeah* and soon everyone was smiling and shaking hands and agreeing to maybe meet in the bar for a drink later, knowing full well none of us would.

It was in the bag or I wouldn't already be in Paris, I knew that. The only one that really worried me was Bill. I knew Bill was supposed to be under the weather but when he showed up for the photo-session I had arranged at the Sacre Coeur the next day, he looked like the ghost of rock drummers past. Dark panda-eyes, hair like a Christmas tree, full alky beard, big beer belly hanging over his spangly rock star belt.

'What the fuck are we doing here?' he kept asking.

'We're getting some shots done, Bill, for your press photos. I'm Mick, your PR . . .'

'I don't care who you are, mate. I want to know what we're doing poncing around in the freezin' fuckin' cold when we should be in the studio working on the album.'

Paul, the tour manager, took me to one side. 'Never mind Bill,' he told me cheerfully. 'He's very musical, is Bill, and when he's got his mind on an album, he can't take it off it. He don't really mind coming out here today for you . . .'

'Paul!' yelled Bill. 'Getcha fuckin' arse over 'ere!'

'Right with you, mate,' said Paul, scurrying away.

Bill looked at him with distaste. 'What the fuck are we doing here?'

Bill had obviously been rocking-out a little too hard and a little too heavy long before I appeared on the scene. Well, that was his business. He was, after all, not to put too fine a point on it, the drummer. Let him rant and rave and let Paul worry about it; I didn't need to schmooze the fucking drummer to get the account.

Then, at about two o'clock in the morning, just as I was drifting off into grateful sleep, the old-fashioned phone by my bed jangled and there was Paul, telling me that Bill would like to 'go over a few things' before I left to return to London in the morning.

'What – now?' I asked, a dark chasm opening beneath me.

'If that's okay, mate, yeah. He really wants to talk to you.'

Christ. I had to get out of my nice warm nest, find my party hat, paste some sort of slave smile on my face and go upstairs and appease the master. For what? A big garden in Hampstead? A regular coke connection? A chance to say, 'I'm in the music business'? Sometimes, at two in the morning, it was hard to remember why anybody did anything.

As I arrived at Bill's suite, the hotel plumber was just leaving. Paul hurriedly explained that Bill's constant vomiting over the last few days had clogged up so many sinks and toilets in the suite that the plumber was having to work round the clock to try and fix them. If we wanted to piss, we would have to go to the public rest room down the hall; the others were all fucked.

'Come in, mate!' Bill called from somewhere inside. 'I've got a treat for you!'

I entered a large pastel-coloured room with a balcony that looked out over to the Eiffel Tower. All the windows were open, letting some darkness into the room. The walls were covered in paintings, large and small, mainly of flowers, with more big flowers on the sofas and curtains. It was like something out of a mini-series. You could imagine Joan Collins swanning in with a glass of champagne in her hand, or some millionaire's dick.

The vibes were all wrong, though. There was a smell of puke in the air. Puke and cigarettes and booze and . . . something else. Quarrels. Outbursts. Things being busted up in the night. I saw his wife first. She was standing in the shadows on the balcony, looking as though she might throw herself off it. She garbled something by way of a greeting, but I couldn't understand what it was. She sounded American and when she stepped into the light I noticed the deep black crevices beneath her small, worried eyes. The fatty jowls at the side of her face made her look like a sad, fat hamster. You wondered what had happened to her, how she had got like this.

Then I saw Bill, slumped on a couch on the far side of the room in his dressing-gown.

'All right, mate,' he said, without looking up.

'I'm all right, Bill. What about you? You all right, mate?'

'I'm fuckin' *brilliant*, mate!'

Bill threw his head back and laughed. Paul laughed, too. We all did. Bill was a crazy, funny guy. We were all crazy, funny guys. But Bill, most of all, obviously.

'I've got a surprise for you!' he said, getting to his feet and tottering over to where a studio-sized hi-fi system was set up. 'You know what I'm gonna do for you?'

I could hardly wait.

'I'm gonna *play you the new album!*'

Bill laughed long and hard again but this time we didn't join in quite as much.

Oh God . . . There are very few things more cringe-inducing than listening to an artist's new album for the first time while the artist is actually in the room with you. Even if it's the biggest pile of shite you've ever heard, you're not allowed to crack on while the poor bastard who made it is watching you out of the corner of their eyes, reading every little twitch for the slightest sign of anything less than total, 100 per cent approval.

And God forbid you actually like what you hear. Then it's not enough simply to sit and enjoy it. You have to jiggle around in your seat, like the magic fever has just gripped you and won't let go. Either way, you have to sit there and think of something to say about it afterwards. 'Hey, that's great!' will not suffice. You have to say *why* it is great. And then you have to listen to them prattle on at length, telling you the *real* reason why it's great.

For the artist, playing their new album to you for the first time is like sharing an intimate view of the parting of the Red Sea. For you, it's like being run over by a two-ton lorry very slowly, back and forth, back and forth, until there is nothing left but an oily, dark stain in the road.

'The only thing is,' said Bill, 'it hasn't got the vocals on it yet. But at least you'll get an idea.'

Oh God, just shoot me in the head now and shove me down the toilet with all the rest of the puke and the shit. The new album without the vocals . . . I must have been a terrible cunt to someone in a previous life to deserve this. I looked at my watch. It said 2.31 a.m. It was going to be another one of those long meetings . . .

*

The best part for me was that by the time Sabbath got to New York in 1980, I had already bailed out of the PR company. They didn't know it yet, but taking *Melody Maker* and *Sounds* to America to do 'on the road' features would be my swansong as Sabbath's PR.

I'd had enough of wiping rock stars' arses while they signed autographs, and in a fit of cocaine jitters I gave up the job and the pad and went back to live with my parents in Ealing. I needed a place to rest up a while. I needed to keep it simple, and I had taken a job as a dishwasher in a burger-and-chips place in Ealing. It suited my needs perfectly. Strange hours, cash in hand, and the kitchen staff were allowed to drink as much beer and wine as they could handle. Not only that, but they left you alone after you'd clocked off and gone home. Compared to the hot-stuff, twenty-four-hour-a-day, seven-day-a-week ballbuster you were expected to be in the music business, dishwashing had a lot to recommend it.

A job in 'the biz' sounds like a dream come true when you're working on the record counter at Woolies and most of your pathetic salary is going on buying the stuff you're supposed to be selling. But there are no such things as 'jobs' in the music business, not real, important ones; there are only lives. To really make it in the biz on even the mundane level of a PR, you have to give up your whole life to it. Leave behind whoever you were when you last bought records for fun, and become someone different. You had to separate yourself from the audience and go backstage and once you went backstage and saw what little there was to see, you could never believe anything you saw on a stage, or on TV, or in a newspaper ever again. Not unless you put it there first, of course. And then you could believe anything, revelling in how magnificently untrue it all was, and what a clever little motherfucker you were.

It wouldn't be so bad if all you had to do was lie, manipulate and steal from the public, like any normal business. But in the music biz you had to do it to the product, too. There is only one set of bastards more gullible than the fans, and that's the stars themselves. You have to speak to them both like children, very slowly and carefully and with a nice happy note in your voice or they simply won't be able to understand you. Even the older, more established ones who like to think they're now beyond all that, you have to treat like fragile china dolls. They break so easily and it's always you or someone like you – we all look the same to them – who has to stay behind and do the clearing up afterwards: paying the cheques; making the phone calls; wiping baby's bottom.

Of course, some of the young guys I worked with in the kitchen played instruments or sang and had already formed bands or were just about to. I made damn sure never to let them know where I'd been at. I remember one was particularly hung up on The Police, who were then on their way to becoming the biggest band on the planet. There was no way I was going to subject myself to the kind of all-round scepticism, jealousy and serial questioning that would have followed any confession that I had once worked with The Police for a few months, in 1978, when they were making their first album. The kids in the kitchen wouldn't have believed me anyway, and even if they had, they wouldn't have wanted to. I didn't want to, either. Fuck that. Dishes and wine and cash at the end of the night – that was plenty to be going on with for now.

Being invited by Sabbath to go to New York, though, was something that was hard to resist. Nobody else at the PR company gave a shit about Black Sabbath by then – they liked the money but actually dealing with the band was deemed far too much like hard work for any of them to want to muddy their own paws with it. So they called me and asked if I'd like to do this one last final thing for them. They tried to make it sound like it was a little holiday they were offering me.

'See it as a way of saying "thank you",' said Big John, the boss.

'How much?' I asked.

'Five hundred,' said Big John, 'plus x-es.'

'I'll take it,' I said.

I had never been to America before and I had a sneaking feeling that if I passed up this chance I might never get another like it. So I told the owner of the restaurant that I was going away for a couple of weeks' holiday. She didn't like it and fired me. There would be other dishwashing gigs.

When we arrived at the Waldorf Astoria a few weeks later, I had exactly five pounds on me; the *Melody Maker* journalist had to pay for the taxi in. But I had arranged for some 'running around' money to be waiting for me when I got there and, sure enough, as soon as we'd checked in, there was a message for me to meet Paul, the tour manager, in his room.

This was in the days before credit cards had taken over completely and I had expected maybe a couple of hundred dollars in cash for my trouble – after all, we were only supposed to be there for the weekend. When I got to Paul's room, though, he counted out twenty-six hundred dollars – worth roughly a thousand pounds in those days. He gave it to me in a big bundle. For some reason I was too surprised to pay much attention to, Paul had decided to give me the company's entire monthly fee.

'Take this back with you and then that's us straight for the next few weeks,' he said.

'Sure,' I said. But as I stuffed the warm, comforting stack of hundred-dollar bills into my jacket pocket, I already knew the money would never make it back to London.

Sabbath were playing two shows at the Garden that weekend – Friday and Saturday. My job was to make sure the interviews got done without too much hassle and that the show was reviewed favourably. For the rest of the time, I was to keep the press as far away from the band as possible.

'Take 'em out and get 'em drunk and fuckin' laid,' suggested Paul. 'Or whatever they wanna do. Take 'em up the Empire State Building – just make sure they don't fall off!' he guffawed. 'Not until they've written their fuckin' stories anyway . . .'

To aid me in this task, I had been given an open tab at the Waldorf and a limo of my own to tit around in. And, of course, I also had the twenty-six hundred bucks. So while the band were sound-checking on the Friday afternoon before the first show, the boys and I climbed into the back of the limo and tootled off to cruise the head shops in Greenwich Village.

Steve, my *Melody Maker* man, was a career writer and already a frequent visitor to NY. Some years later he would move there full time. Steve was a nice guy with a future to consider. He wasn't into head shops. They were strictly for the tourists. So we dropped him off at a friend's place over on Central Park West – the money side of town – and arranged to meet him back at the hotel in time to go to the show that evening.

Pete, my *Sounds* writer, was more like me. Writing wasn't a career for him any more than PR was for me. It was just another ticket to ride. I told him about the twenty-six hundred dollars – a pretty big wad, in those days – and we both agreed there and then to stay on after the Sabbath shows were over and Steve had gone home, and see how long we could make the funny money last.

We made the limo glide along slowly as we checked out the head shops in the Village to see if they had any real legal highs. We ended up spending twenty dollars on a lot of synthetic crap that didn't do it, and ended up throwing most of it away. All except the bottles of amyl-nitrate, which we doused the sleeves of our shirts in. Every now and then you could stick your wrist under your nose, inhale deeply and wait for the spring in your mind to uncoil.

But we soon got bored with that and eventually instructed the driver to take us down to Times Square, where we knew the real action was.

I was told before I went there that New York is a violent, unpredictable place. Watch yourself. Don't walk in the Park at night and don't go down to Times Square. But walking around Times Square after dark, being propositioned by dope dealers, hookers and the more general flotsam that lived on the street there then, I actually felt safer and more at home than I did stumbling around Ealing Broadway on a Friday night, looking for a place to have a quiet beer without getting into a fight.

'Walk around like you own the place, like maybe *you're* the crazy one, and people will leave you alone,' I was told by a photographer friend who had lived there for ten years. 'It's only the tourists and the obvious newcomers who get hassle. Don't walk around staring at skyscrapers . . .'

It was good advice. But Times Square was different. I hear they've cleaned it up now, but back then you only went down to Times Square for one thing: you were either buying or you were selling. Dope, ass, whatever; nobody in Times Square at night was just out walking the dog.

We were peering through the window of a store called Sex Toys when this old black guy with a wooden leg sidled up to us.

'Gen'lemens,' he said, making it sound like a wheeze. 'Gen'lemens, can I innarest you inna little home ennertainment?'

'Why, whatcha got, mate?' asked Pete, sounding far too English. I didn't want anyone to take us for tourists.

'Name it,' said the old guy.

'How about a bit o' weed?' Pete asked.

'Or a bit of coke?' I said.

'Weed, coke, dope, speed, acid, mushrooms, bombers, 'ludes . . . Gen'lemens, I goddit all, ya dig?'

'Okay,' I said, 'what now?'

'You god somewheres we can go?'

We took him to where we'd left the limo around the corner and helped him into the back. He was wearing an old straw hat with what looked like an Red Indian feather tucked into the hatband at the side. His name was Banjo, he said. 'Nod coz I plays it, itz jess ma handle, ya dig?'

We told the driver to drive around and show us some of the sights. Then we buzzed the partition up between front and back and turned off the two-way intercom.

'Okay, what have we got?' I asked.

Banjo leaned over and began unscrewing his wooden leg.

'Christ, what are you doing?' snapped Pete. He was jumpy.

'Be cool, young gen'lemens,' said Banjo.

Then he got the leg off and held it upside down. We looked at it. Then he shook it and about a dozen different little packages wrapped tightly in cellophane tumbled onto the back seat.

'Now,' said Banjo, 'show me wad you got . . .'

*

Backstage, after the show that night, there was the usual queue for the private cubicles in the men's toilet. Why people didn't just do their drugs out in the open was a mystery. Maybe they were worried they would have to share too much out. I could dig that. But it still seemed ridiculous, all this waiting around outside the cubicles in twos and threes, pretending you needed a shit.

Luckily, Pete and I had already been in and gone. Good as his word, Banjo had provided us with a nice little stash. A couple of grams of coke each, a dozen black bombers, and an ounce of the green. He even sold us a little hash-pipe to smoke it with, and we still had about two thousand dollars. What a time we were gonna have once the band were gone . . .

We had done a couple of bombers as soon as we got our hands on them and laid into the weed pretty good before we'd left for the show. All we took with us was the coke, of which we had snorted about a gram by the end of the show. Now we were really iced up and for once backstage at a Sabbath gig didn't seem like such a miserable place to be.

What drugs Sabbath themselves were still into by that point, I couldn't tell. They never spoke about it openly the way most groups would. I suspected Tony was a coke man. He just gave out that feral intensity which long-time coke fiends sometimes have. Geezer, on the other hand, I guessed was probably more of a weed-and-wine man by then. Years later, when we did talk about it, they confessed that they had all been into anything they could get their hands on right throughout the '60s and '70s. But by 1980, in the aftermath of Ozzy's dismissal for being *too* out of it, anything like that which still went on was kept strictly under wraps, and I tried to play it cool as I hovered around the dressing-room.

Being New York, the backstage guest-area was jammed with people. Some I recognised from other bands, some I just recognised from other places. Whatever big city you're in, the people back-stage always tend to look and act the same. Terrified of saying the wrong thing, nervously fingering their backstage passes, they smile too much and laugh too often and stand around like cardboard cut-outs, making bad jokes and hoping someone else will start laughing, too.

That's when you reached for the drugs. Anything to put you out of this misery, even for just a few seconds.

'Enjoying yourself?' asked a blonde girl with large honey-pot eyes.

'Oh, yeah . . .'

'It was a great show, wasn't it?'

'Oh yeah, yeah . . .'

'I think they're even better without Ozzy.'

'Oh, definitely . . .'

There was a pause while we waited to think of something more to say.

3

Fuck the Future

Tall as a vampire and dressed from head to foot in black leather, his fingers, wrists and throat wrapped in a clutter of expensively bejewelled baubles, his dark afro framing his long, sly face like a publicity shot, Philip Lynott played the most convincing rock star I ever met.

Black leather, black smile, but putting out a very mellow vibe, like no big deal, please, just don't touch . . . As the singer, bassist and all-round songwriting baddie in Thin Lizzy, Phil, in his late-'70s prime, was as close to the genuine article as you were gonna get: the romantic, rock 'n' roll gypsy of folklore.

Maybe Hendrix was the original and the best but Jimi wasn't around any more, and Phil really had the rose between his teeth. Standing next to him at some gig or wherever, you suddenly realised you had become invisible. No one else in the room could see you, their eyes were so fastened on Phil. Particularly the women, for whom he embodied a certain age-old fantasy – the boy gone bad for good – which, allied to an easy Irish charm and a filthy sense of humour, made him all but irresistible to them. He was like one of Hemingway's existential bullfighters, and the women who offered themselves to him did so almost ritualistically, knowing he would not be theirs to keep for long.

It was strange how it worked. It wasn't just the usual rock star thing, either. Even Elton John got groupies. Phil had something else going on, too. Something to do with being black and being Irish and therefore somehow . . . outside the rules. *Verboten.* Even for a rock star. And he played on that, stirring up highly eroticised feelings of fear and guilt no café-crème liberal would openly admit to, or be able to resist.

Phil knew exactly what people were thinking as they watched him strut his stuff on TV. On stage, he used to hold his bass much higher than most rock guitarists, who usually opted for the Chuck Berry-Keith Richards round-the-knees routine. I once asked Phil why he did that. Was it simply because he could play it better that way?

'Naw,' he drawled, 'It's so's da girlies can gedda good look at me bollocks!'

'Really?'

'Fockin' right! Don't t'ink da girls don't loik ta look too, you know. Dey look all right! Dey're always fockin' lookin' at fellas' arses and checkin' out da bulge in der trousers.'

He explained how he even got the lighting guys in the Lizzy road crew to bounce spotlights off his groin during the show. I looked out for it the next time I saw Lizzy play and sure enough, there they were – Phil's balls swinging in the spotlight! No wonder the girls used to scream when they saw him coming.

Even the men were a little in love with Phil. Not in an overtly gay sense – though there was that too, no doubt, for some – but there was an under-evolved part of all of us who knew him, if we were honest, that wished we could be just a little bit more like him. Or at least the image he had created for us: the solid stoned groover with the cash and the stash to burn. The lucky black cat who crossed your path. No guilt, no doubt, no problem at all, *baaaby*.

I couldn't even imagine what it was like to truly be that way and I used to watch Phil out of the corner of my eye, searching for clues, looking for signs, excuses. Wanting to know how it worked. Listening to the songs and wondering.

Unlike most rock stars I'd met by then, there were sound musical reasons for liking Phil, too. Partly because I was also Irish – London-born but pure paddy-and-biddy-bred from a couple of escaped Catholics straight off the boat – and partly because they were simply a fucking great band, Thin Lizzy, for me, had always had a little more going for them than most. Particularly post-punk, when the whole concept of the 'rock star' had become laughable.

Lizzy had somehow survived all that, and even the punks held a sneaking respect for them. Authenticity was the key and Lizzy had never lost that, no matter how many times we had watched them on *Top of the Pops*, miming for their supper. The first time I ever clapped eyes on The Sex Pistols, in fact, was backstage at a Thin Lizzy gig, just before the first Pistols single, 'Anarchy in the UK', came out. I was introduced and it turned out Johnny – another London Irish drop-out ready to do anything except find a proper job – was a big Lizzy man too, as were his Pistols sidekicks, Steve Jones and Paul Cook. I didn't know about Glen Matlock; he seemed too foppish, too calm and overfed to really get it. He got the boot from the Pistols soon after for much the same reason, as I recall. I remember laughing when I read that . . .

But that had been in a previous life, back when I was a bottom-rung reviewer for *Sounds*, still living at home and getting shit off my parents for lying in bed all day. Now I was a no-kidding PR with my own pad and my own shit to give. I wasn't sure I liked it and I wasn't sure I didn't like it. But the money kept coming and, though I sensed it wouldn't last, I went with it. I didn't care what it meant.

One of the bands I worked for then were Lizzy-soundalikes Wild Horses, the group that guitarist Brian Robertson had formed after he'd been fired from the real thing for being too out of it even for Lynott. But Robbo and Phil had stayed friends – Robbo always worshipped the ground Phil walked on and could never stop talking about him long after his days in Lizzy were over – and Phil had become a familiar face at Wild Horses gigs, joining them on stage for the encores and generally just hanging out, which is how I first got to know him in 1979.

I did my best not to crack on what a great fan I'd always been, but that's not so easy when you're only twenty-one and still going home at night and playing the records. Especially when you've got a gram or two of Charlie up your nose and a bottle of brandy inside you and you're at that five-in-the-morning stage of the game where dark and tiresome little confessions of that sort are apt to erupt suddenly, like spilt beer, all down the legs of the table and everywhere . . .

So Phil already had my number, even if I didn't have his yet.

Then one night, at a Horses gig at the old Marquee club in Wardour Street, he looked at me with those famously hooded eyes and asked the question that would actually do what rock had always promised it would and change my life.

'Are ya inta a bit o' Fleetwood Mac, at all?' he asked, a lazy smile seesawing across his face.

I was taken aback. People discussing their musical tastes always confused me – especially backstage at a gig, where the subject of music usually fell some way below more conversational dressing-room topics as: 'Who's got some blow?'; 'Who's the chick with the nice tits?'; and the old stand-by, 'Is there a party after the show tonight?'

Being grilled about your musical tastes, though, was like being asked which football team you supported. They were asking for your true colours and while that was okay with football, it wasn't okay with music. When it came to music, I didn't have any true colours, didn't want any. The whole point, as I saw it, was to be promiscuous, to move around and explore, to *listen*. Not just find a groove and stay there, holding the fort like some bomb-brained vet who doesn't know the war's over yet.

Rock, pop, punk, funk, soul, blues, jazz, all that . . . that was just for starters. Greasy kids' stuff, as they used to say. Sooner or later, if I lived long enough, I knew I'd get to orchestras, symphonies, operas. I didn't want to miss a thing and so whenever someone asked me who my favourite band was or what my favourite album was – which, being in the biz, they did periodically – I never knew what to say. How do you explain to some sad, poodle-haired moron who's spent his entire life in a Led Zeppelin T-shirt, or some indie tosser pushing thirty who still buys all the music papers every week, that no such thing exists? They had simply asked the wrong question. When it came to music, the trick was to hate it all, equally, and love it just the same.

'Er . . . well, I like some of the older Peter Green stuff,' I said.

Phil looked at me, unsure of something for a moment, then gave out a low, dry chuckle. 'Oh ya do, do ya?' he said. 'Come 'ere . . .'

I followed him into the tiny Marquee dressing-room. The band was still on stage and there was no one in the room except for a roadie, sitting on the floor writing something down. Phil gave him a certain look and without a word the roadie got up and left, closing the door behind him. Phil pulled a wallet from his jacket pocket, opened it and took out a small white envelope.

He motioned me over. 'So ya loik a bit o' de ole Fleetwood Mac, do ya?' he asked. I nodded but I still didn't know what the hell he was on about.

He carefully unwrapped the envelope. Then, using the corner of a credit card, he skilfully scooped out a large pinch of white stuff and held it up to my nose. We had done a fair bit of coke together at gigs before, so this was not an unusual occurrence. But as I leaned over to snuffle up the gear, I noticed it wasn't quite as white as usual. It was white but it had a dull, sickly hue to it.

'What's this?' I asked, afraid that it would be speed. Coke was fine but speed wasn't, I'd decided. I already had an edge, I didn't need extra; I just liked refining it, which coke and dope could do. Anything else was just mental self-flagellation and I was no longer turned on by simple shit like that.

He looked at me, credit card poised. 'Fleetwood Mac,' he said.
'What?'
'Smack . . .'
'Oh . . .'

I hesitated. I had never done smack before. Up until then it had always been the Great Big No. I had heard all the stories, read all the books, sung along to all the records and built up a fairly detailed mental picture of it. But I hadn't quite seen myself in there anywhere – yet.

'I don't offer dis ta jess annybody,' he said softly.

That did it. Not just the promise of a little chemical diffusion, but the invitation to bond with a genuine '70s rock icon. I had always been a Thin Lizzy man. Now here was Mr Thin Lizzy himself inviting me to join him on a little solo venture. Me and Phil. Phil and me. Not just anybody . . .

I bowed my head and took it all in one snort, then stood back and waited for something to happen. I didn't have to wait long. The rest of me felt the blow before I did. A wave of pleasure like a tide coming in, washing through my body, lapping at my aura, moving like lava up towards my head, lugubrious and unstoppable, where it flowered like a black rose, its succulent ebony petals bursting languidly into bloom somewhere behind my startled, pin-pricked eyes.

Phil scooped out a large pinch for himself, snorted it, then wiped his nose, put the envelope back in his wallet and looked at me.

'Well, whaddaya reckon?'

'Fuckin' great!' I gasped. 'How long does it last?'

'Not dat. I mean, what was da best rec'd Fleetwood Mac ever made – yer man's "Green Manalishi" or "Rhiannon" wit da boiler singin' onnit?'

We both laughed, or at least tried to. We made the faces but nothing came out. We stood there for a while saying nothing, swaying gently on the waves, eyes closed, heads drooping, basking beneath the hot indoor sky. Then Phil roused himself and we were both out of there again, stumbling and reeling, then back standing by the bar like nothing had happened.

Why he had chosen that moment to show that side of himself to me, I didn't know. Perhaps I was the only one left backstage that he hadn't already done the same thing to. Or maybe he was sizing me up as a PR. I really didn't know. Years later, I decided that maybe Phil just liked turning people on. Old-time junkies can be like predatory vampires sometimes, getting their kicks vicariously through others when their own junk-receptors have long since worn out and they can no longer even get high, just maintaining enough of a low-frequency hum to keep the ravages of junk withdrawal at bay. In time, I would get off on a similar kick myself, watching the faces of people who had never tried smack before growing morbid with fascination as I hacked out a couple of ominously brown lines and dared them to do something they shouldn't for once in their mortgage-paying lives, instead of just thinking about it. Then placing a blanket over their shoulders as they knelt by the toilet throwing up. The ones that overdid it anyway, which first-timers, in their enthusiasm, are wont to do.

I was no different and later that first night, at a party for the band in an unnecessarily roped-off section of some expensive shithole in

Knightsbridge, I could feel the smack wearing off. I could feel myself returning to beery disco-reality. I realised I didn't want that and immediately went looking for Dennis the Menace.

Like a lot of people you get tired of hearing about, as a student Dennis had played guitar in a band. The band hadn't made it but instead of putting the guitar away like most of us and forgetting about it, Dennis still clung to a certain image of himself. He wasn't just a drug dealer, he was quick to let you know, he was a musician in his own right and a close personal friend of the band. Any band. Which, while he was hacking them out for free, as he always did for the stars of the show, most bands were perfectly happy for Dennis to be.

I wasn't in a band so I didn't get the here-take-some-home-with-you treatment, but I was the guy to see about backstage passes and tickets and so on, and so Dennis, in his ex-public schoolboy fashion, always made a point of sorting me out early on in the evening, and always at a nice little discount, too. In return, 'The Menace', as he pretended to hate but secretly loved being called, was on the guest-list for everything I did.

'I'm not what you would call a dealer *per se*,' he would explain earnestly while weighing you out a quarter-ounce of coke on his old-fashioned grocer's scales. 'I simply do my best to accommodate old friends and business acquaintances, like yourself, old boy. This isn't actually what I *do*. I'm just getting the necessary funds together to make a new demo . . .'

I don't know what kind of guitar player Dennis was – he gave me one of his tapes once but people were always giving you their tapes and I just threw it down in the corner with the rest of them – but he had a lot of fucking friends, I'll say that. Especially after eleven at night when all the pubs had closed.

'I didn't know you were into the old naughty-naughty,' he said knowingly, when I tugged at his sleeve that night.

'I'm not,' I shook my head. 'I just want to know if you can sell me a bit for later.'

'Well, I don't know, matey. We'll have to see. How much were you looking for?'

'I don't know. A gram?'

'A *gram*? That's rather a lot for someone who claims they're not into it, isn't it?'

'It's not for me, it's for a friend. I'm just gonna have a taste.'

'What, a friend in a band?' he asked hopefully.

'No . . . some writer, you don't know him . . .'

'A writer! No, and I don't want to know him!'

Any mention of the press was always greeted with scorn by the people backstage. It was another way of showing which side of the dressing-room door you belonged on.

'Fuck the press!' cried Dennis indignantly, not that he'd ever actually been reviewed in anything himself. 'One simply cannot trust those cunts . . .'

'Tell me about it. But this guy's into the bad boy and I need to sort him out.'

'All right,' he said, after a pause, as though it mattered what he thought. 'Who is he?'

'You really wanna know?'

'You're right. Just don't bring him near me.'

We entered the men's toilet together, found an empty cubicle, bolted the door, then Dennis pulled out the gear from a pouch he kept tucked down his trousers.

'There you go,' he said, putting the little white envelope in my hand and closing my fingers tightly around it. 'Some good quality China White. Sixty pounds to anyone who wants to know, but to you, squire, a very friendly forty! How's that?'

'Done,' I said, reaching into my pocket.

I counted out the dosh and handed it over. Then I rolled myself a five-pound note and unwrapped the little paper package. I didn't bother to chop out any lines, I just put one end of the rolled-up note up my nostril and stuck the other end straight into the envelope and snaffled some of it up, maybe a bit more than I'd intended to.

'Dear God!' cried Dennis. 'What are you trying to do – kill yourself? For fuck's sake be careful! That stuff's not coke, you know! You have to treat it with a bit of respect.'

Dennis was probably right but some dealers take themselves more seriously than doctors. With his plummy Oxbridge accent,

Dennis even sounded like one. The problem was, like most dealers, he couldn't bear it that no one was really interested in who he was or what he had to say any more, that they just wanted to lay their money down, get the gear and get the hell out of there again. So whenever he sold you something, Dennis tried to push a little of himself onto you, too. The old I-know-something-you-don't routine. Maybe it went down well in the '60s, when drugs still made people take off their clothes and the dealer was the witch-doctor of the tribe, but by the end of the '70s, things had changed. Cynicism had replaced idealism and dealers were treated no better than vending-machines. You put the money in, you made your selection. The words were only words.

Dennis hated that, of course, but I hated all that dealer-as-magus shit, and I couldn't help but take the piss a bit whenever I saw him.

'You think I might OD?' I asked, feigning concern.

'Well, if you do, I don't know you, sweetheart!' he snapped irritably. 'I don't deal with people who don't know how to handle themselves! You OD, it gives me a bad name, don't you see?'

'You're all heart, Dennis. Always looking out for others. I should take you home to meet my mother.'

'Only if she's an absolute peach and I can fuck the arse off her.'

'Oh, you'll love her. She's about your age.'

'You cheeky little cunt, I'm not that old! Anyway, I've had enough of screaming teenagers. They might look all right on the outside but they're a complete waste of one's time, believe you me. They haven't got the slightest idea what to do in bed and all they're interested in is running off with some dickhead from some band.'

'Unlike yourself . . .'

'I beg your fucking pardon?'

'I said, fuck off, man! The last time you fucked a teenager, Elvis was number one!'

It went back and forth and then the tide came rushing in again, the black rose sighed and opened, and Dennis vanished like a bad genie. Just a puff of smoke and then the curtain descending to the stage in slow-motion . . .

*

Like all marriages, heroin has its honeymoon period, too; when, however fleetingly, it appears as though the game has been fixed in your favour, the world remade in your image. When even the sky looks down and has a chuckle at your sudden, unexpected good fortune. You have conquered creation, befriended banality. Kissed the boot and cured your heart. You have won and there is nothing the world can do about it, you're sure.

You were wise at last and after the initial rush had subsided, the first thing you noticed was that all that bullshit about being hooked from your very first fix was just that: bullshit. It took me a good year and a half of snorting and smoking smack, on and off, before I finally felt the first real twinges of full-on physical addiction. For a while, I even began to wonder if they hadn't just made the whole thing up, spreading rumours and lies, keeping the good shit for themselves.

It wouldn't have been the first time. Listening to Lennon shouting and screaming about it on 'Cold Turkey', I was even more convinced. Maybe being strung-out was the only way rich, sanctimonious bastards like that could still feel pain, but it sounded to me like he was getting off on it. The Stones had come a little closer to the truth, I decided, with 'Sister Morphine', still crying like babies, 'cos that was the mournful bluesman thing to do and they hadn't grown out of that crap yet, but at least hinting at what a turn-on it could be to befriend the bad man in that way.

Lou Reed put it best, though, in 'Heroin', because when the smack begins to flow, it's true, you really don't care any more. There was no science to it. It was pure and simple. Smack was just the baddest and the best. Total white-out. And who wasn't into that? Nobody I knew. They might have called it by a different name, but it all smelt the same to me. An up, a down, an in, an out, smack was whatever you wanted it to be. We all needed our hits. And like any other freshly duded-up young arsewipe, all I wanted now was someone to share my new-found wealth with. Someone to help hold the torch while we explored the deepest part of the cave together. Someone who understood shit about shit.

To begin with, Mandy was just another music journalist that I would find myself snorting coke with in the toilets at gigs. I'd read his stuff and knew he was one of the better writers, but I'd snorted coke with a lot of good and bad writers since I'd become a PR and it didn't matter whether they were from *Melody Maker*, *Time Out* or *The Sun*, once you got them inside the cubicle and locked the door, they all acted the same: like sniggering kids smoking behind the bike sheds. It made their night, being hauled off for a little private libation midway through the show. It didn't seem to do their reviews any harm, either.

'I don't usually do this sort of thing, you know,' I recall a brandy-fired old bitch from one of the Sundays telling me as I quickly shuffled a couple of lines out on the little pocket-mirror I always carried with me now. But she rolled herself a nice, tight note like a pro and got it all up in one, no trouble at all.

She even gave my balls a friendly little squeeze as I put her into a cab after the show.

'Call me, okay, darling?' she said.

'Of course, darling,' I said. 'As soon as I've read the review . . .'

My boss at the PR firm, a coke-crazy old-hand from Liverpool that everybody called Big John, had worked in the press offices of several major record labels in London before becoming a partner in the company. Along the way, he'd lost most of his Liverpudlian accent and acquired a new transatlantic one, along with a pretty, American wife to go with it, plus two children, several mistresses and VIP membership to every well-known nightclub in London and New York.

Coke had been the common currency of the music business for as long as Big John, a born PR, could remember, and he loved to pontificate at length on the subject while I sat there snorting his gear and nodding sagely, pretending to take it all in. Coming from the same sort of poor, immigrant background as my own, he imagined he saw a younger version of himself in me, and all calls would be put on hold while Big John sat there chopping them out and putting me in the picture, telling it like it is.

'Coke can write you any headline,' he used to say. It was one of his little catchphrases. 'Coke can turn bad reviews into good,' was another one.

'But it's not bribery, remember that,' he would say, puffing on a joint and blowing irritating little smoke rings across his desk. 'More like a friendly bit of encouragement. Like buying them a drink. You're not making them say or do anything, you're just putting them in the right frame of mind. Creating the right mood. Most of these guys go to two or three different shows a week; your job is to make sure it's *your* show they remember. Or can't remember! Whatever works! And you can't leave something like that just to the band. You have to look after them, hold their hands. Make sure they *enjoy* themselves . . .'

Big John made us sound like a bunch of glorified air-stewardesses but more than once I found myself sellotaping a gram of something to the inside of a record sleeve before biking it over to certain reviewers we knew well on the music weeklies. In those days, there were only four major music titles in Britain – *NME*, *Melody Maker*, *Sounds* and *Record Mirror* – and controlling what went into them was much simpler than it is now, when there are literally dozens of different titles to consider. Not that it doesn't still go on, of course, but perhaps not quite as it did then, or at least not the way Big John and I went about it. And there is at least one former music journalist from those days who is now a major record company executive in London, and is probably reading this right now, wondering if I'm going to spill the beans on him. I'm not, because that would only make him seem as though he was somehow worse than the rest, which he wasn't. He was really no better or worse than any of us. In fact, he was one of the nice guys – honest enough to cut the shit and just want to get it on. Him and Mandy, both.

But I also sensed something else about Mandy that made him appear just a little more human than the rest. He didn't walk around with his TV eye on all the time, recording everything from a safe distance and missing the point entirely, like most music journalists did. He didn't place himself above you in his mind. And he was one of the very few writers who ever offered to actually stick his hand in his pocket and buy some drugs of his own, so that with Mandy it really wasn't just a bribe. It was fun, and he soon became a frequent visitor to the pad in Hampstead.

'What a fuckin' place!' he said when he saw it for the first time.

'What a fuckin' party you could have here!'

We had a standing joke going about throwing a wild party after we'd heard about the one the Stones were supposed to have thrown where they had bald midgets with long lines of Charlie laid out on their heads walking around and mingling with the guests. Any time anybody fancied a toot they simply stopped a midget and snorted one right off the top of his head. As connoisseurs of the socially unacceptable, it was exactly the sort of disgusting image that filled us with glee.

When I showed Mandy the garden, he said, 'Wow, you could erect a big tent out here and have, like, naked serving wenches . . .'

'. . . walking around with big trays of coke . . .'

'Yeah! And you could have a psychedelic punch . . .'

'. . . and invite all the neighbours round for a drink . . .'

'Yeah! And we could video it! It would be like something out of fuckin' *Caligula*!'

A right pair of funny cunts, we thought we were, and so it was inevitable that Mandy would be the first person I invited round to try some of the even more delicious new fun I was now getting myself into.

'Smack, eh?' he said, when I showed it to him. 'And you say you've had some yourself already?'

'Yep.'

'And you say it's good?'

'Yep.'

'How good?'

'*Fucking* good.'

'Right, well, I'm up for it. Excellent! I'm not going to die, though, am I?'

'Sooner or later . . .'

'You know what I mean, though.'

'And you know what I mean. Look, if you don't wanna do some – fine. But me, I'm gonna get fucked up . . .'

I had thrown down the gauntlet.

He picked it up. 'Go on then. Just a little bit to see what it's like . . .'

At first we would simply mingle some smack in with the coke we were used to taking, making little 'speedballs' for ourselves to snort. But we kept cutting down on the coke until we didn't bother with it at all and just went straight for the heroin. It was just better that way. More kick. And as honeymoon periods go, for me and Mandy, the middle of 1979 until about the end of 1980 turned into one long, seemingly endless junk summer . . . not an unsmoked cloud left hovering in the blackened tinfoil sky . . . on the nod and lost in the now . . . we were gone.

We weren't into our serious jazz phase yet, we weren't fixing, and as far as we were concerned, we certainly weren't *bona fide* junkies, as such. We were still just would-be crazy rock 'n' rollers, but let off the leash suddenly, with no urgent need any more to explain ourselves. We had both left home and got jobs. We were up for it. But the music had died on us. Punk was now only there to be poked fun at and new British bands like The Specials, The Selector and Madness were hogging the covers of the trend-obsessed music papers. We felt cut adrift. There was no way born-late hippy-punks like us were going to start dressing up in suits and prancing around in pork-pie hats, pretending to be cheeky chappies and having a so-called social conscience. That really would have been taking the piss.

We liked some of the records but we disdained that whole strait-laced Two-Tone vibe. Given a simple choice between saving the world or saving an ounce of smack, we'd have taken the ounce every time. Fuck the future: the world would still be beautiful with or without the ozone layer; it was mankind that needed saving. But maybe mankind didn't deserve to be saved. Maybe mankind wasn't as important as it liked to think. Maybe mankind was just a smacked-out dream and now the gear was starting to wear off.

Meanwhile, what did we care about the inner city? Let it burn. They could put the flames on the news and we would watch them dance as we sat there sucking up big clouds of dragon's breath. We weren't interested in inter-racial issues, we were into interstellar overdrive. We would meld the white with the brown in our own special way, behind closed doors, far away from the crowd, a very quiet riot. No clubs or gangs allowed.

All the slogans and the promises had arrived too late. We hardly even spoke the language any more. Instead, we got our preferred kicks first from sociologically unsound rock bands with entirely the wrong hair, wrong clothes, wrong music and wrong ideas to be taken seriously by anyone else on the music press. And then, more dedicatedly, from our gradual submergence into the deep wonder of jazz. Our last real lifeline to a world where extra-human values and artistic solace might still be said to exist. Somewhere.

As a result, Mandy, who had never been a big heavy metal fan, suddenly started writing about groups like Wild Horses, Black Sabbath, Hawkwind and Journey, all of whom I worked with as a PR at different stages throughout this period.

Beyond critical belief, in the immediate aftermath of punk, most rock bands existed then like werewolves, somewhere on the edge of our imaginations. Coked-out, sexed-up, bestial, there was something not quite real about them, at least you hoped not. But when the moon came up, there they were. Hairy-minded fuckers, standing at the door, demanding to be let in, the uninvited guests, waiting to show us our real selves the first time we slipped up and said the wrong words; daring us to give in to ourselves and not regret it.

Fashion-wise, of course, they all lived on the dark side of the moon, but at least the rock bands had things in the right order: sex and drugs and then rock 'n' roll. They were the true space invaders. Born to die. Killer queens. All that. And the more shit the critics threw, the more the animals in the cage liked it. Most rock musicians didn't read the words anyway, they just looked at the pictures, then looked in the mirror, judging themselves by the wasted elegance of their profiles, the length of their hair, the size of their cocks.

Wild Horses were our favourites. Robbo's singer and songwriting partner in the band was Jimmy Bain, another hell-raisin' Scotsman who had also achieved a measure of fame in the mid-'70s as the bassist in Ritchie Blackmore's Rainbow.

Two born sidemen temporarily sharing the spotlight together, Robbo and Jimmy were like a double-act. Always dressed as though they were just about to walk on stage, it's fair to say that some of their best performances took place when their guitars were safely packed away. They loved their drugs and not a single day passed when I worked with them that we didn't all get completely out of our fucking heads at the earliest opportunity. Coke, smack, downers, speed, dope, acid . . . there wasn't a drug invented that Robbo and Jimmy probably didn't have a bit of stashed away somewhere in their silver flight-cases. And they were always willing to share it with you. You could relax and be yourself around them.

'There's nuthin' wrong wi' smack,' I remember Jimmy once explaining. 'Ye get a wee bit strung out, like. So what? Nay bother. Ye go tae see thi magic doctor – private, like. Ye bung'um a few notes and tek a few ay his magic pills and – bingo! Sickness aw gone! Back tae normal. People mek too fuckin' much ay it. Smack's nae sweat. Gie it tae me if ye don't fuckin' want it, that's wha' ah say. Gie it tae thi needy . . .'

It was the same with women, and groupies would routinely be passed around in the Horses dressing-room before and after a show. But there was an unspoken pecking order and either Robbo or Jimmy, or someone else from the band, or sometimes all four would have been there before you; the thought of being third or fourth in the saddle was never an appealing one, and, no matter how good it looked at the time, I always passed.

'Ye dinnae know whit yer mussin',' Robbo told me more than once, but I had a horrible feeling I did. Sex was never really my thing in those days, anyway. I was into head-jobs.

And, of course, Robbo and Jimmy loved their booze. For a couple of short-arsed skinny cunts they really knew how to put it away. Robbo's favourite tipple was quadruple Tequila, while Jimmy tended to stick pretty much to the whisky or the brandy. He would bring his own bottle into the office with him and set it down on the table. No matter how long or short his visit, it was always empty by the time he left again.

How and when they ever got around to making music together no one knew. They were permanently fucked up but they were funny with it, too, and they were great at giving interviews. The NME wouldn't touch 'em, of course. Wrong stereotype. But all the others were glad to line up and have Robbo spill cocaine all over them. Not least Mandy, who had never been a big Thin Lizzy fan but was somehow irresistibly drawn to their more fun-lovin' off-shoot.

But then nearly all the journalists that met them went away liking Robbo and Jimmy. One guy who turned up from one of the musicians' mags, *Beat Instrumental*, liked them so much he ended up staying at Robbo's house for three weeks. We looked forward to reading that one . . .

Some of the bands I worked for, though, like Hawkwind, had existed so long outside the bounds of mainstream media approval that if by some miracle it had suddenly come their way again they wouldn't have known what to do with it. I remember their drummer in those days, Simon Something-or-other, had one extra-ordinarily long, black fingernail on his little finger, which he used like a claw to scoop speed out of the little bag he always carried round with him.

'Fuck what they write in the papers, man,' he told me one night. 'I'm glad they don't put us on their covers. Even when they do write about us, they never get it right, man. They're always adding all this other stuff in. All their own shit, nothing to do with us. It's not enough to say, like, yeah, they played really well and the crowd got off on it. They have to attach all this other crap to it. Well, fuck that, man, that's what I say. Here . . . do you want some more?' And the claw would dig in to that little bag again, sharp and black and meaningful in some way that no longer mattered.

The band's leader was Dave Brock, who sang and played guitar. The only surviving member of the original Hawkwind line-up, Dave took great pride in carrying the weight of the band's history on his shoulders. It was the only thing he took more seriously than himself and there was no laughing allowed.

But in the same way that certain pop stars – Phil Collins, say – remind you of bus drivers, something about the greasy unwashed hair, the stringy beard, the decade-old jeans and rancid-looking fingerless leather gloves always made me think of Dave Brock as a dustman. Every time I saw Dave, I just couldn't get the image of him throwing garbage bags into the back of some big truck out of my mind.

Then one morning on tour, before I had learned all the rules, I had approached Brock in the hotel lobby as we were all checking out, and as an attempt at an ice-breaker, I said jokingly: 'The bins are round the back, mate.'

I waited for him to smile or at least acknowledge the joke, but he just looked at me, his expression as inscrutable as the cosmos his music purported to explore. Then somewhere behind his eyes the projector clicked on and the film began to roll.

'You're fired,' he said, and walked off.

Maybe it was just bad biorhythms. I pretended I hadn't heard properly and we carried on regardless, but Dave never spoke to me again.

Of course, some of the older rock bands I worked with then, like Journey, were so out of touch with my own reality that they weren't aware there was anything strange about what they did at all, right down to wearing flared trousers and rambling on in their interviews about peace and love, which was about as far from the centre of things as you could get in London in 1979. But then they were easy-listening, Californian weed-and-wine guys. If there was a little coke going down, too, it was kept very discreet and never referred to outside the dressing-room. Journey had left the street behind a long time ago and they had no intention of allowing you or anyone like you to try and drag them back to it now. Like, what for? Don't you like money, honey?

We sent Mandy to San Francisco to do a story on Journey for *Sounds*. But even Mandy had a hard time summoning up the courage to say he actually liked them in the piece he finally wrote. Instead, he crammed the story with smart quotes from the band and some lively anecdotes about San Francisco. It was a good piece. It made the band sound almost hip. But when they read it, they hated it. They didn't get it. They said they thought he was being 'disrespectful'. I read the piece again. I didn't know what they were talking about. They read the piece again and came back even more horrified. Nobody knew what anybody was talking about.

It was the first time I realised that Americans don't speak or read English, they speak and read American. Subtlety, irony, a caustic wit – these were not much recognised qualities in the reading material of the average American rock musician. The band just saw it all as a put-down. A punk put-down. In short: the PR had sent the wrong guy. What they didn't realise was that the PR had sent the *only* guy. No one else was interested.

I ran into a similar situation not long after with Sabbath's American singer, Ronnie James Dio, who bawled me out backstage at the Hammersmith Odeon one night after some comments made in an interview with him that had run on the cover of *Record Mirror*.

Record Mirror was not known for splashing heavy metal bands across its cover and the fact that I had managed to get Ronnie's wizened visage on there was, for me, a minor PR miracle. It was a pretty flattering write-up as well, and when I marched into the dressing-room that night before the show with half a dozen copies of the mag under my arm, I did so wreathed in glory, I thought. If this didn't force a smile out of them, nothing I did would.

Ronnie very solemnly took a copy of the mag from me and sat down with his reading glasses and began reading. I left him to it. The congratulations could come later. I had stuff to do before the show.

Twenty minutes later I was standing by the backstage door making some last-minute alterations to the guest-list when I got a tap on the back. I turned around. It was Ronnie.

'What is this piece of shit?' he barked. He was holding a screwed up copy of *Record Mirror* in his hand.

'What do you mean?'

'Have you read this?'

'Yeah, I read it. What's the problem?'

'What's the problem?'

'Yeah.'

'You say you read it?'

'Yeah.'

'And you're asking me what the problem is?'

I stood there. I knew it was coming but I couldn't for the life of me think why.

'He calls me a fucking ego-maniac!' he yelled. 'Did you read that? He calls me a fucking ego-maniac!'

'No, I didn't read that.'

'*He* calls *me* a fuckin' *ego-maniac!*'

'Let me see.' I took the paper from him and studied the page but I couldn't find the offending words. I found 'ego' – I think the phrase was 'egocentric' – but I couldn't find 'maniac'.

'Sorry, I can't see where it says . . .'

'You can't see?'

'No.'

'You can't see! You can't read! Am I the only fucking person who can *read*?'

His voice was getting louder. I looked down at him. He was one of the few people who was actually shorter than me.

'Let me ask you something,' he said, his face like thunder. 'Do you think I'm an ego-maniac?'

'No, of course not.'

'Do ya? Huh? Do ya? Well? Whaddaya say, *am I a fuckin' ego-maniac or not?*'

'No, you're not.'

'Then *why* does it *say* I am *right here*? Huh? Huh? Well? Shall I tell you? *Because you're not fuckin' doin' your job!*'

He was screaming at me now, his eyes on stalks. I thought, 'I'm either gonna have to hit him or I'm gonna have to walk away.' I thought about the pad in Hampstead. I thought about the quarter-ounce in my pocket. I turned on my heel and walked away. But the maniac had left bits of his filthy ego all over me. I needed a line.

The rest of Sabbath, meanwhile, didn't seem to be too aware of anything outside their own daily band schedule, and were easily the most miserable and difficult bunch of bastards I'd ever had to deal with. Tetchy, uncommunicative, grim; truly Sabbath were an enigma to me. Commercially, their career was on the up again, the new album had gone Top 10 in Britain and America and tickets for all the shows were selling well, but you would never have known it from the looks on their faces.

Nothing seemed to work for the Sabbath guys any more and having to be around them was like the way someone once described having the flu: it was awful but not so awful you couldn't stand it for a few days. But if you'd had to live with it for any longer than that, you'd have cut your throat.

It wasn't until I was much older that I finally began to piece together in my mind the real tragedy of the Sabbath story, but by then the drugs had long since worn off and I was no longer young enough to care.

Black Sabbath weren't the only middle-aged men who had made some mistakes in their youths and now had an upside-down cross to bear . . .

4

Paranoid

When the comedown came, it lasted forever. Not just the physical symptoms – a dodgy pancreas, a weakened liver – but everything else. The head stuff; the heart. Even from this distance, smoke from the crash still lingers and I've never been able to look out on a clear blue sky since without seeing dark, chocolatey wisps curling around its edges.

There's no such thing as a three-week cure, and it took several attempts – each more painful and prolonged than the last – before I was finally able to rid myself of the physical and psychological straitjacket that smack had become. Having done that, I thought that would be the end of it. I didn't know the real story had just begun.

The first time I seriously managed to kick had been about six months after I'd returned from my trip to see Sabbath in New York, in 1980. The pad in Hampstead was ancient history by then, as was the PR gig, and to begin with I was back living with my parents, signing-on and washing dishes a couple of nights a week for a little extra cash at that burger-and-chips place in Ealing. Hardly the high life, but that was okay. I yearned to just zero-out. I knew I would probably have to kick sooner or later, but the empty, non-committal grind of going to work, coming home, firing up a foil and flipping on the TV was plenty for me. I hadn't watched any real TV in years and hardly recognised any of the shows. It was still crap, of course, but strangely comforting crap. Good for nodding off to.

Meanwhile, Mandy was now the one with the cool pad. He had moved into the spacious top-floor flat in Primrose Hill, with a view overlooking London – the Post Office Tower, all that – and I was now the one who had become the frequent visitor.

Sticky Iranian brown was now our mainman. Following the fall of the Shah the year before, by the end of 1980 London was awash with cheap, strong Iranian smack. Up until then, smooth silky China White had been the mainstay of most dealers we knew, and at £120 a gram smack was still mainly the preserve of those who could afford it.

But with the arrival of the sugary brown Iranian, street prices had been forced down to about sixty pounds a gram, less if you bought in bulk. And where the white tended to be a fairly light ride, heavily cut as it always was with talc and chalk and God knows what else, the brown was much purer and carried a more full-on, lights-out kind of punch. Real heavy stoner stuff. I was mostly broke, of course, but Mandy hadn't forgotten who'd looked after him in the old days and somehow, between us, we managed to maintain our habits.

I knew there were only so many dirty dishes I could wash, or so many times my mother could walk in as I quickly shoved the burnt tinfoil down the side of the chair before I would be forced into making some kind of move. But it was hard to know how else to play out the rest of the game. I'd had enough of the music business, but what else was there that I could actually do? That I was seriously interested in? The answer kept coming back: nothing.

It wasn't just the drugs; I'd always been that way. Once, when I was fifteen, the class was given a special 'careers advice' lesson. We were all given three sheets of paper with hundreds of different jobs listed in long columns on them. Each job had a little box next to it. You had to tick the boxes next to the jobs you thought you might be interested in. There must have been five hundred jobs there – doctor, bus driver, bank clerk, architect, shop assistant, general manager, typist, whatever, whatever. I looked and looked but I couldn't find a single box I wanted to tick. I went through the sheets again, trying to imagine myself as an aeroplane pilot, a garage mechanic, an accounts clerk, a dentist, a greengrocer, a truck driver, a travel agent . . . I tried but I just couldn't see it.

I thought, why doesn't it list 'singer' or 'footballer' or something tasty like that? How about 'film star', 'painter' or 'gameshow host'? And if it didn't list those things then how did it work? Who were the chosen ones who had somehow circumnavigated the need to become something dull? What box did I have to tick for something like that?

All around me, kids were busy ticking jobs. I realised I wouldn't be able to get away with handing back empty sheets. I looked again. Eventually, I found one: 'radio jingle writer'. I ticked it. I sensed that only a complete tosser would ever dream of becoming a radio jingle writer, but I also decided the hours would probably be easy and the pay not bad. I saw myself swanning into the studio late, a cup of coffee in my hand and some aspirin for the hangover, a cigarette dangling between my lips. Pressing some buttons and coming up with nifty jingles for the DJs . . . working with all the greats, Tony Blackburn, DLT, 'Diddy' David Hamilton . . .

It was the same when Mandy suggested moving into the Primrose Hill flat with him. It wasn't really the right move – the part of me I refused to listen to knew that. But it just seemed righter than whatever else was on the page at that moment. I ticked it.

Not as garish or dauntingly palatial as the Hampstead place, the Primrose Hill flat was actually nicer in many ways. There was no garden but it was decently furnished; we each had a good-sized bedroom, plus a kitchen, toilet, bathroom and a large lounge for us to share. The rent was high and left me with nothing to live on, but if you were going to live on nothing, there was no better place to do that than at Mandy's.

Mandy was a salaried staff writer by then, but he only ever spent the absolute minimum amount of time at the *Sounds* office and most of the time we just sat about the place, chasing the dragon and listening to jazz. Although we were every-day guys by then, a gram split between us would last a good couple of days, and though I still had my money worries, for a while the living was safe and easy.

Mandy even had a girlfriend, to begin with, a beautiful eighteen-year-old blonde called Trixie that he'd met at some party. Intelligent, fun, sophisticated for her age and not a bit turned on by smack, what a smart, sexy babe like Trixie was doing with a complete cunt like Mandy not even she could have told you, I'm sure. But the world is full of smart, sexy babes wasting their time on complete cunts, older and more fucked-up than them. Like me, she adored his spiteful sense of humour, but it took a while before she realised he wasn't always joking.

He used to have a polaroid camera and he had taken literally hundreds of shots of Trixie naked or 'in various states of undress', as the tabloids say, which he used to pass around the room like holiday snaps as she sat there fidgeting in her seat.

'Mandy!' she'd cry. 'For God's sake! They're supposed to be private!'

But Mandy wasn't listening. He just sat there chuckling and passing over the shots. 'What d'ya think? Not bad, eh?'

I looked. Lots of masturbation shots, sometimes with his dick in her mouth or with various objects – pens, combs, toothbrushes – shoved up her arse. Lots of cum shots.

'Yeah, nice,' I said.

He looked at her. 'You have a beautiful smile, my dear.'

'*Oh, fuck off! Fuck off! Fuck off!*' Trixie screamed and ran from the room.

Mandy just sat there chuckling. 'Seen this one?'

I looked. There she was again. Horrible junkie spunk all over her sweet baffled face. I quite fancied her myself . . .

But as the days and nights slid by and my money and all the records and books I was prepared to sell from my collection had finally run out, I began to envy Mandy his easy lifestyle, his handy expenses and his regular monthly dollop of cash straight into the bank. I began to think about getting back into writing myself.

When I had first started out as a reviewer on *Sounds* I was nineteen and still thought of rock journalists as artists in their own right – the ones worth reading, anyway, like Charles Shaar Murray, Nick Kent, and the bad daddy of them all, Lester Bangs. Consequently, I would spill blood over a three-hundred-word review of second-division Clash clones at some half-empty shithole in publand, dragging the whole history of late-twentieth-century pop into it. I used to sit there on the floor in my bedroom, writing it all out in longhand, a dictionary by my side, looking up words I didn't know the meaning of but which just looked good together on the page.

Once, when my typewriter was broken, I had asked if I could type up one of my reviews in the *Sounds* office. It was the first time I had ever sat in there with the staff guys, the editors and the feature writers. I feigned indifference but my stomach quivered as I sat down and began typing with one finger.

As I began working, one of the guys whose picture always ran next to his by-line, a pretty-boy know-all named Phil Silverbum, came up and stood behind me. Silverbum was one of those guys with all the right clothes (the blue Lewis leather jacket, the tight-fitting black 501s, the faded White Riot T-shirt) and all the right records (Costello, Clash, a sprinkling of Marley). One of those guys who always knew the right thing to say; what the word was, who'd knifed who in starland this week. He was a little tin god straight out of the punk gift shop and I didn't know how to handle him at all.

He stood behind me eating an apple, reading over my shoulder. He chewed very slowly and deliberately; and as I typed, each drawn-out bite, each exaggerated swallow was like a slow running commentary on what I was writing. I felt his eyes over my shoulder, weighing, judging, discarding . . .

Finally, I finished. I whisked the paper from the machine and stood up like I knew what I was doing. I turned around to face Silverbum, as though just noticing he was there. He was shorter than me, which meant he was short, but his face came at you from a much larger screen hovering somewhere above.

'I get it,' he smirked. 'You're into bubblegum, right?'

There was a certain kind of self-consciously cutesie '60s American pop that the critics had dubbed 'bubblegum', and there was the pink glob of sticky chewiness that kids blew bubbles with and stuck to the underside of chairs and tables. And then there was whatever the hell Silverbum was talking about. I didn't know what the fuck, just kinda nodded. I sensed he was merely baiting the hook. That some show of superiority was being called for.

I waited for the punchline but either it never came or I had already missed it. Silverbum just looked me up and down, smirked some more then turned his back on me and began talking to someone else. I realised I had failed some sort of test, and that whatever my review said now, it didn't matter. I just didn't have it.

Then living with Mandy, watching him work, pecking at his typewriter while crouching on the floor of the lounge, surrounded by blackened pieces of tinfoil, I began to get a better idea of how it might be done. I was amazed to discover that Mandy never did more than one draft of anything, not even cover stories. 'Just bash it out, check the spelling and hand the shite in,' he advised me. 'Don't think about it, just crank it out, boy! You can do that!'

That was easy for him to say. As a writer, it was obvious reading even his most mediocre, bashed-out stuff that Mandy had at least found a groove. All he had to do now was be there by the machine and the words would come. He just had to fill in the blanks where the song titles and all the other dull stuff would go.

But then you read some of the bad ones, which was most of them, and you realised he had a point. There was no big deal in writing for *Sounds*. It was more like a comic than a music paper. You only had to look at the Letters pages to see that. Punk v Heavy Metal. Mods v Skins. It was just what's-your-favourite-colour done up in late-'70s drag.

It certainly wasn't like trying to write for the rigidly pseudo-intellectual *NME*. As a reader, I preferred the *NME*; it was always light-years ahead of *Sounds* or any of its other rivals, but, in truth, by 1980 I really couldn't understand a lot of what was being written in there any more, let alone try and emulate it. Post-punk, the *NME* was at the peak of its pretentiousness, and I'd never been to university, I'd missed all those student union bar debates. And though I still enjoyed reading Tony Parsons ripping into some broken-down old punk-archetype like Dee Dee Ramone, I didn't know what the fuck someone like Ian Penman was on about. One of the speed-pimpled, post-irony new breed, I sensed he had a genuine take on things, but he was so stuck on his own genius nothing else come through, just the exuberant, speed-spiel verbosity. I mean, the kid was all right but someone please just shut him up for five minutes. I'm trying to listen to some music here . . .

Besides, I didn't *just* like A Certain Ratio and Orange Juice, I liked Thin Lizzy and Black Sabbath, too. That meant I was damned forever as far as the *NME* was concerned. Just another reject who didn't have the brains for it.

I decided to call Alan Lewis, the *Sounds* editor. Ironically, in the early days, I had once asked Al why he didn't give me any interviews or features to write, why I only ever got little reviews to do, and he had told me straight: 'Because you don't write like a *Sounds* writer, you write like an ex-*NME* writer. You write like you've got a dictionary by your side.'

That was when I knew I would never crack the code. But the years in between as a PR had also helped demystify the process; working with so many writers, spending so much time in the toilets at gigs and at parties shovelling coke up our noses, it gave you a much more realistic perspective.

With very few exceptions, most of the rock journalists I'd met were a disappointingly ordinary bunch, generally of less-than-average intelligence. For all their thousands and thousands of words on the subject, none of them seemed to have much idea of what rock 'n' roll might actually be about. Ten years before, they would have been asking for the singer's favourite colour. Now they felt obliged to enquire into his soul, questioning his integrity, his political allegiances, or lack of, and judging him by how far up or down he lay on the new barometer of taste that punk had helpfully erected for them.

That they themselves – Mandy, Nick Kent and one or two others excepted – would have been equally at home working behind the counter of a bank hardly mattered. They had us believing that rock had to mean something or it simply wasn't worthy of our enjoyment. And you needed a music paper to tell you which was which – the rock that meant something and the rock that didn't. They never seemed to grasp that it was not meaning anything at all that made the best rock music so infinitely compelling, so irresistibly erotic, so electric and must-have-now-able.

The feeling you got from a good rock song was like a reminder of a place that existed long before words did. It was like having a good stinking curry shit. You just liked it, the smell of it, the feel of it shooting out of your arse, the sound as it hit the pan; it was ecstasy. When you put it down on the page it always seemed vain and hopeless to say so, but rock really was hoping to die before you grew old; wanting to destroy passers-by; the firestarter twisted firestarter; being here now. Not changing anything but breaking everything down, making your particles sing, your soul dance, not for the good of it but for the *now* of it, good or bad, up or down or just rammed up the side. Having it off . . .

Some got it and did their best to explain it, but most just didn't have a clue. It was all there in the opening seven seconds of 'Metal Guru' or 'Pretty Vacant' or whatever, but the critics didn't know how to say that, so they waited for the singer to open his mouth and concentrated on that instead.

Some, like the great Jane Suck, could do it but she would have frightened Charles Bukowski. Her first ever interview for *Sounds* was with her idol, Iggy Pop, and when she got there she jumped straight onto Iggy's lap and pledged to throw herself out of the window right now, if he just said the word. Even the Iguana couldn't come back from that. Jane was simply *too* real, *too* street. She ate Burchill for fucking breakfast. Then, later, she dropped the 'Suck' from her name and it was like Samson losing his hair. She was still a good writer but something had gone from the work. She was no longer as frightened or as frightening.

Then there was Nick Kent. The dark prince. What hadn't he written, done, been, said, thought, lost, won that wasn't great? Nothing I could think of. Tall, rakishly handsome in a thin, per-manently stoned way, his black raven's hair cut like Keef's and streaked with cat-piss yellow, paint-chipped fingernails, badly applied make-up, chandelier earring, the whole bit, Nick Kent was the man who invented the term 'elegantly wasted', not just on the page but in real life.

I first set eyes on him during one of his brief, periodic visits to the PR office to blag some free albums, as he tended to do every couple of months. He never remembered me from the last time but I always used to pack him up a nice little bundle, knowing full well they were going straight to the Record & Tape Exchange store just up the road. Like any other junkie, Nick was always short of 'the old ackers' as he called it, and selling free promotional copies of albums had become a useful form of income.

Only once did he ever actually interview any of the bands I represented, a retro-rockabilly outfit from London called Whirl-wind. He spoke to the whole band for nearly three hours in a side-office down the hall. When I asked if I could get him anything before the interview started, he looked at me out of the corner of his half-closed eyes and said, 'Tea and cigarettes. Lots of tea – with honey – and lots of cigarettes.'

We sent someone down for sixty Rothmans and told her to keep the tea and the Gale's coming. Afterwards, when I asked the band how the interview had gone, they seemed unsure.

'It was weird,' one of them said. 'He just sat there with his eyes closed . . .'

'. . . and he didn't have a tape-recorder . . .' said another.

'. . . he didn't even take notes . . .'

'. . . just said he'd be able to remember it . . .'

'. . . I dunno, weird guy . . .'

But when the interview ran in the NME a few weeks later, the band were amazed. As far as they could tell, Nick had captured their voices perfectly. There wasn't a quote out of place. Weird guy, all right . . . Much later, he too reinvented himself, and though his voice was still strong, it had lost its frantic edge. He'd started doing interviews with his eyes open again and though you had to allow the man his personal victory, the writing would never be so valiantly corrupted or as wilfully blissed-out again.

Well, we all get old, move on, fuck up. Sometimes when you gained something new you lost something old, and, given a straight choice between being the greatest, most tortured artist in the world and being a happy, over-indulged old fuck who never writes a word, only an idiot nothing really bad had ever happened to would not choose the latter . . . the easy chair by the window with the gear all laid out nice on the table next to you . . . the phone that never rings . . . the days flowing easily, uninterrupted, into night . . .

But Nick, Jane, Mandy and one or two others, they were the exception to the rule, even in the early-'80s before AIDS came along and turned us all into eunuchs. The truth was, most rock journalists were the literary equivalent of dishwashers. They had the easiest, dirtiest job in the kitchen, and the more I thought about it the more I decided there was no reason why I couldn't churn out the suds just like the rest of them.

So I smoked a foil and called the *Sounds* office. 'Listen, Al,' I said, 'you know I've always been a *Sounds* man.'

'Er, yes . . .' he said uncertainly.

'Well, since I stopped doing PR I've had some time to really read the magazine again, to really study it, and the thing is, Al, without meaning to sound big-headed, I honestly think I could write the arse off most of the people you've got working for you right now.'

'Oh, yes?' he said, his interest only vaguely sparked. Al had worked with some good ones in the past – Jane, Giovanni Dadomo, Jon Savage, real bluff daddies. I knew what he was thinking.

'Listen,' I said, 'I know what you thought of my stuff in the past, but that was two years ago. I've been working non-stop in the business since then, and I know a hell of a lot more now than I did then, and I've got good contacts now, too, and I've got into writing again, and I think I can really bring something to the magazine that maybe the others don't have.'

Silence. Then, 'Hmmm, well, the proof of the pudding is in the eating, of course,' he said, distractedly.

'I know, so listen, what I wanted to say, Al, is give me one story to do – a decent-sized feature, just one story – and I promise I'll deliver. I'll show you what I mean. What do ya say?'

Al didn't sound too convinced and, looking back, who could blame him? How many times over the years must he have suffered versions of this same rap from other young dickheads looking to come in from the cold, looking for the free ride? And if he had put the phone down at that moment, too busy to be bothered with my bullshit, I wouldn't have blamed him for long. A couple of weeks later I'd probably have laughed about it. The day I got loaded and called old Al Lewis up at *Sounds* and told him how great I was! *Hahahahaha!*

Instead, he surprised me by asking what I had in mind. My great idea was an interview with Phil Lynott – as seen from 'the inside'. Hardly earth-shatteringly original but it was the best I could come up with and, when Big Al said yes, I nearly burst out laughing. It wasn't until he said yes that I'd realised he wouldn't say no.

Now all I had to do was write the thing. I fired up another foil and thought about that . . .

*

Well, the article had gone in and it was fairly standard, the sort of thing that could have been written by anybody on the magazine. It hardly lived up to the billing I'd given it to Al, but Lynott had provided me with a few good quotes and, with Lizzy just about to ride the charts again with their *Chinatown* album, Al seemed pleased enough to let me do another story for him. To my surprise, I very quickly began to get regular features to write and albums to review. Mandy was right; the trick was to smoke a foil, close your eyes and let your hands do the work for you. Interviews were especially easy to write up. All those quotes. You just had to hang it in a nice little frame. Make it fit. It was easy and reasonably honest work. I started to get into it.

Suddenly, I was making money again, too. Not in the same league as my days as a PR but enough to make the Primrose Hill place affordable at last as well as keep up my increasingly large habit. The more work I got, the more I loved to sit there smoking foils while bashing away at the typewriter; it made everything flow just that much easier. But the more I smoked the more I had to buy, and the more I had to buy the more I had to work to pay for it . . . and so on. That was my excuse, anyway.

Mandy was more honest. He didn't need any excuses. He just loved it to death. He used to sing a little song he'd made up as he unwrapped a fresh foil and tapped a little of the good brown out onto it:

> '*Oh, give me the gear*
> *that makes you feel queer*
> *One little smoke*
> *to give me some poke*
> *Oh, give me the gear*

that makes you feel queer
High as a kite
no, I don't give a shite
Just give me the gear
that makes you feel queer . . .'

He even had me singing it and, even today, whenever I'm doing something monotonous, I still find myself humming it sometimes, softly under my breath, forgetting for a moment. *Oh, give me the gear that makes you feel queer . . .*

When I made the decision to kick the first time, I did so because I had to, not because I wanted to. Following a complimentary article I had written for *Sounds*, I had been asked to write a book about Split Enz, the band from New Zealand which featured the brothers Tim and Neil Finn, better known these days as former members of Crowded House.

Split Enz were huge in New Zealand and Australia at that point and had enjoyed a brief success in Britain and America with their 1980 album *True Colours*, which included the hit song, 'I Got You', sung by Neil. Now the band wanted to put out their biography. Something about the article I had written had rung a bell somewhere, I suppose, and they decided I was the boy to write it for them. Not knowing the first thing about writing books but feeling unduly flattered, of course I said yes.

The idea was for me to travel with the band for three weeks on their first tour of Europe, in the summer of 1981. My first thought was to go to a doctor and have myself put on a maintenance programme, allowing me to legally carry at least some methadone around with me. But the tour would be criss-crossing European borders every few days and there was no way I was going to go through the ordeal of having to explain to a never-ending parade of customs officials that my medicine was purely for my health. I realised with a sense of impending doom that the only way I was going to be able to make a three-week tour of Europe was to do it straight.

I would have to clean up. Well, maybe that was no bad thing. I was still only smoking then, and going from what friends in similar situations had told me, it would only take a couple of weeks to get completely straight. I hadn't learned yet that smoking is as potent and addictive as fixing – maybe even more so in some cases. Something about the ritual each involved – the cooking up of the gear and the special funnel used, either for smoking or injecting with – just made it all so much harder to stop. There was much more to say goodbye to. Some junkies, when they were trying to kick, would cook up sugar and water and fix that when they got too strung out. It was the needle they craved almost as much as the gear itself.

But I didn't consider myself anywhere near that far gone yet, and I didn't foresee any real problem coming off, at least for a little while. It might even be fun, I reasoned, being straight again. And I had never written a book before.

There was a private doctor in Harley Street that we all used, all the musicians and managers and publicists and whoever else had a problem at the PR company. His name was Dr Jewel and we would joke and say: 'He's a real diamond, that Dr Jewel, worth his weight in gold he is!' And everybody would laugh. Everybody that wanted some.

Dr Jewel was the musician's friend; the original Doctor Feelgood. And, in the early days, feeling bruised and busted from another long coke bender, me and Big John would get a cab down to the doctor's office for one of his famous shots of B_{12} – mega-vitamins and other shit to which the boys used to swear the Doc always added a drop of coke, not just that street shit, either, but the real 100 per cent pharmaceutical stuff.

You'd pay him twenty-five pounds and he'd plant one of these beauties into the cheek of your arse and within moments you'd feel like a new man. That was the hype, anyway. We'd certainly feel chirpy enough in the cab on our way back to the office. But once we got there, we felt so good that the first thing we usually did was get the coke out again and hack ourselves out a couple of celebratory fat ones, and so it was impossible to tell what was doing what to our systems.

Then, when I got into smack, the B_{12}s just seemed like a waste of time and I began to see the doctor less and less. For twenty-five quid I could buy myself a day on the brown. Not even the best coke would cut through that and confuse you over where the kick was coming from.

But I'd heard Dr Jewel was also good at helping you get off the gear and so, soon after agreeing to write the Split Enz book, I booked myself an appointment to see him again. He tut-tutted dutifully as I outlined the situation, but it seemed to be more out of boredom that genuine affront. The good doctor had seen and heard it all before. He hurriedly wrote me out a prescription, I handed over the cash and hustled down to the nearest Boots to get it filled.

I returned home to the flat that day armed with my new cold-turkey kit: a large jar of little white pills called DF-118s, 'for the withdrawal symptoms', explained the chemist, a kindly old Chinese woman who seemed happy to discuss my 'symptoms' the way she would any other common ailment; a bottle of black-and-blue capsules that turned out to be high-strength Librium, 'for the depression'; and a bottle of triangular-shaped pink pills, 'to help you sleep'.

I had three weeks until the Split Enz tour began in France, in May, and I was determined to make it. I smoked my last foil that same night and the following morning I began by swallowing eight of the DF-118s – highly concentrated tablets of codeine, which metamorphosed in the liver into minute amounts of morphine, hopefully providing just enough of a junk charge to waylay the worst of the withdrawal symptoms.

I didn't know if they would work or not, but kicking without having anything at all to ease the symptoms was simply out of the question. There had been a couple of forty-eight-hour stretches where something had happened, something unexpected that made something else go wrong, then something else and something else . . . times where I'd been left clinging to the floor, unable to sleep, unable not to sleep, completely out of gear and with no possible way of getting any. Very bad vibes indeed. Even though I still had only a mild habit compared to the fearsome beast I would later breathe life into, being left cold for a couple of days without gear was enough to let you know all you needed to know about heroin withdrawal.

Every joint in your body ached, not just your elbows and your knees, but your fingers and toes, your ankles and wrists, your shoulders, your neck, your face. Your whole being ached with a dull, gnawing pain that came from somewhere within, scraping at you. You could feel the meat squashed against your bones; your innards slopping around like ships in a gale. Your eyes burned and watered, as though you were crying, and your nose streamed with green snot, as though it, too, were crying. And then the awful sweats, the incessant hot and cold flushes, and – my pet hate – the horrible, violent shiver that climbed up your back and dispersed itself across your shoulders like an electrical charge. Meanwhile, all the clogged-up shit you hadn't been able to pass for weeks suddenly loosened itself and began avalanching out of you, and when you weren't on the toilet squirting your guts out, you were on your knees throwing up into it. It was at moments like this that you began to understand what they meant in the old days when they talked about that old monkey climbing up your back. It was at moments like this that you realised you would now do anything for a hit; that you had become a real pro.

But, then, just when you thought you could stand no more, the gear would always arrive, like the cavalry on the horizon, bugles blaring, and everything would be fine and dandy in junkie town again. Until the next time; for no matter how much you guarded against it, you knew there would always be a next time. Life was just a cunt like that.

I was to begin by taking eight DF-118s every few hours the first day, then seven every few hours the next day, then six, then five, and so on, until I got down to none. It seemed simple, and, sure enough, the DFs kept the worst of the sickness at bay. There was still some muscular pain, very slight, but no throwing up, no diarrhoea, and no snakes in the bed. The DFs were good stuff.

What they couldn't help you with was the unexpected depression. It would hit you in huge waves of almost unbearable nostalgia, just lying on the bed, staring at the ceiling, remembering things you thought had been forgotten . . .

. . . *Saturday afternoons, I used to lay the green felt Subbuteo pitch out on my bedroom floor. I had my own team, Ealing Albion, white shirts with green stripes, and we were fighting for a place at the top of the First Division table. We didn't win every game but we were tough, we never gave less than 110 per cent right up to the final whistle. Our speciality was coming back from impossible scorelines to win 4–3 or 5–4 in injury-time, the crowd going wild . . . In the background, the radio on, listening to Fluff . . . I liked the part where he read out the letters. 'Dear Fluff, please play more Sabbs, more ELP, more Genesis . . .' It made you feel like part of the club, to know what he was talking about. I wasn't quite that – too many long, fizzy Rick Wakeman solos – but listening to 'album' music, as I used to think of it, presented in such a way, somehow lent a grandeur to it that I had never perceived before. I loved the way he segued in all the riffs with great splashes of classical music. I had always hated classical music – it smelt of party political broadcasts and religious programmes. But listening to it on Fluff sparked an unwitting interest that would not surface properly for many years but was begun there, nonetheless, on those lost afternoons, now always wintry in my mind, when I tuned into Fluff in the hope that he would occasionally switch from playing colossal bores like ELP and Yes to something a little tastier, something maybe by Free, Deep Purple or Led Zeppelin. Or best of the lot, of course, the mighty Sabbs. 'Dear Fluff, please . . .'*

Then, when I stopped playing Subbuteo, I stopped listening to the radio and got into reading the music papers . . . Bowie was the man, he was the nazz. Being a sucker for loud guitar music, I always felt The Man Who Sold the World *was a far superior album to* Ziggy Stardust *or anything else he had done up till then, and although the music press detected a difference, for me Ziggy and Ozzy and Geezer and Ronno were interchangeable. They all played a kind of sonic, doom-laden rock, littered with sci-fi references and occult connotations, and it filled me with wonder . . . my hair dyed red and cut in the Aladdin Sane pompadour . . . then listening, shocked, to* Low *. . . on another kind of comedown this time, a speed comedown, and somehow it had all added up: the bleak, depressed vocals, the half-baked pop songs that collapsed in an exhausted heap halfway through, the teeth-grinding guitars and windy synthesisers . . . Most disturbing of all, the idea of not using proper lyrics on side two, but having the vocalists merely 'scatting' gibberish that just sounded right. At first, I was* *appalled, because it proved that words meant nothing and words were still sacred to me then. Words on Bowie albums, especially. But there was something there; you could hear it if you listened carefully. Something broken and irretrievable that could not be expressed any other way, and I began to see that sometimes there was simply nothing left to say, nothing that would make sense any more by the time it reached your ears . . . just the sounds of drowning . . . My father's face, red and menacing, following me up the stairs. 'Oi'll teach ye a lesson ye'll nivver fergit!' Undoing the buckle on his belt and winding the leather tightly around his knuckles . . . 'C'mere, ye little bastard!' His drunken friends whom I had somehow offended laughing and joking in the background . . . the chink of glasses being emptied and refilled . . . Tom Jones and 'The Green Green Grass of Home' on the record player . . . the sound of him coming up the stairs . . . my mother calling after him, 'Leave da boy alone, dadda, he meant no harm, sure!' That old familiar love song going round and round in my head . . .*

The Librium didn't seem to help at all. If anything, it just made me more morose. After the third day, I just stopped taking it. I sold the bottle for a tenner to a speed-freak drummer who I knew could use them. As for the sleepers, they were good, they did the trick. I just wished I had asked for some more before I left for the Continent. Insomnia would plague me the entire time I was away, an unexpected hangover of my still recent withdrawal.

It all took so much longer than I had thought. The fact that Mandy had no reason to kick and so went about his business as per usual hardly helped. Sitting there watching him gulp down a foil piled high with brown bought fresh from the dealer that morning was almost too much to bear and I took to hiding in my room, where more than once I found myself silently weeping. It seemed so unfair. I felt locked out. Why on earth had I agreed to write this fucking book anyway?

But the DFs did their stuff, and by the end of the first week I was down to just one every four hours. By the end of the second week, I had stopped taking them completely. I was straight. I could feel it. Looking in the mirror for the first time in weeks, I even thought I could see it. Junk gives the features a strangely blurred characteristic. Now it was like my features had been defrosted. I could smile convincingly again. My voice no longer sounded like a Dalek's. Like the sinner I was, I had been born again.

Ten days later, I was out on tour with Split Enz, convinced the worst was behind me. But things started to go wrong almost from the moment the tour started, and I soon regretted my decision to take the trip on.

The Split Enz guys were nice people – sincere, intelligent and very talented. They had just one fault: a crippling inferiority complex. They had first sprung to the attention of the British music press in the mid-'70s, when their *Python*-esque humour and surreal post-glam make-up and costumes saw them dubbed 'the weirdest band in the world'. Encouraged by the response, they had set up base in London and for a couple of years were considered almost cool. But then, like so many promising 'progressive' popsters of their generation, they had been swept off the page by punk, their fey, whimsical theatrics made to look hopelessly outdated next to the spit-and-vomit of equally theatrical but more explosive new weirdos like The Pistols, The Clash and The Damned.

They had relocated to Australia, licking their wounds. Now, four years on, they had reinvented themselves as clean-cut if still faintly psychedelic pop stars; huge at home in Australia, well known in America, and still major headliners in Britain. But, because of their pre-punk past, they would never be fashionable again, and for the older members of the group, singer Tim Finn in particular, that was a burden they found hard to bear. Musically, visually, in the late-'70s Split Enz felt they were at the cutting edge of pop, and yet they were treated like Hawkwind by the UK music press. Older guys, out of touch, not one of us.

None of this mattered while the band were touring in Australia or America, where they were treated like the real-deal they had always believed themselves to be. But the closer the band got to Britain, the more their bitterness betrayed itself. To make matters worse, they had never toured Europe before and the name Split Enz was not well known there; and while the date-sheet featured a number of theatres and good-sized concert halls, it was also padded-out with plenty of no-hope-saloons, the band booked into little clubs and gymnasiums that barely held two hundred people.

'This is a complete waste of fucking time,' Tim would announce every so often to no one in particular. The band weren't even making any money on the tour. It was costing them two thousand pounds a day just to keep the show on the road. I remember because he said it so often.

Meanwhile, far from being completely over the withdrawal jitters, I found I was unable to sleep for more than two hours at a time. Most of the band were dedicated dope smokers, so that was all right, I thought, I can blast my brains out on good, strong hash during the long hours on the bus every day, and belt back the booze during the show every night. But instead of knocking me out, the dope and the alcohol merely left me in a permanent daze.

After the fourth day, I couldn't get a grip on things at all. I didn't know where to begin, couldn't remember what it was I was supposed to be doing there. Nobody had said anything but I assumed they expected me to start interviewing people or something, to start scribbling notes. But I just couldn't get into it. The pen always felt like a mallet in my hand and the very thought of having to start fiddling with the tape-recorder and start picking my way through the entrails of the Split Enz story sent me into giddy fits of gloom every time I stopped drinking and smoking long enough to think about it.

Then little things kept happening. I was supposed to be interviewing Tim, but Tim was also suffering from some unmendable depression and he kept cancelling and rearranging, then cancelling again, until I just gave up. For different reasons, neither of us wanted to know. Well, that was fine with me. I had my seat on the bus. I'd just keep looking out the window, watching the world zip by.

The only one who was really game was Neil, the younger Finn brother. We were the same age, had grown up on the same records and books, knew the same jokes, all that, and we got along well. I tried taping something with him one afternoon but when I played the cassette back in my hotel room that night I couldn't understand a word either of us was saying. We had been talking on the bus and all you could hear was the roar of the engine.

The whole thing was just fucking doomed. I lost interest. I

thought I'd never sleep again. I did what I could. I kept drinking, kept smoking, kept counting the days till I could get back to England and sort myself out, and not just with pissy little pills this time, either . . .

*

Needless to say, I never did write the Split Enz book. I never even started it. Instead, the band disappeared back to Australia and I returned to Primrose Hill and tried to forget all about it. I never heard from any of them again.

Mandy handed me a welcome-home foil. 'I thought you might appreciate this,' he said tenderly.

'You're not fuckin' joking!' I said. I felt like crying. I took the foil and lit it, glad to be back at last where I belonged.

But even after the Split Enz fiasco, I still hadn't learned my lesson. Being off the brown for a few weeks, I had convinced myself that I didn't have to have a habit again, that I could just be a weekend junkie. Cruising on the good stuff only when I could afford it. What I was after, I decided, was a cushy number. Freelance writing was good but you never got expenses, you never got holidays and sick pay. I fancied something with lots of holidays and sick pay.

Which is how I ended up taking a job as press officer at Virgin Records. It started out all right, too. I was smoking but I wasn't hooked again yet – not physically. So I was able to go out boozing with the boys. I soon learned that boozing with the boys was a crucial part of record company life. Unlike an independent PR, who lives or dies by his cuttings, a record company PR picks up his salary and expenses each month no matter who's on the cover of the NME. Consequently, a record company PR does all his best work outside the office, chatting in the corridors with more influential members of other departments, like A&R and Marketing; plotting destruction at lunch-time meetings which stretch into the afternoon and evening. In short, a record company PR's most worked-on product is himself. That's why most of them are such fucking plods.

Well, I could plod, too, if that's what was required, and for a while I got used to having my back slapped. But the gear kicked in much faster than before – having been hooked once, it always works that way, I discovered – and within a few weeks of taking the job I was disappearing into the office toilets half a dozen times a day for a little 'wake-up' foil. I told myself it was the only way I could stay awake at their meetings; the only way I could work up the enthusiasm to make those calls to all those journalists who didn't give a fuck about whatever piece of shit record I'd just sent them; the only way I could make it on any meaningful level whatsoever.

And that was all right, too, for a while. Vicky, the secretary, used to joke about my weak bladder and started referring to the toilets as 'Mick's office'. I played along, thinking I had it all covered. Which is how it might have stayed if I hadn't then got into fixing. Fixing brought a whole new set of problems to the job. For a start, there was all the paraphernalia: the spoon and the lemon juice, the cotton and the matches, and of course the gear and the syringe. I ended up spending longer and longer in the office toilets.

I began to run out of veins I could hit in my arm and had to start working my way further down my wrists until both my hands were covered in track marks and sores from the times where I'd missed. For weeks, I walked around with bandages on both hands, in a pathetic attempt to conceal the scars all over my wrists and hands. I claimed I'd fallen down some steps at a party and sprained both my wrists. Nobody really believed me but the truth was far too horrible for any of them to guess at and so, for a while, I just played the enigma. The guy who never rolled up his shirt-sleeves, never wore shorts, never showed himself, not even on the hottest days.

And I was forever sending company messengers out on their motorbikes to pick up more gear for me, going down to reception to pick up the little packages, as though they were important correspondence. Then sliding off to the bogs for my hit, gone another twenty minutes while I poked and prodded for a vein in my hands, my arms, my legs, anywhere I could get the blessed needle to go. Just to get it in. Just to carry on. One fix at a time.

It got so bad I couldn't even take journalists out on the road to write stories about the bands I was meant to be looking after without having to build the entire schedule around my inability to go longer than about three hours without a fix. I remember taking some poor sod from one of the weeklies to Liverpool to review a band I worked for, and when we got there I took a bad fix in my hotel room and came down with cotton-fever. It's what happens when a minute strand of cotton ends up in your vein along with the junk. If it gets to your heart it can kill you. But most often, you just begin to tremble violently and feel sick. Cotton-fever, we called it. It was deathly but once you had it there was nothing you could do except hang on in there. But you needed a handful of aspirin and a few hours in the dark to get through it. There was no way I was going to be able to stand on my feet and go to a gig.

God knows what it must have sounded like, but I phoned the journalist in his room and told him I wasn't going to make it. I told him I would reimburse him all his costs, his beer money and taxis and so forth, but that I had been suddenly stricken, chucking up everywhere, and that the hotel doctor had told me I had to stay in bed. Or some goddamned thing. I was too strung out to know what I was saying. I didn't care what he thought, just so long as he left me alone.

Anyway, he went to the gig and I stayed behind at the hotel, rattling on the bed like a broken-down engine. I blacked out and when I came round it was morning. The atmosphere on the train ride home that day was kind of cold, but the review still ran and it was a good one. Job done, I decided.

The worst, though, was when I took my old pal Phil Silverbum, who was now writing for *Smash Hits*, to interview Ian Gillan, the former Deep Purple singer who was then signed to Virgin as a solo artist. Some years had gone by since the days when Silverbum used to intimidate me on *Sounds*, and the drive out to Berkshire, where Gillan lived, had been a surprisingly pleasant one. We had chatted about this and that. Silverbum could be a charming, funny mother-fucker when he wanted to, and I got so carried away I forgot to take the fix I had planned to have at the service station which we stopped at for some lunch. By the time we got to Ian's house, I was sweating heavily and the ice-cold fingers of junk withdrawal had already begun crawling up my back like a big, pink crab. I needed a hit.

So once Phil and Ian were settled in the lounge, drinks poured and tape rolling, I sloped off to Ian's toilets. Once inside, I bolted the door and went about my business. I was as quick as I could, but there were times when it seemed you just couldn't hit a vein. I began to sweat even more heavily, the perspiration drip-dripping onto my hands as I tried and tried again to slide the needle home.

No luck. I must have been in there for forty-five minutes before I finally found one in my leg. I wiped away the blood, took the spoon and the matches and the lemon and whatever and thrust them all into my jacket pockets. I turned the taps on and threw some water on my face. I looked into the mirror above the sink, wondering.

When I came out, the interview was already over.

'Had a good shit, then!' Ian joked, but he didn't look happy.

Silverbum just looked at me incredulously. 'Er, I'm ready to go if you are,' he said.

Then one morning, as I arrived at the office and collapsed in my chair, I noticed something on my desk that sent a shiver up my spine almost as bad as junk withdrawal. There, jutting horrifyingly out of the middle of my desk like a miniature lightning rod, was one of my needles.

All the needles I used were disposable orange screw-tops that you placed on the syringe before taking your hit, and I recognised it as one of my own immediately. How it had got there, though, left like a signpost on my desk saying JUNKIE, I didn't like to think about, but I had to.

Someone had obviously found it. I must have dropped it on one of my frequent back-and-forths to the toilet, but how they had known whose desk to stick it into, who it belonged to, was what worried me.

I checked to see if anyone else had noticed but for once I had arrived at the office early and there were very few faces around just yet. Whoever had put it there must have done so the night before, after I'd left.

I reached over and pulled the needle out of the wood. I took it to the toilet, wrapped it in tissue, then hid it in someone else's bin.

I didn't know what else to do. Then as the others arrived for work that morning, I waited for someone to say something, for something to happen. I had my story ready: I knew nothing. But by the end of the day, no one had said anything, nothing had happened, and that's when I knew they were all in on it. Even the toilet walls had eyes.

It was a bad omen. I realised that whatever happened now, it was no longer just up to me.

5

Turning Japanese

Time was short. Nothing had been said yet but I knew: I could either quit the job or quit the gear. I didn't want the job, I wanted the gear. But I knew I would never be able to afford what I wanted without having to do something I didn't. It was just the way of it.

I could barely afford the gear, as it was. By the time my salary and expenses had gone into the bank every month, what didn't go on the rent was already owed to whoever I'd been buying my gear from lately. You tried to keep up a network of regular dealers as a safeguard against ever running short – the junkie's worst nightmare – and as a way of avoiding being palmed off with too much crap. It's only when you start buying regularly that you realise just how much really bad stuff there is out there, and when you absolutely relied on it to keep you cool, you simply couldn't afford to take too many chances. So it paid to shop around, but it all cost money and the only way I'd been able to keep up was by selling some of the promotional albums I was supposed to be sending out to journalists.

Each night I would wait until everybody had gone home, then I would gather up twenty or thirty albums from the cupboard in the press office, place four or five each in various large, fictitiously addressed, brown envelopes, then carry them downstairs to reception with me, as though I were just dropping them off at the post-room. But reception was nearly always empty by then and I would walk straight past the post-room and out the door, into the street and away to safety, striding up Portobello Road towards the Record & Tape Exchange in Notting Hill Gate with as much gusto as my sweat-drenched, guilt-ridden body could muster.

I'd get maybe forty or fifty quid for them – enough for about three-quarters of a gram – then catch the tube to wherever I was off to that night to score. There was no time for pleasantries and as soon as I'd got my hands on a bag, I'd be out the door again, scurrying off like a hungry rat. No matter how sick I was, I always liked to wait until I got back to my own room at the Primrose Hill flat, where I could be alone, before taking my evening fix. It was my only moment of peace in another long, battle-weary day with my head down in the trenches of non-smack conformity, and I cherished it like a baby, cooing softly to myself as my eyes began to close and my nightmares unravelled like old video-tape, worn through by too many recordings . . .

But now the vibes at work were turning nasty. Not long after I'd discovered the needle poking accusingly out of my desk, they had introduced a mysterious new rule in the office about keeping the albums-cupboard locked at night. And my boss, a former journalist himself who had risen through the Virgin ranks to become a minor player, began picking through my expenses regularly, questioning every bike-messenger booked, every so-called lunch I had apparently had with journalists, every drink allegedly bought . . . Not only were all my little avenues for raking in extra cash being steadily closed off, but there was something in the air, something malicious, and I felt it circling, getting nearer, throwing its shadow over me.

With great reluctance, I decided I had no option but to try and kick again. With the warped logic of the true junkie, I cheered myself with the thought that being straight again would mean I'd be able to keep the job and go back to doing gear occasionally. And because I wouldn't be so hung up any more, I would really feel it again.

Things would just be better. I had it all planned. The Christmas holidays were coming up and I would go and see the doctor, get a script for some DFs and sleepers, then head off to my parents' place in Ealing, where I could kick in relative peace. Christmas gave me the perfect disguise. Over-stuffed on booze and turkey, nobody at my parents' house ever moved far from their armchairs in front of the telly. The fact that I would be sitting there pale-faced and semi-comatose for a couple of weeks was more or less expected.

Then, just as I thought I had it all worked out, fate took a hand in things. I used to go to the same place most days for lunch, a cheap and overcrowded working-man's café round the corner from the office that I liked because you never saw any of the other Virgin employees in there. It wasn't swanky or expensive enough for them, but it was here that I'd have an occasional meal – always the same thing, a grilled chop with some lettuce and chips. The rest of the time I existed on Twix bars, up to a dozen a day, and two or three large bottles of Lucozade.

About a week before Christmas, I was in there one lunchtime and I couldn't finish my meal, which was unusual as I practically wiped the plate clean with my tongue most days. For some reason, I just couldn't manage it. Something about the smell of the meat and the grill turned my stomach. Even the chips tasted bad, like chewing a ball of wool.

When the woman who worked behind the counter came to collect my plate, she looked at me quizzically. 'Are you all right, dear?' she asked. We had become familiar in the way you do sometimes with shopkeepers you see a lot.

'I think so,' I replied. 'Why?'

'It's just that you look a bit peaky, dear,' she said, a genuinely worried look in her eye. 'You look a bit yellow, dear.'

'Yellow?'

'Yes, dear. You don't look well at all. I'd go and see my doctor, if I were you.'

I walked out of there and for the first time I realised that the lack of energy and general feeling of unsteadiness I'd been grappling with for the past few days had nothing to do with how much gear I might or might not have had in my system. I realised suddenly that I felt quite ill. I couldn't think why, but I staggered back to the office, feeling worse with every step. When I got back to my desk, I collapsed into my seat.

I picked up the phone. 'I'd like to make an appointment to see Dr Jewel, please.'

'When would you like to see the doctor?'

'Right now, please.'

'I'm sorry, sir, the doctor is not free today. He won't be free again now until Thursday.' It was Monday. I simply couldn't wait that long.

'But this is an emergency!'

'An emergency? What kind of emergency, sir?'

'Life or death,' I said, trying to sound grave. But it just sounded ridiculous and for a moment I felt like I was in a movie. A very bad movie. Then that passed and I remembered that, no, this was the real thing, baby.

She somewhat reluctantly agreed to let me see Dr Jewel at the end of the day. I got a taxi straight over and sat there in the reception area waiting. There was nothing else to do. I thought about a fix and I just felt sicker. That's when I knew it was bad.

The doctor took one look at me and there was no doubt in his mind. 'My dear boy, what have you been doing to yourself?' he asked, but he knew.

*

I never did make it to my parents' place that Christmas. I called my mother and gave her a load of bollocks about having to go to Scotland at the last minute with some band; tried to make it sound go-getting and impossible to turn down; told her I'd call again when I got back in the New Year; that I'd bring her back a present.

She still sounded disappointed. She knew I was lying even if she didn't know why. But I couldn't let her see me like that. I had turned a deep, sickly yellow colour. Not just my skin, but my eyes, my fingernails, my tongue, the soles of my feet . . . Even my shit was a radiant amber colour and when I pissed it was like squirting thick yellow paint down the toilet bowl. I had a wank one day and discovered my sperm was a sickly green-yellow colour, too. It looked like snot, only it was coming out of my cock, not my nose.

Turning Japanese, I found out they called it. Other than that, I didn't know too much about hepatitis. I knew that rock stars came down with it sometimes, along with that other disease that rock stars got: 'nervous exhaustion'. And though I had my suspicions, I wasn't even sure how you caught it. Some said you could get it from a toilet seat – the same ones who probably now say you can get AIDS from kissing a lesbian. Joe Strummer claimed he got it when someone in the audience gobbed at the stage and it landed in his mouth and he inadvertently swallowed it (though how a person suffering from hepatitis came to be pogoing down the front at a Clash gig was never explained). And then there were those who had been to India or the Pyramids or wherever and said they had got it from drinking the wrong water. I tried to think of all the wrong water I might have drunk in the past six months . . .

It was left to Dr Jewel to spell it out for me. 'It's a very serious illness,' he explained excitedly, once he got the blood tests back. 'But it's not hepatitis B, so that's a stroke of luck.'

'How do you mean?'

'Well, B is a killer, you don't want that.'

'No . . .' I thought about it. 'What do you call this one?'

'This is a non-specific form of hepatitis.'

'And that's better?'

'Well, better than B. But it's still not very good news.'

I felt a fool asking but I had to be sure. 'And . . . how do you get it?'

A smile spread across his face. 'Well, I expect you'll be able to tell us that. There are really only two ways you can become infected with this particular virus: either by the use of infected needles, or by having sex with someone who's already got the virus or is a carrier.' He looked at me expectantly. 'Have you slept with anyone recently that might have had hepatitis, or been a carrier, perhaps? Hmmm?'

I shook my head. I hadn't slept with anyone for two years.

'Well,' he said gleefully, 'you're a very silly fellow for allowing yourself to get into this mess, that's all I can say.'

He asked me to take my shirt off and to lie down on the couch. He began prodding at my side. 'Ah, yes,' he said, 'I can feel it. The liver has enlarged significantly.'

He took another blood sample. I noticed he always hit a vein straight off and couldn't help but admire his technique. He was a good doctor.

I lifted my head. 'So what's the cure?' I asked.

'Cure?' he said. 'My dear boy, there is no cure! You'll just have to be nursed back to health as best we can. That means either coming into hospital right away . . .'

'I'd rather not,' I said. 'Unless I have to.'

'. . . Well, either that, or promising me you'll confine yourself to bed for the next three weeks – at least. Here, I'll give you this,' he wrote me up a script and tore it off the notepad. 'And you can come back and see me in three weeks. In the meantime, definitely no drugs. Particularly heroin, do you understand? Your liver simply won't be able to tolerate it, at this stage.'

'No drugs,' I said. 'I promise.'

'Good,' he said, doubtfully. 'Now, is there anyone at home to look after you?'

I thought of Mandy, sitting there cooking up a fix, a good one. 'Oh, yes.'

'Someone reliable? Hmmm?'

'Yes, I think so.'

'Good. Because you're going to need all the help you can get.'

I don't remember the actual withdrawal. It had always seemed such a big thing before, but now I was too ill with the hep even to notice it. The symptoms were somewhat similar anyway and I had no trouble keeping my promise to the doctor: I wouldn't have been able to get off the bed even if I'd wanted to. And I really, really didn't. Knowing there was no longer any quick easy fix available to help snap me out of it, I just lay back on the bed and waited for it all to come down.

As a nurse, Mandy was hardly ideal. He managed to open a can and heat me up a bowl of soup a couple of times at some point during the first few days, as I recall, but when he saw me throw it all back up again a few minutes later, I suppose he no longer saw the point and simply gave up. The only other thing he had to offer was what had put me in this predicament in the first place. Nothing made sense any more. He kept his door closed.

We both did. It was winter, the days were short and dark and you hardly noticed their passing. But I must have been delirious because now they simply toppled over, the nights blinking past like the lights of a train. I lay in bed surrounded by rolls of toilet paper, little bottles of medicine and an array of saucepans and basins doubling as sick bowls. The doctor had prescribed some super-strength milk-of-magnesia-type stuff, along with the usual trancs and sleepers – though no DFs, this time – but it didn't seem to help. I got so used to throwing up it became like lighting a cigarette, habitual and banal.

Christmas came and went, I think. I don't know if Mandy stayed in the flat or went back to Wales to see his parents. Most of the time during those first unreal days, I lay there barely conscious, not sleeping, just dreaming . . . *sticking it in, like a cock, waggling inside you, just sticking it in, seeing the blood leaving your body, just sticking it in and sticking it in* . . . Followed by moments of sudden, achingly acute clarity . . . waking up abruptly to darkness, not knowing if it's night or day, looking around with curiosity at the misshapen shadows on the walls, then noticing the sick bowls brimming over by the bed, smelling them . . . the feel of the yellow-stained sheets, warm and wet, beneath my back, the blankets tangled round my yellow arms and legs like badly tied rope, my head a dusty attic, full of cobwebs and old, unopened boxes . . . fighting off waves of nostalgia at the sound of a car door slamming shut in the street . . . sad for my tree-less, undecorated room . . . sorry for my mother, hurt more by what she didn't know than what she did . . . listening for the lonely sound of the train whistle Burroughs had warned of . . . then hearing it blowing somewhere far off in my tiny, TV mind . . .

I would prop myself up on one elbow, light a cigarette, take a few hungry puffs, gag, then put it out again. The hep even stained your taste-buds yellow. Trying to piece it together, I surmised that I must have left the bed occasionally, if just to stagger to the toilet, but when it happened, or how, I was not able to recall. Some bits never come back to you. Then I would fall back on the bed exhausted, just lying there, glowing in the dark, feeling the sickness hovering in the room like a heavy green mist.

I had never been so totally out of it before, never felt so completely done in. Hep had smack all beat; now this *was* a trip. The thought never occurred that I might actually be dying. I just thought I was riding it out, waiting for the storm to pass. I came from an age where we believed they could cure everything except cancer, and even that they could now do things with, you heard some amazing stories . . . And, anyway, drugs didn't kill you. That was just something they gave to the masses, who liked it all set out nice and easy for them. No, it wasn't the drugs that killed you, man, it was all the rest. The dirty needles and the dirty laws that forced you to use 'em. The tricks you had to pull just to keep yourself interested. The hep would pass; nothing else would.

*

It was several weeks before I was finally well enough to be able to go back to work and by then it really was all over. I wasn't the only one at Virgin who had figured out by then that hepatitis had nothing to do with toilet seats or dirty glasses and I was only back at my desk a few days when I was taken into a side office one night after work and given the news I had been waiting for since the beginning.

'I'm sorry, but we're going to have to let you go,' said the boss, his face stern, compassionless. 'We've had some disturbing reports back from some of the acts you've been working on, and there are some other things I think you know about that we don't need to go into . . .'

It was only a crummy job, I didn't even like it that much. But to lose it like that, especially after so long spent getting well again, hit home surprisingly hard. In one way it was a relief not to have to go in there any more and put on a big show every day. But being sacked for being a junkie, even I knew that was not good and the walk up Portobello Road to the Gate that night was a long one. I was crying so hard I couldn't see in front of me. I wasn't crying for the job, I was crying for me and for Mandy. I was crying because I wanted to make it real.

Then the tears dried up and I began to see again. So much for being straight. By the time I got back to the flat I was no longer confused about anything. Mandy wasn't home yet, but I knew he'd have some gear stashed away somewhere. We had reached the stage before I became ill where we were hiding our gear even from each other. There were no rules left by then and we were convinced the other would steal it without a second thought if he could. But I had not touched gear for months and Mandy had gotten careless.

He kept all his shit in a kitsch little First Aid kit he'd found with a big red cross on the side. Usually, the First Aid kit would be squirreled away somewhere absolutely unfindable. But as I entered the lounge my eyes took me straight to it, sitting unopened on the floor next to the couch. I didn't give it a second thought, just went straight to it and unfastened the catch. It flapped open and a large gram-packet of the brown and half a dozen new needles and a syringe still wrapped in cellophane spilled onto the floor. My hands began to shake as I found myself an old spoon and some juice and began cooking up a hit. I hadn't had a fix for over four months and I decided to treat myself to a real goodie. I tapped some brown into the spoon and then tapped in some more. It looked good, lumpy and strong. I got a semi-hard-on. I wasn't heterosexual or homosexual, I was heroinsexual.

I tied up my arm and found a vein immediately. Hello, old friend . . .

When I came to, Mandy's face was peering intensely into mine. 'Mick! Mick! Wake up!'

I felt like someone was trying to get me out of bed 'cos I was late for work. I tried to push him away.

He slapped me across the face, hard. *'Wake up, you cunt!'*

I suppose that did it but I was so tired, I just wished he'd leave me alone.

'You fucking bastard!' he yelled, shaking me by the shoulders. *'I thought you were fucking dead!'*

It took time, but I started to come round. And when I did, I felt good. What a hit! *Pow!* I began rummaging through his album collection, looking for something to play. Something *up*.

I couldn't understand why he was looking at me like that. 'You don't know what happened, do you?' he said. 'You had some of my gear, didn't you?'

I looked at him. His face looked strange, frightened.

'You had some of my gear, didn't you, you cunt? And then you fucking ODed!'

'I what?'

'You fucking ODed! I walked in the fucking room and you were sitting there cross-legged with your head splat out against the floor. Your whole body was limp! The needle was still sticking out your fucking arm, you cunt! I thought you were dead, I swear to God!'

I looked down at my arm. He'd taken the needle out but I saw the fresh red mark, and the smear of blood. I couldn't put it together, the horror and indignation on Mandy's face and the great feeling I had inside, they just didn't go together at all. He was spoiling things.

When I awoke the next day, though, and Mandy went through it with me again, I couldn't believe it had happened, that I had been so stupid. I had fallen for the oldest trick in the book: getting straight for a few months then cracking and having a hit, but measuring out the same amount of gear you used to take, before you got clean. More junkies have died that way than any other.

Sacked and overdosed in one day. What the fuck was wrong with me? Maybe I had better stay straight. So, at first, I tried, or at least I thought I tried, just to be a joy-popper. A once-a-week man. But those other six days dragged by like old TV repeats and within a few weeks I was as hooked again as I'd ever been.

Although I was no longer jaundiced, it would be some time before my body fully recovered from the long-term side-effects of the hep and I wore two long, yellow streaks down either side of my face for about eighteen months afterwards. I was thinner, too, than at any time since my speed-freak teens, and I noticed that I got drunk more quickly than most people, and that I got stoned on much smaller amounts of gear than I used to. At first, I attributed the latter to my recently withdrawn metabolism reaping the benefits of temporary detoxification. But even after I got hooked again, it took only half of what Mandy and I had once barely been able to scrape by on to send me juddering right through the floor.

Having a weakened liver could have some benefits after all, it seemed, and I began to regret having wasted so much time in the past on trying to quit. I had tried and tried the straight life and it just didn't work for me. Now I had been booted out of the club: unclean. Well, okay. Mandy had never tried to kick and never would. He wasn't bogged down by guilt or even doubt, and once again I found myself thinking maybe he knew something I didn't . . .

The next twelve months seemed to go by like twelve days. Or maybe just one long day into night. I signed on, washed dishes occasionally, sold gear with Mandy, and gave up all pretence of being anything other than an out-and-out junkie. I didn't write any more but I read like a monk. Dostoyevsky, Burroughs, Crowley, DeQuincy, Miller, Machen . . . anything I could get my needle-scarred hands on that had that certain dark junkie vibe to it. Favourites like Art Pepper's autobiography, *Straight Life*, or Anne Rice's *Interview with the Vampire*, were kept by the bed and read and re-read like bibles.

Reading also helped avert my eyes from my crumbling surroundings. The Abbots never ventured up the stairs to our floor, and the flat, which had not been cleaned or vacuumed for years, had begun to take on a life of its own. Beneath our feet, the carpet had vanished beneath a thick, webbed mat of garbage, from discarded old needles and syringes to empty, sour-smelling milk cartons, filthy ashtrays, old take-away cartons, dirty cups, hundreds of old sweet wrappers and left-over magazines and newspapers, just piles and piles of blood-stained rubbish, all trodden down and moulded onto the floor.

In the kitchen – the least visited room in the flat – the sink was piled high with every single piece of crockery we had once used, all sitting in about eight inches of pungent, shit-brown water. Neither of us had been able to bring ourselves to wash up for months and there was now some form of life swimming around on the surface.

We left it. We never went near the kitchen any more anyway. We had run out of everything long before you'd even thought of asking for it. We had the essentials: several lemons, cotton-wool, an array of blackened dessert spoons and at least one big box of matches, all the items you needed, bar the smack itself, for cooking up a fix. Food-wise, however, the cupboards remained bare, the cooker like some relic from a previous life, and, without my little café to go to every day, I began to live entirely on chocolate bars and Lucozade.

Anything more would simply have required too much effort.

It was a similar story with the bathroom: if the toilet hadn't been in there, I'd hardly have gone near it at all. Like most junkies, I could not bare the touch of bathwater against my naked skin. Sitting immersed in it became a nauseating prospect and for the last year or so that I was on the gear I stopped washing completely. If I was going anywhere important, I would brush my teeth, wash my hands and try and run a wet comb through my hair. But I was never usually going anywhere except to score and so most days I didn't even do that.

It was the same with clothes. The nearest laundrette was just a couple of hundred yards up the road from where we lived but, somehow, much as I fretted over it, I simply could not dredge up the necessary energy and enthusiasm to put the filthy clothes and rotting bedsheets into a plastic bag and carry the whole appalling bundle up there. I truly felt the effort would have been too great and so, for over a year, I wore the same T-shirts, the same socks, the same jeans and underpants and everything else, over and over, spraying them with cheap deodorant and hanging them out the window 'to air' rather than go through the physical and mental torture of actually staggering up the road to the laundrette with a big, heavy bag on my shoulder, swimming in my own sweat and cursing my misfortune.

God knows what I must have looked and smelled like on those few occasions I did wander out the door, but things were at least simple then. We'd never heard of AIDS. It was just around the corner but we didn't know that. We hadn't been told about it yet. And even if we had, so what? AIDS, cancer, car crash . . . strictly for beginners, all of it. When you're fixing four or five times a day, every day, you know you're putting something at risk. You might lose an arm, as one old-timer I knew did; you'll certainly lose teeth and maybe your hair, as many of us did. Or perhaps it's something more serious. Because the gear suppresses the function of the pancreas – part of which is to maintain the correct level of sugar in your bloodstream – when you come off, the pancreas has usually been inactive for so long it simply no longer works. This can lead either to long-distance pancreatic cancer or, in most cases, a highly unstable little organ that needs regular stimulus – i.e. food – to keep it ticking over.

And then there's the liver. As any former hepatitis sufferer will tell you, you never get over the yellow peril. Liver cancer at twenty years' remove is the norm for the big Hep B boys. Others of the 'non-specific' variety like myself merely have to put up with the sallow, yellow-tinged skin of a dead fish for a few years, but even then you have to look after yourself. Drink lots of water and walk slowly.

These days, of course, the risks involved in being a junkie are even greater, but I notice that the number of people willing to roll the dice and gamble has not drastically decreased. If anything, having more to lose has only deepened the appeal of smack and there are now more needle-using junkies around than ever before. That's because there *is* a romantic side to smack; it *is* glamorous. The bigger the taboo, the deeper the thrill in breaking it. So when people ask: was the film version of *Trainspotting* likely to make young people go out and try smack for the first time? The answer is: of course it fucking was!

Every kid lives his own movie; the projector's always running in his head. And it wasn't for the Americanised Scots accents and overly theatrical acting that they queued in the streets to see *Train-spotting*. It wasn't even the bit where Renton dives down the toilet and swims in his own shit – a moment of supposed 'magic-realism' that was, for me, the most realistic scene in the entire movie. People went to see it for those gorgeous, ectoplasmic moments where he's depicted taking a fix. It's the equivalent of the moment in a slasher movie when the creature with the eighteen-inch blade and weird face-mask finally reveals itself; or the bit in a porno flick where they finally reach penetration. *Sticking it in . . .*

But *Trainspotting*, the film, was kids' stuff and unworthy of the book it paid mere lipservice to. Cool soundtrack, nice-looking boy in the lead: they made it into a pop video. As a film, *Pulp Fiction* caught the real adult-oriented romanticism of smack much better. From Travolta's suave three-gram gangster grouching-out at the wheel of his car, to the dealer's ice-cream-and-monster-movies-at-2 a.m. home-life, it was a much more aspirational and true-to-life account of a world where smack is not about moral choices – everything has side-effects, not just heroin – but merely another expression of the same free will which forced them to look beyond the law for their limits, their reality, in the first place.

You can moralise but, when you do so, you are evading the real issue. Would I have shared needles if AIDS had been on the menu in those days? Not at first maybe, but sooner or later, under the right circumstances – the middle of the night, say, and no other works available, a fairly normal scenario for most full-time junkies – of course I fucking would. And so would you if you were sick and they were the only works available. You would do a lot worse than that to get what you needed when the time came.

But those are Big Things. Stuff you really don't give a fuck about when you've got a spoon cooking in your hand. Mainly, it was the little things that brought on the despair – the inability to have a good shit, for instance. All junkies suffer from constant constipation. Not shitting for weeks on end soon becomes the norm; reaching down between your knees and trying to pull the shit out of your arse with your own hands as ordinary a part of your day, after a while, as tying your shoelaces.

But the most important and difficult thing always was finding the money. Having sold everything else, I began working my way steadily through my precious jazz collection. The rare Japanese imports and limited editions were the first to go as they always fetched the best prices. Soon, though, I had blitzed my way through the lot, nearly two hundred albums, collected so carefully over a three-year period, all gone in less than a week. None of that stuff about jazz and junk going together mattered now. I'd discovered there was only one thing that really goes well with junk and that's more junk and more junk.

The typewriter went next, then my watch, my rings, my record player, TV, radio, all my books. I even managed to sell a big bundle of dirty clothes for a £20 bag to the old lady of one of the dealers I knew. She had her reasons for wanting them but I wasn't listening when she told me them. I wasn't interested in reasons any more.

*

Despite my poverty, only once during this time was I tempted back into writing: out of the blue a little heavy metal magazine that was just starting up rang and asked if I'd be interested in interviewing Ozzy Osbourne. Two thousand words for fifty quid. Not much by freelance standards but nearly a gram by smack standards. Writing wasn't what I did any more. Like everything else, it simply required too much effort. But the magazine had said they would take a simple Q&A and I thought of the fifty and went for it.

I agreed to meet Ozzy a few days later at the Mont Calm hotel in Marble Arch. In the bar. It sounded easy enough but I wasn't really looking forward to it.

I had met Ozzy once already, at a stag party for Jimmy Bain, back in 1979, just before I had begun working with Sabbath. The party had been held at a big rehearsal room in north London . . . sound-stage with instruments all tuned and ready for when the musos wanted to start getting it on; different coloured girls hired to perform numerous sim-city sex acts at predetermined intervals; plenty of gear floating around . . . When Ozzy arrived, he was immediately escorted into a side-room 'production office' where he was personally 'sorted' by Dennis the Menace. Then when he finally staggered out of there, everywhere he went he seemed to have a couple of blokes either side of him, trumped-up cab drivers they looked like, but one of them would always appear to have a steadying hand on Ozzy's arm, or tucked into the small of his back, turning him this way and that, laughing at all his jokes even when no one else did.

It was all very formal; he didn't just mingle like the rest of us, he was taken around to meet everybody one at a time. He looked like a prize ape being led around the room for the edification of the assembled guests.

When it came to my turn, we'd hardly said hello before it all came tumbling out. 'I was given ninety thousand dollars and told to fuck off,' he said, his eyes staring past me. 'Left to fuckin' die, I was! If it wasn't for Sharon, I'd be out selling fuckin' hot-dogs!'

This was shortly after Ozzy had been sacked by Sabbath. 'Sharon' was Sharon Arden, daughter of the infamous music-business figure, the self-styled 'Al Capone of rock', Don Arden. It was she who had scooped Ozzy up from the gutter where Sabbath had left him and was now, slowly, putting together a solo career for him. Not that Ozzy had bothered to explain any of this to me. He just assumed everybody was up on the plot. Ozzy had been a rock star for so long he'd forgotten what it was like not to have the whole world revolving around him.

'I mean, what would you have done, eh?' he asked. I noticed he was drooling.

'Well,' I said, 'I don't know. The same as you, I expect.'

'Fuckin' right, mate! Fuckin' right! Fuck the lot of 'em, that's what I say! Fuck the fuckin' lot of 'em!'

His handlers started laughing and I did my best to join in. Then they moved him off somewhere else. 'Ninety thousand dollars they gave me,' I heard him saying as he shook the next outstretched hand.

Later that night, Jimmy and Robbo and Phil and Ozzy and who-ever else was there all got up on the stage and blasted their way through a few raggedy-arsed numbers while the rest of us stood there gawping. They played some Lizzy tunes, a couple of Wild Horses numbers, a few Stones and Elvis things . . . It was strange, there was no 'audience' as such, not really, it was just a bunch of mates naffing around with each other at a party. But the minute any of them got up and started playing, they just couldn't help them-selves, they started doing all the moves and shaking their hair and getting right into it. Which just proves that the biggest fans of all are always the ones on the stage.

None of the boys knew any of the Sabbath songs, except for 'Paranoid', so they played an especially long version of that. I must admit, it gave me quite a tingle. The moment Ozzy's hand touched the mike and the band struck up those unmistakable opening chords, you'd have thought he was on stage at Madison Square Garden. He fucking ripped into it. Headbanging, peace signs, jumping up and down on the spot like a demented Zebedee, the whole kit and caboodle.

At the end, we all gave him a big cheer and started applauding. Ozzy just ignored us. He looked confused.

'He's da fockin' man!' said Phil, grinning in admiration. 'He might be a bit fockin' loopy but he's an original, d'ya know whaddamean?'

Maybe. I had certainly once thought so. But meeting him, or at least whatever version of him was on display that night, even witnessing his almost psychotically intense performance of 'Paranoid', I found the whole thing surprisingly unsettling. I couldn't put my finger on it, but there was something disturbing about being around someone so apparently fucked up. Not just on drugs, but on the real killer: life.

Then later, when I met and started working with the rest of Sabbath, Ozzy's general demeanour, in retrospect, seemed less strange. To a greater (Bill) or lesser (Tony and Geezer) extent, they were all like that. Maybe it was something in the water in Birmingham. Something dark and stinking and . . . black.

So the thought of meeting Ozzy again and actually trying to interview him was not an entirely cheery one. On the other hand, once upon a time in the long ago, I would have given anything for such an opportunity. For me, in the early-1970s, Black Sabbath were a truly mysterious, possibly even dangerous, proposition. Bowie may have begun his shows in those days with the Beethoven overture from *A Clockwork Orange*, but it was Sabbath who were the ultimate in scary, futuristic rock bands. Alice Cooper, with his snakes and eye-liner and toy dolls was a pantomime-dame by comparison, and nothing freaked the fourteen-year-old me out quite so much as going to see Ozzy and Sabbath play live for the first time.

As though they were from some parallel dimension where things were similar but essentially different to our own world, everything Ozzy and Sabbath played and did on stage in those days came at you sideways, backwards . . . wrong. They all wore big crosses around their necks, and certainly there was a kind of weird religiosity about their manic, finger-pointing performances. But it was clear that whatever they were on, it obviously had very little to do with boring '60s conceits like peace and love. These bastards meant business. You felt it.

Nobody smiled. Little or no talking between numbers; everything deadly serious. Especially Tony Iommi, the moustachioed guitarist who stood centre-stage, playing it left-hand, solemn, pitiless. He had lost the tips of the fingers of his left hand in a welding accident in the car plant where he worked as a teenager, and he had replaced them with home-made plastic tips he had constructed himself from melted-down washing-up liquid bottles and little strips of leather. It meant he couldn't actually 'feel' most of the bizarre notes his fingers were concocting. But everybody else could. They wrapped themselves around you like unwanted friends and clung to you afterwards like bad memories.

Tony was King Riff.

And unlike Bowie, who always claimed 'Ziggy' was just a mask that had grown too tight, 'Ozzy' looked like a proper mental case who didn't know what it was to pretend. On stage, he didn't stand in the middle like most singers, he stood to one side, and he didn't sing so much as let out the pain, flashing mournful peace signs and jumping up and down hopelessly, a mad dog at the gate.

But by the time Ozzy had been fired from Sabbath, I was past caring. I'd bought my last Sabbath album, *Sabotage*, in 1975. Whatever Ozzy did now was after the fact, as far as I was concerned. But then he did a strange and wholly unexpected thing. Recruiting the services of a blond, twenty-two-year-old wonder-kid guitarist from California called Randy Rhoads, Ozzy recorded two fantastic solo albums: *Blizzard of Ozz* and *Diary of a Madman*.

Randy had co-written all the material with Ozzy and both albums are now rightly regarded as groundbreaking releases in heavy-rock circles – the best proof of which is that most of the songs, along with the Sabbath back catalogue, still make up the bulk of Ozzy's live show today.

Better still, though, both albums had been sizeable hits in Britain and America and suddenly Ozzy had become a huge star in his own right. An unexpected turn of events, especially given that Ronnie James Dio, Ozzy's successor in Sabbath, had recently fallen out with the band and quit. Just as Sabbath's career seemed to be plunging into turmoil, Ozzy's career had taken off like a rocket.

The only blight on the horizon had been Randy Rhoads's terrible death in a plane crash that same year. Not only had Ozzy lost the creative linchpin behind his new solo success, he had also lost the first real friend he'd made in years. I found out later that when Randy died, Ozzy decided to call the whole thing off and retire on the spot. But Sharon, who was now not just his manager but also his fiancée, wouldn't let him. The way she saw it, she told me later, Ozzy stopping then would have meant two deaths.

As usual, Sharon was right and so Ozzy drafted in another guitarist, the first of many Randy clones he would unearth over the years, and carried on. By the time I caught up with him again, at the end of '82, he was just about to do two sold-out shows at the cavernous Wembley Arena in London. If anything, Randy's death had focused even more attention on Ozzy's new solo career. But it was plain he was still grieving over his loss, which perhaps explains why the interview we did that day didn't exactly go to plan. Neither of us was in the best shape for it.

I had decided in advance that the best way to handle it was to go in, get some quick quotes, and get out again in under thirty minutes. If anybody asked, I had a tight deadline. Just to be on the safe side, I got to the Mont Calm early that day and made my way to the toilets, where I settled myself down in one of their plush cubicles and cooked myself up a nice, easy hit.

That done, I made my way to the bar purposefully to meet Ozzy. When I got there, the room was empty except for Ozzy's table, where five or six people all sat around drinking and smoking and laughing just a little too loud.

I walked over and a smoky hush descended on the table. I ignored it and decided to make straight for Ozzy, only when I looked I couldn't see him. I stood there, puzzled. Then one of the bunch, a podgy-faced geezer with dark, cropped hair and a braying Brummy accent looked up and said: 'Awright, mate. What can we do for you?'

'Er, I'm looking for Ozzy,' I said, not really looking at him, just addressing the table generally.

They began tittering. 'Well, you've fuckin' found him, old bean!' said Podgy.

I looked again and realised my mistake. It wasn't Podgy who was talking, it was Ozzy! The last time I'd seen him he'd had long blond hair. I found out later that he'd actually shaved his head bald some weeks before and had only just started growing it back. It had been the end of an American tour and so outraged was Sharon that she immediately had half a dozen blond wigs made up for him to wear on stage, one of which he obediently donned each night for the remainder of the tour, usually pulling it off to uproar from the audience halfway through.

I explained who I was and what it was about. Ozzy lapsed into silence. I grabbed a chair and sat down. The table became quiet again. 'Go on, then,' said one of them, 'ask him something he's never been asked before!'

Nobody else had been introduced but they all seemed to have broad Brummy accents. All apart from one stringy-looking git at the end of the table, who sounded a bit more like me. Him I did recognise. He stood up. 'Pete Way,' he said, extending his hand.

Pete had been the bass player in UFO, one of the bands the old PR firm had looked after in the '70s, back when UFO were still a big deal in America. But the band had collapsed into drugs and despair at the start of the '80s and it turned out Pete had recently auditioned and got the job as Ozzy's new bass player. Well, well, small world, etc.

We shook hands and Pete ordered me a drink, and gradually the vibe at the table turned a shade warmer. But only a shade. Pete was obviously still a newcomer, too, and a southerner at that. They hadn't quite made up their minds about him yet.

'Well,' I began. 'What have you been up to lately, Ozzy?'

'Fuckin' 'ell! Is that the best you can do?' one of them chuckled. A moron with a red beard. Ozzy just sat there silently, staring off into space.

'I see you've cut your hair,' I said. 'Why's that then?'

'Well done, mate. That makes you the fiftieth journalist today who's asked him that!' sniggered another. The boys had obviously been hard at it all day.

I started to launch into another question and Ozzy suddenly sat bolt upright. He leaned forward so that his lips were almost touching the tape-recorder and then, very softly, he began making little *ooh oohhh ooohhhhh* sounds, like a chimpanzee. The others started joining in. Soon the whole table were screeching and chattering like monkeys.

When it eventually died down again, I tried one more. 'How did you and Pete end up getting together then?'

But again, even before I could finish speaking, the whole table erupted in violent animal noises. Not just monkeys this time but chickens, horses, dogs, pigs . . . Ozzy started flapping his arms like a bat. 'I'm just gonna come on stage and bite the heads off the fuckin' lot of 'em!' he declared. Then he looked at me, as though just remembering I was there. 'And you,' he said, pointing his finger, 'you'll be fuckin' first!'

The boys loved that one. *Hahahaha!*

I turned the tape-recorder off and put it back in my bag. 'Right, well, I think I've got enough,' I said. There was some more tittering, then they just sat there waiting for whatever was going to happen next. I decided they would have to wait without me . . .

*

The end came quite unexpectedly one morning as I sat on the floor by my bed trying to have my first fix of the day. As usual, I was having trouble finding a vein but I'd long since lost my impatience with such things and merely sat there diligently prodding away.

I'd sold the big mirror that had once sat on the wall opposite my bed, so it wasn't that, but somehow I caught an unexpected glimpse of myself sitting there, holding the syringe, my arm tied tight with a belt. I looked idiotic, sad and small. I tenderly touched the bruises on my arm, ran my finger lightly down the track marks that led all the way to my knuckles, noticing the absurdity of the lemon on the floor, lying next to the black spoon. I looked at my arm, so thin and torn-looking, and I began to feel sorry for it.

Great waves of guilt and sadness engulfed me. I realised I didn't want to put another needle into my arm. But I knew that I'd be sick without it and that I had no choice, so I dug it in again and eventually found a vein. The chamber filled reassuringly quickly, but I almost couldn't bear to watch. I felt sickened. I sent the plunger home with my thumb and, despite the hit, for the first time I began to feel let down by myself. I couldn't remember what had happened, how things had got to this stage. But something fell into place inside me, like a book slotting back onto the shelf, and I knew I couldn't carry on any more. Didn't want to. I'd had enough. Not just of the smack but of the whole fucking lonely deal. I wanted out.

I told Mandy but Mandy had heard it all before. He looked at me impatiently. Then I told him I was leaving the flat, too, and he really thought I'd lost my marbles.

'But why?' he kept asking, his voice a mixture of genuine puzzlement and contempt. 'I get it that you want to be straight, but why do you have to make such a big fuss of it? Why does it mean you have to move out?'

'Because, if I stay . . .' I started.

'Yeah?' he said, almost daring me to say it. 'Yeah?'

'Well . . .'

'Well, what?'

Did he really not know?

'Because if I stay, I'll die!' I blurted it out, somewhat surprised to hear myself actually saying it. I hadn't imagined I'd ever put it so bluntly.

'What d'ya mean *die*?' he asked, disgusted. 'Who's dying? I'm not dying! Are you saying you're dying? Is that it?'

He looked like a child surrounded by bullies in the playground. He really did not get it at all. It was the first time I'd realised. For me, smack was something I had more or less abandoned life in order to explore. For Mandy, it was the opposite. Life had been a barely tolerable battle against anxiety and boredom until smack had come along and liberated him from it. Now he wanted to keep it that way. For ever and ever.

'I don't mean I'm dying, Mandy. I mean, I just can't live this way any more. I've got to get away, that's all.'

'But why? How can you die if you're not fixing? What are you going to OD on? Life?'

It was worse than trying to end an old affair. Quitting was one thing but moving out was seen as a kind of rejection. A betrayal. There was simply no explaining it to him, and as I bundled up my few remaining bits and pieces into a plastic carrier bag, Mandy sat on the floor shaking his head in something like a state of shock. He simply couldn't understand what the problem was. I had a feeling he never would.

'See you later,' I said, as I opened the door.

'Yeah,' he said.

I left in a hurry. I'll never see him again, I thought, and I was very nearly right. We would bump into each other from time to time – I remember running into him coming out of a bookshop on the Charing Cross Road and we shared a taxi to Camden, and I remember the heavy, musty smell he gave off, like an old coat that had been left out in the rain. But after the first year or so, I only ever saw Mandy once more.

It was more than a decade later. My car was being repaired and there was a Tube strike and so, for once, I found myself riding the bus into town – the 207. I didn't notice him when I got on, but the look on his face – one of stoic, almost manic calm – when I did finally recognise him told me that he had most certainly seen me.

But he had said nothing, and it wasn't until he got off at a stop or two before mine and I gazed out at the stooped and ragged figure shuffling back down the street towards me that I realised what I was looking at. His face hadn't changed (pinched, pissed-off, perspiring) and nor had his walk (getouttamyway) but everything else had. His hair looked like it was painted on and he had a preposterously large red beard that sprouted out of his face like a grotesque, knotted plummage. He was wearing old plimsolls and clutching a torn white plastic carrier bag. He looked like he was in a hurry. I wondered what for . . . and then I remembered.

*

I couldn't bring myself to face the doctor yet again, so I arranged for someone else to go for me. Louise was one of the good old girls, past her prime and track marks up to her arse, but a heart of lavender. She was from the '60s, had once fucked Keith Moon, Eric Burdon, all that, and was a well-known face on the scene until punk or something else had come along and somehow she'd got left behind.

Lou had been a junkie on and off for most of that time, which is how I'd met her, and in exchange for half the DF-118s the good doctor prescribed for us, she was happy to keep going in my place for as long as it took. She was relatively clean herself at the time, but she knew she could sell the DFs and, sure enough, after we'd milked the doctor dry for a few weeks and I found I still needed more, she began selling me back all the stuff I'd just given her. I didn't mind. At least she was trying to help.

'You can sleep on my floor for a few weeks until the DFs kick in,' she told me. 'But the minute you start preaching about how good it is to be clean again, you're out! Got it? I'm too old for all that shit.'

'Don't worry about me, darling,' I said, not confident at all. 'Three or four weeks, I'll be fine again.'

Six months later, I was still there. The DFs were long gone and so were the worst of the withdrawal symptoms, but I sensed there might be more to it than that and hung on to my mattress by the door for as long as I could. I knew Lou had gotten used to the company, and I relied on that to see me through. She was good at conniving ways of keeping your mind off the unmentionable. We smoked a lot of dope, drank a lot of wine and listened to lots of old Nick Drake records, sitting there playing backgammon on the bed together.

Once, far too stoned on some sticky black Nepalese Temple Ball she had gotten her hands on, we ended up in the bed together. Lou was big and heavy, twice my size and nearly twice my age. I didn't care. She had been decent to me, the first person to be so for some time, and yet she hardly even knew who I was. That's real kindness.

Burning Spear was booming out of the stereo as we rolled around on the bed, giggling like half-wits. Then I had one of her large, milky breasts in my mouth, trying to squash as much of it into me as I could, my hand between her legs, probing. She was dry so I licked my fingers then put them back. Now she was wet and she took my hardening cock in her hand and guided me in. I began sawing away. It was 1983. I had not fucked anybody since the '70s. I gave her five or six quick stabs and came immediately, my cock jerking around uncontrollably inside her like a maddened snake. Then I collapsed on top of her, unable to move.

Mainly, though, we watched TV. But even that Lou was able to bring a certain ambience to. They began a rerun of the *Brideshead Revisited* series, and she would go out and buy half a dozen quail's eggs and a half-bottle of sparkling white wine for us to have while we watched. Then another time they were showing *Key Largo* and she turned up the central heating in the flat to full, closed all the windows, and we sat there doing our best to sweat along with Bogie.

I didn't want to say anything that would get my arse kicked out the door, but inside I felt a certain elation building. Not only was I clean, but I was convinced there was no way on earth I was going back to it now. I had seen the light, brothers and sisters, and like any recently converted sap, I was dying to tell everybody all about it.

But I knew if Louise caught me spouting that shiny-happy-people shit, I'd be out the door, and that would mean finding a place of my own to rent, which would mean getting a job and dah dah dah . . . I may have been straight but that didn't mean I had to be stupid.

Or did it? It was the '80s, after all, the most stupid decade since the '50s. People, it seemed, were prepared to pay good money for almost anything, as long as it was dressed right. And the more stupid, the better. Look at Duran Duran. Look at Bowie and 'Let's Dance'. Look at JR and Joan Collins and Margaret Thatcher and Ronald Reagan . . . What a vulgar, unconvincing bunch of arse-sucking stupidity.

Maybe there was something in that. Maybe I could find a way to sell my own inanity. I rolled a joint and thought about it . . .

6

Bored Again

I had been straight for nearly a year, signing on and working on the side for a catering agency in Acton. As far as the catering boys were concerned, my name was Michael Black and my story was that I'd been living in Ireland for the past couple of years, working in restaurants and pubs. That's why they'd had so much trouble finding my National Insurance Number and P45. Well, you know what those bastards are like over there. Probably lost it on their way to the pub. It meant that I was always paying Emergency Tax on my wages, which meant taking home a little less each week than I should, but that was all right. I had the dole to fill in the gaps.

As a 'kitchen porter' – catering jargon for dishwasher and general dogsbody – I got sent out to a lot of different places: hotels, offices, factories. But once there I found they were mostly the same: dull, unimaginative little worlds run on strict hierarchical lines – the tall-hatted chefs and their pink-fingered apprentices at the top of the table, the grubby-aproned kitchen porters at the bottom, and all the fat, older women gossiping and laughing and scheming in between.

I usually sat with the women at tea-breaks, smoking cigarettes and listening to them prattle on about their husbands, their children, their pets, what someone said, what someone should have said, on and on, their mouths barely closing, even for food. They had few doubts and many certainties, and I tried to imagine their husbands climbing into bed with them every night, still getting it in the ear as they pulled back the sheets. No wonder the pubs and the madhouses were always full.

But it was cheap, easy work, with no extra demands on you once you'd fled the place each day. The best time was when I got sent to Richmond ice-rink for a couple of weeks. I was on the evening shift, working on my own in the kitchen, just a couple of the women on the counter out front. Mainly, the kids wanted crisps, chocolates, cigarettes, Cokes, all the stuff you got from the counter. The only time I was needed was when they wanted chips. The menu offered all kinds of things – steaks, sausages, chicken, ribs, fish – but all they ever wanted was chips.

The rest of the time, there wasn't much to it. I started buying a little quarter-bottle of vodka on my way in every afternoon, to help pass the time. Every now and then I'd nip into the toilets for a quick slug of the voddy and a fast cigarette. Then I started bringing a book into the bogs with me. I began to spend longer and longer in there. Some habits were harder to break than others.

By the end of the two weeks, I was so drunk, I didn't give a fuck. I stood at the chip-fryer, fag in mouth, a half-empty bottle of voddy on the table next to me, a book in one hand and a large basket of hot greasy chips in the other. Nobody said anything. Then, before I left, I took half a dozen large steaks from the freezer, a couple of frozen chickens, and a dozen or so beefburgers and wrapped them all up in a bin-liner and placed them in my bag. I didn't even bother to hide them but still nobody said anything. It was the best job I'd ever had. (When, some years later, I heard they were going to tear the old ice-rink down, I was very sad. A new, more efficient world is not necessarily good news for everyone.)

After that, things went downhill at the agency. Most proper kitchens start work somewhere between six and seven in the morning, which meant dragging your poor, disbelieving bones out of bed somewhere between five and six. It was an almost impossible hurdle to overcome, and every day that I actually managed it was like a wicked miracle to me. Completely distraught, utterly bewildered, I would stagger down the icy black streets of dawn towards the tube station like a man shot through the head by an arrow. I was always terribly hungover and the train journey in would be a nightmare – constantly falling asleep and missing my stop, then blacking out on the train coming back again and missing it a second time. Once, I woke up back at the station I had started at, but on the train going the other way. I didn't know what the fuck. Just accepted it. Life without heroin was full of surprises.

Some mornings when I awoke, of course, it was simply too much. A gun to the head would not have made me move from that warm, dark spot. Let the job go to fucking hell, I thought. I'd had my turn. I wouldn't even bother to phone in sick, just grope for the off-switch on the alarm-clock without opening my eyes, then turn over and go straight back to sleep.

It was winter, dark and cold out there, and I began to miss more and more days. The agency was not happy. I got a bad name and they started farming me out on the 7 a.m. to 3 p.m. shift at Heathrow Airport, known as one of the worst jobs on the books.

It was this big, aircraft-hangar-type building, only it didn't house aeroplanes, it was just one big kitchen. All the in-flight meals for all the various airlines were made there. It didn't matter which airline you went on, or what class you flew, whatever they gave you originated on a tray somewhere inside this building.

More like a factory than a kitchen, it was a big, twenty-four-hour-a-day operation, divided into three eight-hour shifts. My job was to scrub the giant-size pots and pans they cooked all the food in. Some of the pots stood almost as tall as a man, while the sinks were four-foot-deep moats which you stood guard at, up to your shoulders all day in heavy industrial detergent and hot, greasy brown water. They were hard motherfuckers to get clean, too. You went through pad after pad of tough wire-wool, scraping the skin off your hands, losing your nails, burning your skin, and still you could not get them quite clean. You moved on, hoping no one would notice, but sometimes they did and the pots would be brought back for you to scrub again.

It was hopeless and insane. There was no time for lingering in the toilets, either. The dirty pots and pans would stand in a tall hill beside you, and when you finished your shift, no matter how many you had scrubbed or how tired you were feeling, the hill never seemed to get any smaller. Sometimes it appeared to have grown even larger. It was a most discouraging sight to send you on your way home each night, knowing you had just brutally murdered eight hours of your life, apparently for nothing. Every time I heard or saw a plane go by, I imagined shooting it down.

The only alternative, as ever, seemed to be to try and get back into the music business somehow. I thought about it once or twice but just couldn't see it. *Sounds* were unlikely to offer me a third crack of the whip, and all of the others were out of the question. I hadn't read an *NME* for years. I hadn't bought a record for years. I didn't even own a typewriter.

No, fuck that. Those days were through. There had to be something else. But before I could figure out what it was, I'd let go of the reins again and let somebody else decide for me . . .

*

Her name was Maria, but it could have been almost anything. Celibate for most of the four years I had been a junkie, I longed not just for sex with a beautiful woman but for some kind of . . . *involvement*. I was twenty-five and most of my new-ish, straight-ish friends had girlfriends or boyfriends. A couple I knew had even got married. I wasn't that far gone yet, but I was looking for something. Then I met Maria – Spanish Maria, they called her – and I convinced myself I'd found it.

Poor Maria. She was beautiful, dark, Mediterranean, with long, dyed-red hair: a walking male sex fantasy. Even the gay boys stopped and stared in shocked admiration as she sauntered by. She looked like the young Sophia Loren. Women, too, could not take their astonished eyes off her. The whole street shook with her vibrations. But that had been the case since she was a child. Maria knew there was no great talent in beauty and, to her credit, she aspired to be something more than just a goddess.

She was a painter, she said, and had just been accepted for a place at St Martin's School of Art. She was twenty-four, a late starter, and determined to make up for lost time. She was also a speed-freak and an alcoholic, but I hadn't figured that out yet.

We never officially moved in with each other; we just met at a gig one night, got roaring, singing drunk together, and woke up in the same bed the next day. Maria was sexy and funny and quite intelligent, and I was very pleased. What she saw in me, I didn't like to think about. I had been honest about my recent past but it had just rolled over her. She was more interested in the parts where I'd met and interviewed rock stars. I tried to explain that I wasn't into that any more and that my working for the catering agency was merely a convenient bolt-hole while I rested up and decided what else to do. But she couldn't get into that at all. Instead, she always introduced me to her new college friends as 'a writer'. But then they would ask what I'd done lately and I'd watch their embarrassed expressions ice over as I tried to explain about being a kitchen porter and resting up and so on.

Maria hated that and I quickly realised I would have to do something about it if I wanted to hold on to her. And I did, I did. I was crazy about the fucking bitch. I knew she didn't feel the same way about me – she'd told me so enough times. But knowing it wasn't 'real' love only made me want to fake it more. I had become diseased by her. Worse than any smack addiction; neither Mandy nor any doctor would be able to help me now.

I clung on and, as the months passed, I got used to Maria coming home later and later each night from college. She was always drunk, of course, always out of her head on speed, and always surrounded by at least two or three of the younger art-school boys she was now hanging out with. They were always very fashionably dressed, very good-looking, very relaxed. They would loll about the place smoking dope and making clever jokes about Clemente and Schnabel and a lot of other modern art-whore types I'd never heard of. I didn't know shit about art but I knew exactly where this crowd was coming from. None of them would ever end up as a kitchen porter.

And they were always about to go off somewhere . . . Amsterdam, for the Van Gogh museum, Paris for the Pompidou Centre, New York for a shot of the real thing . . . and so on and so forth. Maria lapped it up. I was pleased for her. I just felt bad I didn't share her enthusiasm any more, her innocence, her ignorance. I had arrived too late, that's all. Now, somehow, without noticing, I had become the oldest guy in the room. I wasn't sure I liked it either but there it was.

Then, a few mornings later, half-running down the road in the pissing 6 a.m. rain, late, late, late for work again, still drunk and waiting for the hangover to kick in, my piles killing me, I started to think maybe I'd missed something here. Taken it all a bit too seriously, perhaps. Or just allowed my smack habit to soil my attitude. If Maria and her paint-smeared college brats knew so fucking little, why was it my arse running down the road in the freezing cold every morning? When did I get to do *my* paintings?

Then that day, as I stood there at the moat, I moved the giant pots around in my mind and tried to scrub away the shit to find some of the happier memories from my time in the biz . . . celebrating my twenty-first birthday at the Savoy, nipping at strawberries and cocaine with Phil and Robbo . . . seeing my writing in print for the first time in *Sounds*, my name in black at the top of the page . . . jumping through the TV screen to America and other places that had now returned to being out of my reach . . . getting into the most expensive shitholes for free . . .

I knew that if I allowed myself to think too long about it I would talk myself out of it. But I also knew that Maria would be impressed by all that crap, and decided not to look any further than that. Somehow, I had to find a way to give it another shot. And to hell with the hell of it.

I thought it over, what I could say. I still had one or two names and numbers left in my address book, if I could find it, that would still probably take my calls, and when I got home that day, I got down on my hands and knees and dug it out from under the bed with all the rest of the crap. It was the first time I'd looked through it seriously for years . . . caressing the dry pages with my puckered dishwasher's fingertips . . . *hmmm, hmmm* . . .

I lifted the phone and dialled. It rang. I don't know what else I expected. Then, when I'd finished that call, I picked it up and made another. I was getting busy. I was getting real. When Maria came home from college that night, I'd show her something she hadn't seen before . . .

*

Using a similar rap to the one I'd given Alan Lewis on *Sounds* all those years before – I've been in the biz, I'm great, I could write you stuff that your other guys can't – I'd actually talked two different magazines, *Time Out* and *Kerrang!*, into giving me something to write for them. Of course, it helped that the people I'd spoken to were both old drug-buddies from the PR days, but I didn't bother to mention that part to Maria and it's fair to say she thought I was pretty fucking far out for a couple of days there, at least while the novelty lasted. We even fucked a couple of times, an increasingly rare privilege, by then, for her to bestow on me.

The *Time Out* piece involved a phone interview with the singer of a new band from Manchester called The Smiths. Their second single, 'This Charming Man', had just been released and, like everybody else, I admired both its black, northern humour and its ringing, guitar-shaped sound.

Morrissey was not yet the household name he would later become, and when I asked him for his full name and age, he sighed deeply. 'Stephen,' he said dolefully, 'but I'd rather you didn't put that in the article. I've not been Stephen for a very, very long time now.'

'And how old are you?' I repeated.

'Oh . . . somewhere between fourteen and forty,' he replied coquettishly.

But that was as witty as he got and after talking on the phone for twenty minutes I got the impression of a moany Mancunian as nondescript as his band's name, sitting alone in his room listening to old Velvet Underground albums and watching *Coronation Street*. I yawned and cut the interview short. They only wanted 750 words anyway.

When Maria got home from college that night, I told her about it.

'What was he like?' she asked eagerly.

'Oh, you know,' I said, 'boring.'

'Oh, come on!'

'What do you mean?'

'I bet you loved it!'

'What?'

'I bet you loved it, sitting there, chatting away with a pop star.'

'He's hardly a fucking pop star.'

'Yet! Did you use this phone?' she asked, pointing.

'Obviously.'

'Oooh!' she said, and picked up the phone receiver and started rubbing it against her crotch. 'Oooh!' I couldn't tell if she was joking or not. Or maybe I could but didn't want to.

The *Kerrang!* story involved a face-to-face interview with Trevor Rabin, the new guitarist in Yes. Rabin was from South Africa and as a teenager he'd been in what he described as a 'South African Bay City Rollers'. Then, in the late-'70s, he'd released a couple of solo albums where he sang and wrote all the songs and played all the instruments. They were all right, if you liked that sort of thing. After that, he'd made it for a while as a producer, which is how I'd first met him, briefly, when he produced the first Wild Horses album. Now, four years on, he was in the reformed Yes. Well, well. What a guy. A career musician.

We were to meet in Rabin's room at the Kensington Hilton. Maria would take some snaps. I hadn't asked the magazine or the record company and I wasn't entirely sure of the arrangements, but Maria had gone on and on about it and at least she had a camera. I hadn't owned a tape-recorder since I'd sold my last one for a gram. The camera, I felt, would at least lend an air of authenticity to the proceedings. Something I knew I would have difficulty summoning up on my own.

I needn't have worried. I could tell by the way Rabin's face lit up the moment he caught sight of Maria that he wasn't about to turn us away. Sometimes beauty can be cold, aloof, insurmountable. Maria's wasn't like that. It was warm and inviting. She just looked like sex. She had come in her eyes. And, like the rest of us, Rabin saw it immediately.

Six foot, puppy-faced, tanned, late-twenties, limp-dick handshake, familiar in the way of pampered sidemen not as used to the spotlight as they would like you to believe, Rabin ushered us into his room like long-lost friends, distant cousins maybe, from the poor, cross-eyed side of the family.

He offered us a drink and I started to warm to him. Beers for us;

Diet Coke for him. Then the nearly famous guitarist propped himself up against the pillows on his bed, I perched myself at a table by the only window, and Maria cat-crawled around the room with her camera, the three of us pretending we knew what we were doing.

I produced a pen and a sheaf of papers and very carefully wrote at the top of the first page: Trevor Rabin interview, Page 1.

'What, no tape-recorder?' he asked, all business suddenly.

'No, I prefer to take notes. Tape-recorders can lie,' I said as a joke, but he didn't get it. Maria shot me a glance: *don't blow it.* Snap, snap. Rabin nodded and let it go.

I sat there firing questions. Nothing tricky, of course, mostly stuff I reckoned Rabin would expect to hear, then making as if to write it all down, scribbling down one- or two-word gibberish I vaguely hoped I would be able to make sense of later. The interview went on for nearly an hour. Long by my standards back then. Towards the end, I ran out of paper and had to ask Rabin if he had any. He did.

My clearest memory was of Maria kneeling on the bed, leaning backwards, her miniskirt riding up against the tops of her thighs. It was an interesting technique: showing him her knickers then taking pictures of him trying to pretend he hadn't noticed. You could tell he liked it, too. He sat there on the bed sucking in his cheeks and smiling like somebody enjoying the smell of his own farts. Snap, snap, snap.

As we left, Rabin asked Maria for her phone number. 'So I can look over the shots, see if there's anything I might want to buy off you.' When she only gave him the number of her college, I didn't know whether to be pleased or not. I am not the jealous kind but very little about Maria pleased me in those days, particularly when it came to other men. I had answered the phone to too many already.

Downstairs in the Hilton lobby, we let all the pent-up, fussed-in air out of our lungs and decided to treat ourselves to a proper drink. Large ones. I knew through experience that most of Maria's pictures were doomed to be out of focus or in some other way unusable, and I had no idea yet whether I would actually be able to fake a story out of the encounter. But there was an odd sense of triumph in the air. We'd done it, that was all. Now it was over, for better or worse, and we were going to have a drink and celebrate. Think up what to tell our friends.

We sat down on two stools at the bar, lit cigarettes, ordered drinks and looked around.

'Wow,' Maria sighed.

'Wow, what?' I said.

'Wow, just . . .' She shrugged her shoulders and smiled, her eyes glittering like cold, distant stars. Clearly, Maria had been impressed by the experience. She submerged a hand into the vortex of her hell-red hair and crossed her legs.

'You've got to admit, he's a pretty amazing guy,' she said.

'You think so?'

'Definitely! Why? Don't you?'

I shrugged manfully. 'Why? Because he's a rock star?' It was no stupider than any of the questions I had asked Rabin.

'Oh, come off it!' she laughed, tail flashing like a cat's. 'You mean just because he's rich and handsome? Girls like that!' Her laughter was full of come, too.

I decided to keep the peace and keep my mouth shut. Maria regarded me with womanly contempt.

'Whatcha think I'm gonna do, run up there and jump into bed with him?'

I could think of her doing a lot worse than that but I decided not to say any of it. Outside there was still some daylight left but I could already see the evening dwindling before our eyes.

*

It took me three weeks to write the story. Two weeks to find someone with a typewriter I could borrow and a week to actually sit down and rap it out. In the end, I borrowed a crusty old Remmington from a reluctant aunt of Maria's. Several of the key-caps were missing but the ribbon was still good and though it hurt your fingers to type certain letters, if you wanted it bad enough you could make it work. I wanted it.

I had moved out of Lou's place some months before. She had started getting into the gear again and once when I came home from the pub with some friends she was face-down on the floor, out cold with the needle still in her arm. As chance would have it, one of the guys I'd brought with me was a medical student at Charing Cross and he immediately went to work. Taking the needle out of her arm, he rolled Lou over on her back, tilted back her head and began giving her mouth-to-mouth resuscitation. Then he stopped and began pummelling her chest, then back to her mouth again, then her chest again, then her mouth. I thought: 'She's not gonna make it.'

Then, just like that, she began breathing again, her large, heavy breasts rising and falling rapidly as she sucked in air. I wanted to help but I couldn't move. I had turned into a statue, transfixed in the gory moment. She started to come round. She smiled up at me and said something, but I couldn't stand it and walked out. I thought of the time it had happened to me. What would Mandy have done if I'd stopped breathing?

I just couldn't handle it any more and a week later I'd moved out of there and into a small, one-room bedsit in Chiswick. It was next door to a pub, and after I'd met Maria we got into the habit of going into the pub, ordering our drinks, then taking them back to the little room with us on a tray. The night I started to write the Rabin piece, I bought two pints of Guinness in the pub, then walked back to the room, a glass in each hand, and set them down by the Remmington. I rolled myself a joint. Made it a good one. Lit it. Inhaled, exhaled.

I began typing . . . *'Trevor Rabin is a man of many parts, but none more demanding than the one he is about to play in the reformed line-up of Yes.'* I stopped and looked at it. What shit, I thought. That'll do!

I carried it on for a few days, giving it an hour here and there whenever I had a drink in my hand, or a smoke. I did my best to say something of my own, but it was never going to be easy. Rock magazines are hardly the place to allow one's true feelings to show through, even if you knew how. Instead, I grab-bagged something together that I hoped would (a) show what a useful wordman I could be, and (b) please God, ensure a steady stream of similar such assignments in the future.

What I couldn't decipher from the notes I took or couldn't remember, which was a lot, I made up. Who it was or even what it was I was writing about was no longer the point. It was all about trying to prove to Maria that I was an artist, too. That I was worth one of her fucks.

Then it was done. My favourite words – 'The End'. I delivered it personally, eleven pages of A4 along with a handful of Maria's black-and-white prints. It was lunchtime and nobody was there but the editor's desk was pointed out to me and I left the package on it, wrote a brief hope-ya-like-it bit of grovel on the envelope and walked briskly out the door, suffering from that peculiar deflated feeling you always get whenever a piece of work, no matter how good or bad, is finally handed in. I was back in the half-world. Nothing doing; nothing to be done. Except wait.

I checked my pocket for change, decided I had enough for either a pint or a packet of fags. I sensibly decided on the fags. (I always found it easier to blag drinks than fags.) Bought 'em and lit one up. Found the tube. Made it home. The next morning I was up again at six, wondering if I'd dreamt the whole thing.

Then the *Time Out* piece ran and they gave me an album to review. Maria flipped. She took a photograph of the page, then blew it up to giant-size, stuck in on a canvas and began painting over it. She turned it into a collage she called *Fame*. Then a few weeks after that, the *Kerrang!* piece ran. Four pages of words, but not one of Maria's pictures. That soured it for her but, in truth, I was glad. This was my trip. A little envy might go a long way . . .

'It's a crap magazine, anyway,' she said, tossing it on the floor. Maybe. But it was a crap magazine with four pages of my words in it. There would also be a crap cheque to come, too. Things were looking up.

*

After the Rabin piece, the magazine had a brainstorm and asked me if I'd like to interview Kate Bush. Kate Bush in *Kerrang!* would be 'off-beat', they said. Not something you'd normally expect to find there. Therefore, they wanted someone not entirely connected with the magazine to do the piece. I thought it was a great idea, of course. Whatever you say, boss.

We were to meet Kate at her dance-studio in south London, me and an alky photographer I knew called Roy. We drove down in Roy's old car, smoking joints and nipping at a bottle. Roy knew even less than I did about the current music scene but he loved photographing women. He talked about the tricks he used to make them look even more beautiful in photographs.

'If they haven't got very big tits, you get them to bend over and squeeze their elbows together,' he explained. 'Or if they're starting to knock on a bit and they've got a lot of lines on their face, you make sure not to light them from above, but from below. That way the lines don't show as much. And then I use a very fine silk stocking over the lens, which makes their skin look even more creamy and perfect.'

Roy had it all worked out. He was another kind of artist. Then when we got there, we were so mellow from the dope and the booze, and Kate was so nice – big tits, not many lines – I completely forgot what it was the magazine had told me they wanted me to ask her and went off on creamy little female tangents like whether she hennaed or crimped her hair (no), or whether it was just naturally red and gypsy-ish (yes); whether she danced at clubs the way she danced in her videos (no); whether she would like children (yes, one day); and whether animals had souls (yes).

She kept trying to drag the conversation back round to music. 'I really like that last Def Leppard album,' she said at one point. But neither Roy nor I had heard it ourselves and we just sat there grinning, trying to think of what to say.

'Could you ever see yourself making music that was a bit rockier?' I asked eventually. 'Say, like Def Leppard?'

'Oh, yes,' she replied earnestly. 'I don't think I'd ever do anything that was out-and-out heavy metal, but I can definitely see myself getting a bit heavier in the future, yes. I love the sound of the electric guitar.'

I couldn't help but smile. She was trying so hard to be helpful, yet all I really wanted to ask her was if I could kiss her, just once, full on the lips, my mouth on hers, my hand on her breast, squeezing her . . . just to see what that would be like. I began to understand what Maria had said at the Hilton a little better. It would be a major turn-on to fuck a star. Like fucking the television. Like fucking God. Or, in this case, a goddess. You could see how easily it could be mistaken for being the ultimate attainment.

I asked some more questions: do you pray (yes), do you believe in marriage (depends), will you ever perform live again (no more tours, no). I finally ran out of ways to keep her talking, to keep her looking into my eyes. Then Roy took over. Kate didn't need the tit-treatment but he had her bending over anyway, dirty bastard. I began to see why 'celebrities' hate being interviewed and photo-graphed so much. You really can't trust the press. None of us. Not when it comes to pop music and not when it comes to anything else. We all arrive with something in our heads and whatever you tell us it's just a little more paint to squirt at the canvas and push around into the shapes we want – how we want and when we want.

As the interview was for *Kerrang!* – some record company dick-head had probably waved a demographic at her manager that told him something like 70 per cent of heavy metal fans also buy Kate Bush records – Kate had probably been expecting a couple of anoraked eighteen-year-olds. Instead, she got a couple of bish-bash-bosh merchants masquerading as journalists, out for a lark and making it all up as they went along. But she wore it well and when we left that day she told us to make sure we sent her some copies of the magazine when the story appeared. Who was she trying to kid? I almost felt sorry for her. Such a nice girl.

'Nice smile, nice personality,' said Roy, as we drove away. 'And very nice tits. A photographer's dream, really,' he smiled. That made both of us photographers. I rolled another joint and he uncapped the bottle. We drove along smiling and feeling pleased with our-selves like two cunts with the cure for cancer.

When I came to write the article, I really tried to throw some-thing into it this time. Not real feelings, of course, but something that would make the story stick out even more than just the fact it was about Kate Bush. I didn't really succeed, but the whole thing was daft enough to grab the readers' attention, and letters began pouring into the office, either praising the article to the high heavens or demanding my head on a stick. From an editorial point of view, this was gold dust, and suddenly *Kerrang!* was on the phone every week with something new for me to do. Not just features but reviews and other bits and pieces. It was the most work I'd done as a writer since the old *Sounds* days.

Kerrang! at that point was still just a fortnightly magazine, so it didn't mean a lot of money, but it was still more than I was getting as a kitchen porter, and the day I got the cheque for the Rabin piece – £160 – I called the agency and told them to take me off their books. There would be no more six o'clock mornings for me.

Writing for *Kerrang!* was, in essence, just another portering gig; better hours, better fun and better pay, for sure for sure, but still no more than a glorified stop-gap until I could figure out some other way to make it. I was nearly twenty-six. I didn't want to see myself writing for 'The Bible of Heavy Metal', as it billed itself, for any longer than I had to, and at first, all my work was done at long distance. Albums would arrive in the post. They were all by bands with names like Thunder King and Head Hunter and they were all so unbelievably atrocious I couldn't bring myself to listen to more than a minute or so of each track. I'd never heard so many terrible albums in one go and I would sit at home with the knackered old Remmington, smoking joints and thinking of ways to describe this ridiculous rubbish.

I knew I'd have to be careful, though. I noticed that similar-sounding albums got pretty good reviews elsewhere in the magazine. I reminded myself that it didn't matter what I actually thought of the albums, the bottom line was not blowing the gig. In the end, I used to just flip a coin. Heads – it's great. Tails – it's shite. And whatever it came up – heads or tails – would be the review I would write. It was fantastic fun. Mad little 250-word poems about rock and what it meant and what it didn't mean, with as many drug references as I could cram in and whatever else was passing through my weary, addled mind. Then I'd take it down to the photo-copy shop, duplicate all the pages and post the originals to the magazine.

Mostly, it was gibberish, but the cheques kept coming and I got to stay in bed longer and longer. It was even better than Richmond ice-rink. The only time I had to go anywhere was when they asked me to review a gig. It was easy money but I always hated having to go to gigs. If it was the Hammersmith Odeon or one of the other big theatres, you weren't allowed to buy booze during the show in those days and that meant bringing in your own, which was a drag, 'cos then everybody hassled you for some and you still ended up dry. And if it was a club and you could get served, it was still bad because once the band came on, everything else – conversation, jokes, a little back and forth – it all had to cease for the duration. Everything stopped for the band and I always hated that. Someone once described golf as a good walk spoiled. For me, gigs were always a good night out ruined.

The first one they sent me to was Judas Priest at the Hammy Odeon. Don't ask me what album they were promoting or what tour it was, they were lucky I turned up at all. I couldn't interest Maria in the other ticket so I took Gianni, an Italian friend who didn't know what he was letting himself in for. Gianni was a smooth soul boy and a dedicated clubber. His drug was clothes and I don't know what sort of 'show' he thought we were going to but he met me on the steps of the Odeon wearing a new, three-piece Armani suit, shiny black shoes and a tie. A gold cigarette-holder waved from his mouth. Sitting in the booth at some nightclub at three in the morning he'd have looked magnificent. There would have been an unbelievably beautiful girl sitting on either side of him, pressing their long teenage legs against him. Here on the steps of the Hammy Odeon, however, surrounded by the metal hordes, he looked like the enemy. Several large members of the tribe – beards, belts, Viking haircuts – were already sniffing round him suspiciously as I arrived.

When we handed in our tickets at the door, the bouncer looked at him and said: 'You sure you're in the right place, mate?' Gianni just nodded, very pleased with himself. 'I have come to dance!' he cried, then sashayed past the bemused bouncer, and into the dark, smoke-filled hall. Gianni always loved to be the centre of attention, even if it was just from a bunch of long-haired, denim-clad Neanderthals. This was going to be a good night, he decided. I wasn't so sure.

I had to laugh though when the show began with the much-anticipated explosion of noise and lights and Gianni's poised, suited form was lit up momentarily, standing solemnly in the front row, taking it all in. He looked like Dr Livingstone surrounded by his hairy savages.

He was determined to get into it. 'Let the ceremony begin!' he cried, as the band began roaring into the first number.

The only person in the whole place who looked more ridiculous was the Judas Priest singer, Rob Halford. Rob hadn't come out of the closet yet – not publicly, at least (we would have to wait another fifteen years for that) – and maybe it was because of the frustration of that, I don't know, but the way he dressed and the way he strutted about the stage back then was pure gay biker.

Dressed from head to foot in tight black leathers, he arrived on stage on the back of a motorcycle, wreathed in dry-ice and revving it up as though he were about to ride the damn thing straight out into the audience. But there was never any danger of that. Rob was far too much the old pro. The bike was just part of the costume, dear. Something to get the kiddies going and as a gift to the photographers.

His hands wrapped in black studded gloves, a ridiculous New York policeman's cap perched at a jaunty angle on his bald head, Rob thrived on Making An Entrance. As the smoke cleared and he climbed off the bike and began pacing about the stage, you noticed the ensemble was topped off with a pair of naff sunglasses (the type cool dads wear) and that he was holding a long bullwhip, which he would thrash the lip of the stage with every now and then.

The rest of the band were your standard metal sidemen. They all wore versions of Rob's leatherman kit but without the more obviously gay accoutrements such as the cap and the whip. They were Old School. Lots of hair sculpting and lots of practice in front of the mirror. You could tell. They had two guitarists, and when one crossed to the left, the other crossed to the right. Sometimes they stood together, headbanging over their guitars in unison, or sometimes they stood back to back. The bass player looked older, heavier, and didn't move around as much, just swayed his body back and forth from the waist up. He had a big moustache and he looked like a pub landlord. It didn't matter. The show was action-packed with big, booming beginnings and long, strangulated endings, the lights and explosions going off non-stop throughout. They had their moves worked out and they made them. It was like watching an old video. You could have wound it backwards or forwards as much as you liked, it would always be exactly the same.

All around us though, people were freaking out, throwing their heads and their arms around like this was the real thing. It was confusing. I couldn't decide which of us was having the more authentic experience: me in my boredom, or the rest of the audience in their apparent rapture. Even Gianni was getting something out of it that I wasn't. I decided it must be me.

'Let's get out of here,' I said, grabbing Gianni by the arm.

'But I'm just getting into it!' he protested.

'Fuck off. You're just taking the piss. Let's go.'

That was a hard review to write. Apart from the fact I missed most of the show, I still didn't know whether it should be a good review or a bad one. I decided to go with the kids. I smoked a joint and phoned the review in off the top of my head.

'You really liked it then?' said Malcolm, one of the guys I used to speak to on the phone up there.

'Yeah,' I said. 'It was rocking.'

'We didn't see you at the after-show party. We saw you arrive with, er, that bloke you came in with . . .'

'My girlfriend's brother,' I lied. 'He'd never been to a rock show before but he really liked it.'

'Oh, right. Well, anyway, we came looking for you after the show but we couldn't find you.'

'Yeah, I had to go. Gianni – my girlfriend's brother – had to get up early for work the next day.'

'Oh, right. It was a great show, though, wasn't it?'

'The best I've seen in a long while.'

*

The easiest gig of all was when they sent you to review a film. I went to the first couple, but they were nearly all dull Sunday-morning preview screenings in Soho. You only got paid about twenty pounds for a film review and I soon hit on a better plan. I started giving my preview tickets to friends who would get a buzz out of going maybe once or twice. Then when they got home, they would ring me and tell me all about it and I would rattle something out from there.

It was a great plan but it came unravelled the time I sent my mate Deadly Pete – so called because of the 'deadly' nature of his personality – to see *Supergirl* for me. When we spoke on the phone the next day, all he could say was, 'Yeah, it was great, yeah.'

'So what actually happened then?'

'Happened? Well . . . I don't know. You saw her fly and all that, you know . . . and there were some baddies.'

'Tell me about the baddies.'

'Er, there were two of them. No, three of them. No, er, no, three, yeah. And they were great, you know.'

'No, I don't know. Great in what way?'

'Oh, you know, funny and that.'

'What were their names?'

'Oh, blimey, what were they . . .?'

Jesus Christ. Even I couldn't cobble anything out of that. I went down to the newsagent and bought a copy of *Time Out*. Turned to the film pages. There it was. A review of *Supergirl*. I read it and wrote out something much the same. Handed it in.

'That *Supergirl* review you did was really good,' Malcolm told me the next time we spoke.

'Yeah?'

'Yes, excellent. Would you like to do another one?'

'Yeah, sure.'

This time it was *Conan the Barbarian*. There was no way I was going to sit still for that fucking old tosh. Luckily, *Time Out* was a weekly mag, so the *Time Out* reviews always appeared first. I became a regular reader of the film pages. Sometimes, just for the hell of it, I would deliberately say the opposite of what the *Time Out* reviewer had said. But the details – director, plot, gossip, so forth –

and any other general points of interest were always the same. It was such a cosy number I couldn't believe I was the only one who'd ever thought of it, and I wondered how many of the big day-to-day boys, the newspaper cunts, got up to similar stuff. Well, you can't be everywhere at once, can you? And I still had Maria to contend with.

Then one day when I rang in, the guys at *Kerrang!* asked me if I had any ideas of my own for stories that I wanted to put forward.

Ideas? Hmmm, tricky . . . Ideas were not really my thing. Putting a match to it was usually my best idea. In every sense. I just wanted a job that didn't waste you too much. The same as anybody.

'I'm easy,' I said. 'What's coming up that's big?'

7

Free Money

It was the morning of Live Aid, in Philadelphia, and despite our vicious hangovers we were getting ready to feed the world. Thankfully, there was no Geldof-figure in America to bore us with their tantrums, but still it was wearying the way every person you met felt obliged to mouth some staggeringly repulsive guff about what a 'great day' this would be. Let the crowd send all their money to Africa, then go back to their racist little lives. So what? The crowd would always love a circus. Me, I wanted to stay in bed and watch the other channel. Fat chance. As usual, the job had gotten in the way.

This time I had some really big pots on my hands. Along with Led Zeppelin, Crosby, Stills & Nash, The Who, Status Quo and several other old grizzlies, Ozzy and the three other original members of Black Sabbath had agreed to reform especially for the occasion, and in exchange for a four-page feature in *Kerrang!*, Sharon had flown me out to Philadelphia to meet up with Ozzy and accompany them all to the show.

We were staying at the Four Seasons hotel – us and all the others like Simple Minds, Bryan Adams, The Pretenders, The Power Station, The Thompson Twins . . . The crowds outside were kept at bay by security and the really big boys like Bob and Eric and Jimmy and Keith were nowhere to be seen. We might be feeding the world, but that didn't mean we would be changing places at the table.

'I know it's for a good cause but, to be honest, I don't really care,' Ozzy had admitted when we spoke on the eve of the show.

I had discovered that, once you'd got past the sad clown façade, Ozzy was one of the very few rock stars who always told you exactly what he thought. He was the first person I'd met since Mandy who really knew what a bucket of shit the whole business was, and wasn't afraid to express it. He was fearless – not through arrogance but more just a certain weariness. He hadn't just bought the T-shirt, it was his fucking picture on it . . .

'It's like my father used to say: during the war, everyone was friendly and helped each other, but as soon as the war ended they were back to being pricks again,' Ozzy said. 'And I bet there'll be people at the show who'll be telling each other to go fuck themselves again the next day.'

Did it matter, though, as long as the money was raised?

Yes and no. 'The thing is,' he said, 'they'll get the money, and food will be taken over and they'll feed them and they'll still fuckin' starve again! Because the money, no matter how much is raised today, won't last forever. I think that not only rock 'n' roll groups should do this, but industry, too – the IBMs and GECs. They should say, "All right, one week a year our output will go to charity," whatever that might be. I mean, they spend hundreds of millions on nuclear defence, but would they ever say, "Okay, let's save a hundred million today and feed these fuckers"? That's nothing to the government – it's not a piss in the ocean! It's like giving a tramp a dime. But, no, they'd rather burn leftover supplies of wheat than stop people dying. They crush billions and billions of apples back into the ground because of surplus stocks . . . I mean, I know it's only apples and they'd probably be bored stiff sitting back in the old desert eating a ton of fuckin' apples, but it's better than a fuckin' pile of dirt, ain't it?'

It was a poor joke, perhaps, but Ozzy wasn't the only artist who had expressed serious doubts about the true validity of the Live Aid concerts. Huey Lewis and the News, who were then huge in America, had actually pulled out of the show at the last minute after reports had been aired in the US that many of the supplies the London-based Band Aid Trust were sending to Africa were being left to rot in dusty, unguarded docks while more 'important' deliveries of weapons and ammunition were unloaded first.

And if Michael Jackson, Stevie Wonder, Dionne Warwick, Lionel Ritchie, Quincy Jones and all those other black supercats that regularly thanked God on their albums had thought enough of the project to record the buttock-clenching 'We Are The World', why didn't any of them put themselves forward for the actual show? Was it because they hadn't been asked? Or was it that they'd been asked but had turned it down?

Either way, something strange was going on here. If I'd been any kind of a reporter, I would have tried to dig a little deeper, perhaps, tried to unearth a few ungnawed bones. But I wasn't just any kind of reporter. I was Tarzan, swinging through the trees, grabbing at the first vine that came to hand, anything just to keep moving, keep me up there . . . above ground . . . yodelling.

I wasn't really interested in knowing anything except what time it ended and when I could leave. Ozzy was the same. Having just come out of the Betty Ford Clinic a few months before, he was still clinging to sobriety, but the ordeal of getting back together with the others in Sabbath, even for just three numbers, was starting to tell on him. You could see it in his bright, eager eyes as he watched us downing beers and shots in the hotel bar the night before the show. He looked like an animal in pain, suffering in silence, hoping the humans wouldn't notice. I gave him another month, tops, before he caved in and started drinking again.

In the meantime, just as it always had been, Ozzy's main line of defence was his sense of humour.

'I've still got me own bar at home,' he told me. 'Except it's got no booze in it. It's all Diet Cokes now, and I ask you, what's the good of having your own bar at home if you can't have any beer in it? It's like having a dartboard with no darts! That's what my life is now,' he said, looking round, 'a pool table with no balls . . .'

Being a natural-born comic had not only helped Ozzy dodge the blows in the school playground; it was what had given him the confidence to feel he could get up on a stage and entertain people. He'd always been one of those kids with a crowd around him, either laughing at him or hitting him.

As he once told me, 'I know I'm no fucking brain surgeon. I'm not what you'd call a really heavy songwriter. I'm not even that great a singer. It's not exactly what I'm known for, put it that way. With me, it's all the other stuff – the mad fucking stuff. That's what people think of when they think of me. Biting the head off a fuckin' bat! Getting pissed and getting stoned and arrested . . . all the crazy stuff. I don't mind. I only mind when they go on about Devil-worshipping and all that fuckin' crap. That really does my fuckin' head in, that does. Other than that, they can say what they fuckin' like, mate. It's probably true, most of it, anyway . . .'

*

Because the London Live Aid show had begun at midday in England – 7 a.m. Philly time – the American show had to start at some unbelievable time like eight in the morning.

I sat on the bed with my English muffin and clicked on the TV.

'Good morning, children of the '80s,' said Joan Baez from the stage at JFK Stadium, standing there like a schoolmarm waiting for ninety thousand well-brought-up young Americans to return her greeting.

They did. 'This is your Woodstock,' she said, like Mommy giving out the graduation presents, 'and it's long overdue.'

They loved that. It may not have meant much, but it was just what they wanted to hear. And Joanie being a living relic of that fabled world they call the 1960s, and this being America, where any excuse to indulge in sentimental, self-congratulatory old cock is welcomed with open, pleading arms, they went wild for it. They ate it up and made themselves sick on it, then bayed for more like the polite, eager-to-please children they were. 'Yeah!' said America, 'Awright!'

But in some strange way, the old girl was right. At thirty to fifty dollars a ticket for a globally televised one-day event policed by armed guards, Live Aid summed up the true spirit of rock – that is to say, of white Westernised society – in the '80s as surely as Woodstock had come to symbolise the same for the '60s. Only where then it had been 'peace' and 'love', the buzzwords now were 'money' and 'self-promotion'.

Nobody in the crowd would be taking their clothes off at Live

Aid. This wasn't really trippy, muddy, bare-titty Woodstock; this was just the new feel-good TV, with compères and ad breaks all pre-sold and built in; every ad-libbed link as tightly scripted as an episode of *Dynasty*.

Yes, the starving of Africa would be getting their money's-worth, but it was still a two-way street, like any other modern '80s deal. The artists at Live Aid may not have been paid for being there, but they *were* getting something in return, something even better than money to a bunch of rock stars already awash with cash: they were getting *fame*. You didn't have to be Paul McCartney to see Live Aid as an opportunity for massive, worldwide self-publicity on a scale previously undreamed of. And while it may, at least on paper, have been about feeding the world, Live Aid also helped feed the careers of all the major star turns we still remember best from that day.

The last time either Bowie or Jagger would have a No.1 single, with their Duran-ish cover of 'Dancin' In The Streets', Live Aid also temporarily resurrected the careers of Queen, Status Quo, Adam Ant, The Who, Elton John and many others, not least, Geldof himself. Who would remember Bob now, other than as the big-headed, mouthy twat from the crappy Boomtown Rats, if it hadn't been for Live Aid?

And it wasn't just the oldies who got the treatment. Live Aid made U2, particularly in America, where Bono's down-on-one-knee histrionics went down a storm. The band were already big, but Live Aid sent them supernova, and, like Sting, who would also forever after be associated with 'big' causes, U2 would never be starved of anything they wanted ever again.

What Ozzy and Sabbath were getting out of it, though, was harder to tell. A place in the history books? Or was there some-thing else cooking? Were the band planning to do as Deep Purple had the year before and cash in with a big reformation tour? An appearance on the bill at Live Aid would certainly have been the perfect platform for making such an announcement.

But Ozzy was adamant: 'No fuckin' way, mate!' he shook his head.

I pushed him for more. He rambled on a bit and then he finally got to it. 'At the end of the day, I have to ask myself: if Black

Sabbath had done as well as I'm doing now and kept hold of Ronnie Dio in the group or whatever, and I was where they left me, down and out in a fuckin' LA bar, would they give everything up just to bring me back into the group?'

He looked at me. We both knew the answer to that one . . .

'Christ,' he said, 'do you know how many years it took me to get out of that fuckin' mess with Sabbath? And all these cunts who do get back together, don't ever believe that it's for any reason other than the fuckin' money. If there was another reason, they'd never have called each other cunts and split up in the first place. No, bollocks to all that! I've got enough to worry about trying to kick this drink thing, you know?'

Ozzy and Sabbath were due on stage at the ludicrous time of 10 a.m. and I left my room that morning, still blinking into my hair, just as the TV showed Joan launching lugubriously into 'Amazing Grace'. I winced and looked forward to another long day.

Apart from the Zeppelin and Dylan crowds, who would arrive in limos, everybody else was being ferried back and forth from the hotel to the stadium in little white transit vans. Just as we were about to close the doors on ours, a middle-aged man with fair hair and long Elvis Presley sideburns came lumbering breathlessly up to the van and asked if he could squeeze in with us. We all moved up one and the van drove off.

'I'm Martin Chambers, by the way,' he announced.

'Oh, aye,' said Bill dolefully.

'You know? From The Pretenders?'

'Oh, aye. What do you do?'

'I'm the drummer.'

'Oh, aye.'

The van lapsed into silence. It was still early. There wasn't anything to say yet.

Martin leaned across the seat. 'You're Ozzy Osbourne, aren't you?' he asked.

'That's right, mate.'

'So the rest of you must be Black Sabbath,' he said, turning to look at me.

I nodded.

'I've always loved that song you did . . . "Paranoid", is it?' he asked, still looking at me.

'Go on, Mick. Tell 'im all about it,' Bill chuckled darkly.

Martin still hadn't got the joke, but sensed he'd gone wrong somewhere. Tried too hard, perhaps. Phew, those heavy metal guys!

He tried again. 'So what are you doing – just three numbers like the rest of us?'

'That's right,' said Ozzy with a straight face. 'But we've got a special surprise worked out for them. For an encore we're gonna come on and do "Food Glorious Food".'

The rest of the van began to titter. Martin looked vaguely disturbed. Then Ozzy broke into song: 'FOOD GLORIOUS FOOD! HOT SAUSAGE TOMATO!'

We all joined in. Martin smiled but wasn't sure. His face was contorted, like a man trying to have a shit. And failing. Then that quietened down and Bill started talking to Ozzy about the baby girl Sharon had recently given birth to.

'Were you there for the birth?' Martin asked.

Maybe he was nervous but the guy simply couldn't take a hint. Ozzy decided to give him another one.

'Was I fucking there?' Ozzy parroted. 'Was I fucking ever! Fuck me!' he cried. 'They tell you all about being there to hold the old lady's hand and help her breathe and all that shit, and then you get there and it's like a scene from *The Exorcist*! Blood and fucking guts everywhere! The doctors were on about giving her drugs for the pain, I was like, fuck that, give 'em to me! You fuckin' need something to get you through that, I tell you!'

Martin was like most people. They never really knew if Ozzy was joking or not. They never really would . . .

*

But at least Ozzy sober was someone you could be with. After our encounter at the Mont Calm three years before, I had planned never to set eyes on the fucker again. But then Lynn, an old friend of mine from our Virgin days, had begun working for Sharon, who was now Ozzy's wife as well as his manager. When I'd told Lynn what a disaster my last meeting with Ozzy had been, she had insisted I try again. I was like, no way. But she kept on. Ozzy wasn't anything like I pictured him, she said. He was one of the good guys. A real scream. I'd just got him on a bad day. Sure.

Reluctantly, though, just to please Lynn, who really was one of the good guys, I agreed to wipe the slate clean and meet up with Ozzy again some time. One fucking monkey noise, though, I warned her . . . But she promised: no monkeys. I almost believed her.

It had been in Rio de Janeiro, at the start of the year, that we finally got together again. Ozzy had been on the bill at the first ever Rock In Rio festival and I had been there covering it for *Kerrang!*. While we were there, Lynn decided to arrange a lunch for me with Ozzy and Sharon; a little meet-and-greet down by the pool at their hotel on Copa beach.

It was a beautiful, smog-ringed day. Ozzy had only been released from the Betty Ford Clinic a few weeks before and though still fragile, his sense of humour had returned along with several of his marbles, and it turned out to be a surprisingly entertaining lunch.

Ozzy ordered chicken curry. 'And don't forget to leave the head on!' he told the waiter but the waiter didn't get it, just smiled and smiled like he didn't know what the hell.

It was the first time I'd really spoken to Sharon and I discovered that she could be almost as good a storyteller as her old man. They certainly had a few tales to tell.

Before she met Ozzy, Sharon had worked for her father, Don, who had been managing Sabbath when Ozzy was fired from the band in 1979. Don Arden had been a notorious figure in the music business since the early-'60s, when he worked as a promoter on the type of package tours which were typical in Britain at the time: multi-act bills featuring old '50s rockers like Gene Vincent, Bill Haley and Eddie Cochran, with a few local acts shoe-horned into the nether reaches of the bill.

By the mid-'60s, Don had his own management company and booking agency, representing a whole slew of artists like Mickie Most, The Small Faces and The Animals. He also had a name for being a hard man – a reputation encouraged by Don himself – and stories about him have passed into music-business folklore. Led Zeppelin's infamous manager, Peter Grant, was an early protégé and it was from Don that Grant was said to have picked up the habit of always taking a gun with him into business negotiations. Then there was the time Don was reputed to have had rival manager Robert Stigwood held out of his office window by his legs for daring to try and lure The Small Faces away from him.

Don's son, David, who also worked for his father for a number of years, later told me that while it was true the old man always carried a gun, it wasn't just to meetings. 'He carried it with him everywhere!' he chortled. 'He probably even took it to bed with him . . .'

But the Robert Stigwood incident, though it almost certainly happened, had always been exaggerated, David said.

'I've no doubt the old man did go round there with a couple of heavies,' he said. 'But I doubt they held him out of the window by his legs. They probably just shoved his head out the window and showed him the ground and told him that that's where he'd end up next time . . .'

David had been in the family business since the mid-'60s. Sharon, a little younger, arrived on the scene in the early-'70s when she began working as 'personal chaperone' to singer Lynsey de Paul, whom Don was also then managing.

'We were sharing a hotel room together and by the end of the first tour, I hated her!' Sharon laughed. 'I thought she was a stuck-up little bitch and I'm sure she thought exactly the same about me. Then one night when I was drunk, I'd decided I'd had enough, and I got hold of her suitcase and peed in it!'

These were Sharon's Wild Years. 'I was the original little rich bitch,' she smiled. 'The mouth I used to have on me! People used to run when they saw me coming!'

'They still fuckin' do, some of 'em,' smirked Ozzy.

Later on in the '70s, Sharon had also worked with ELO, another band Don managed. At that time they were fronted by Jeff Lynne and were one of the biggest-selling acts in the world.

'Oh, God!' she sighed. 'It was like running an old-age pensioners' club! They'd all been around for years and all they ever wanted to do on tour was sit in their rooms doing their knitting. We were touring all over the world, going to places most people would only dream of going, and here I was stuck with these dreary old geezers who just weren't interested. I thought, I'll go out of my mind if I don't get out of this!'

Ozzy had been Sharon's way out. Still working for her father when Sabbath booted him out, Sharon had come along and offered to help Ozzy rebuild his career at a time when most other professional pundits considered him dead meat.

'Ozzy had always bugged me,' she said. 'Because he was lazy, he was insecure and . . . dumb! And that bugged me about him because I knew that he had so much more potential there. And he didn't even know his own strength. He'd always been bullied, all his life he was bullied, and so he had become the way most people would become when they've been bullied non-stop. He was like a squashed man. But I knew he had just so much more in there, and I was just trying to kick his arse into shape.'

At the time, Ozzy had been living in an apartment at La Park, a seedy, second-string hotel in West Hollywood, working his way through the ninety thousand dollars the band had given him when they told him to fuck off.

'A typical day for me at La Park went like this,' he recalled. 'Get up, start sniffing cocaine and start drinking lots of beer. I mean, lots of beer and lots of cocaine, and lots of rude women walking about the place. And I just idled my sweet time away doing what the fuck I wanted. I never used to go out. Never. I spent so much time in this apartment, just sitting around and getting completely out of my head, I knew every inch of the walls, the ceilings, the floor . . .

'I had this gas fire in one of the rooms, and it used to come on automatically – puff! Big jet of flame shoots out of the grate. I spent so much time sitting on the couch waiting for this thing to come on that it got to the point where I knew exactly when it was about to happen, down to the very second. So what I used to do, whenever there was a new chick over, was to start ranting on at her, telling her that all that stuff about black magic and me was true, and just as she was on the edge of beginning to believe what I was telling her, I'd suddenly stick my arms out in the air and – puff! Big jet of flame shoots out the wall, and the fire comes on! If they managed to survive that without a heart-attack, I'd let 'em hang around for a while . . .'

Sharon's arrival on the scene had soon changed all that. Now, five years on, not only was Ozzy a bigger star than he'd ever been in Sabbath, he was also the father of two infant daughters, Aimee and Kelly, and, post-Betty Ford at least, surprisingly clean.

It was an almost unbelievable transformation in his fortunes and neither he nor anyone else was in any doubt whatsoever as to who was responsible for it.

'When we first met,' said Sharon, 'we were both drinking and it was just insane. Being with Ozzy meant waking up with a raging hangover every day. Then one morning, I thought, we're never gonna get anywhere like this. At least one of us has to be straight, and I knew it wasn't going to be him. So I stopped there and then. That was it.'

'It was unbelievable,' said Ozzy. 'I couldn't do it, personally. Just stop cold like that. But Sharon did and thank fuck she did! 'Cos if it had been down to me, we'd both be out selling fuckin' hot-dogs now!'

They sat there grinning at each other. Sharon reached over and squeezed his hand. He looked pleased. It wasn't often you saw such a happy couple. It was almost inspiring.

'She's not only a great wife and manager,' he said, 'she's also a great mate. Of course, I have to say that 'cos she's sitting 'ere . . .'

Clearly, though, they'd had their troubles, too.

'Some of the worst, most violent fights I've ever 'ad 'ave been with 'er!' said Ozzy, jerking his thumb. 'Far worse than any bloke you might have a punch-up with. She's fuckin' vicious, she is!'

It was Sharon, of course, who had forced Ozzy to enter the rehab clinic. Despite my own habitual recoveries from heroin, the only professional help I had ever sought was purely for the withdrawal symptoms. All the other stuff – the psychological angle, the wanting-to-fuck-my-mother, all that stuff you can't actually see (at least, not at first) – I had never gone in for any of that. How did it work, I wondered?

'Oh, you know,' Ozzy said vaguely. 'They talk to you and try and get you to see that what you're doing is fucking things up for you.'

'Therapy classes, you mean?'

'Yeah, and different things . . . I remember them showing us films of people spending their lives doing all the bad things, like drinking too much and snorting too much coke. They would be like these little soap operas where you see this guy and his wife going to a party, then the guy gets totally fucked up out of his head on booze and things start falling apart in his life. But that bastard tickled me! He was having such a good time at this party, I started cheering and clapping every time he chucked one back or snuck off for a sneaky line. That's when they decided to ban me from attending the film classes. I was enjoying them too much!'

'Does that mean you have to give everything up then? You can't just quit the booze and get into smoking a bit of dope?'

'No, you've got to give up the lot, mate! That's what they say, anyway.'

I began to feel for Ozzy. I knew how hard it was giving up just one thing. Giving up the lot . . . I knew that I would never have been able to handle that. Who would?

'Wouldn't it be better to be fucked up and at least partly happy, though, than be straight and bored out of your mind the whole time?'

He shook his head. 'I don't know, mate. I'll have to get back to you on that one.'

He looked at Sharon.

'Ultimately,' he said, 'you've got to want to stop fucking up your life. You've got to want it. They can give you all the pills and potions in the world, which is what I had at first, but if you don't want it to work then you needn't worry – it won't. And if you're taking a pill as a substitute for a drink, you're still as fucked up as you were on the drink, except now it's a pill. I'd rather have a drink myself . . .

'What's that smell?' he said suddenly.

'I don't know,' said Sharon, 'but I'm eating it.'

'Oh God, you're not eating it if it stinks like that, are you?' Ozzy wrinkled his nose. 'It smells like someone's crapped their pants!'

'It might be the olives,' I said.

'It could be the cheese,' said Sharon.

'Smegma!' cried Ozzy. 'It smells like somebody's guts got hit!'

Sharon leant over to sniff the cheese. 'I think it smells quite pleasant, actually,' she smiled.

'Well, you can rub it round your arsehole then, can't you?' he giggled and the pair of them dissolved into fits of laughter again. Even the burnt Brazilian sun looked down and laughed. It was a sunny, laughing world.

Somewhere up above us, music began blaring suddenly from one of the balconies. It was 'Green Onions' by Booker T – but loud.

'That'll be fuckin' Rod Stewart again!' Ozzy groaned. 'That cunt's being playing that same fuckin' record for two days now. I'm gonna swing for 'im when I see 'im!'

The music was so loud, there would be not be many more questions that day, I realised. I threw my last couple of cards down on the table.

'When do you think you'll decide you've had enough of this?'

'What, retire, you mean?'

I nodded.

'Put it this way, I've got a house in London but I'm never there. So that's my dream for the future: to eventually get home, close the door, put the stereo on and that's it . . . Play pool in my pool-room and sit in my bar with no drinks . . .

'Sharon keeps saying to me, "Do you want to be singing when you're forty?" But I don't know. I keep saying to myself, "I'll give it another two years, I'll give it another three years." But until there comes a day when the band stop giving people fun, until the kids stop having fun, until I stop having fun, I'll probably keep going. It's too fuckin' late to stop now, anyway, ain't it? And I've got a lot of respect for the kids. They get on your fuckin' nerves sometimes, but if it wasn't for them there wouldn't be a Rod Stewart, there wouldn't be an Ozzy Osbourne, there wouldn't be a Queen, there wouldn't be any of us poncing around like pricks! As long as my band don't look like a darts team on stage, that's all I worry about, do you know what I mean?'

Yeah, I knew.

I couldn't resist asking, though: 'When was the last time you did a gig straight?'

'Oh, I've done gigs straight before,' he shrugged. 'Up till about halfway through the last American tour, I was straight almost every night. But towards the end I was getting up fucked up again every night. So would you, after nine fuckin' months, old bean. But that's now one of the things I've vowed I won't do. It's the easiest thing in the world to be a cunt all your life. It's somebody else's turn now to be a cunt. I don't wanna be a fucking douche-bag that goes up there every night, a fat, boring old fart . . .'

*

Sabbath's actual performance at Live Aid was incongruous, to say the least. While 'Children of the Grave' bore some passing resemblance to the subject matter that day, it was hard to see what 'Iron Man' or 'Paranoid' had to say about the plight of starving Africans, even in the most metaphorical sense.

In truth, the band looked old, out of synch. They looked like what they were: a dusty relic from a bygone age. Ozzy, who hadn't sung live since Rock In Rio six months before, was breathless and overweight, his dull imprecations to 'Go fuckin' crazy!' again hardly reflecting the desired aims of the rest of the show. His double-chins were starting to take over. Never mind. Sharon would soon fix that. The rest hardly seemed to matter; it was just enough that they were there.

Then, suddenly, it was over. The band were led off the stage and whisked back to the dressing-room area. It wasn't even 10.30 in the morning yet, but we'd been there, we'd done our bit. Now we had the whole fucking day to get through . . .

Well, if you saw it on TV, you know the rest. The only relief in the boredom, for me, was when I was introduced to David Crosby. He was short and round, like Danny DeVito, but older and much more wasted. I'd been told he was on his way to jail on guns and drugs charges – looking at a five-year stretch, they whispered every time his back was turned. When I spoke to him he certainly had the look of the condemned man.

'Hi, how's it hangin'?' he said, as he dropped his limp, warm hand into mine and allowed me to shake it. His eyes were small and black and they didn't look out at you, they looked in.

'I guess this must remind you a bit of the '60s,' I said.

'What?' he said, the eyes not moving, just floating in his head like dead fish in a tank.

'The '60s. You know?'

'The Beatles?'

'No, the '60s! You know? The '60s?'

'I don't know what you're talkin' about, mister,' he said. And for a moment there, you could tell he probably didn't.

He waddled away, looking agitated, an old fat guy with no hair left and a ratty white beard, just the red bandanna tied around his head to remind you he had something to do with music . . . Looking at a five-year stretch. Poor motherfucker. Someone should have tried to feed him. He really needed it.

I would have but I was a clean machine by then. Except for the booze, I was so straight I could hardly bend over to wipe my own arse. Booze was just easier and more readily available than gear. Booze and dope, and, if someone else was laying it out, maybe a little coke. I could always sweat it out again in the gym. A nice, healthy, '80s kind of sweat.

Maria was now just a memory, as we both always knew she would be one day. The ending had been completely predictable – I had finally caught her out fucking some other (younger, more arty) guy. But knowing it was inevitable hadn't meant it hurt less. It may even have hurt more. I'd been storing up the pain of my expected betrayal for so long that when I finally let it out, it ran like a pathetic river right over me.

I nearly drowned in it, too. I lost the room in Chiswick, and for a while I was sleeping on friends' floors and couches. I would just turn up on their doorsteps with my portable typewriter in one hand and a plastic carrier bag full of my crap in the other. I'd stay as long as I could, then move on when they were sick of me.

One night, it was getting late and this guy I was hoping to see wasn't in. Either that or he'd got wind of my plan and wasn't opening the door. I'd already stayed there a couple of times before and I sensed hostility whenever I spoke to his girlfriend on the phone. I walked around, not knowing what to do. I found myself in the park. It was night but the gates were still open. It wasn't that cold, the moon was up and though it was dark you could see all around. I appeared to be alone. I found a park bench and sat down. I was tired. I could hardly keep my eyes open. Living on other people's kindness meant living on other people's time. It wore you down. Having to fit in with everyone else. When did anybody ever try to fit in with you? I felt my eyes closing . . .

Then a bolt went through me and I sat upright suddenly. I caught myself just in time, and I got up off that bench and moved out of the park as quickly as I could. So that was how it happened – you just ran out of places to stay, places where you really wanted to go. And so you ended up living at the bottom of the well . . .

But even love is a drug you can eventually kick and it would play no more part in my life in the '80s than smack would. There would always be sex but love was something that would grow more mysterious with the years. I just didn't want to go through the comedown again. Instead, I found myself a nice, designer girlfriend, Belinda (veggie, thin, uptight) and a nice, designer flat to live in (a one-bedroomed loft in Hammersmith) and I allowed the rest to go fuck itself while I did like everyone else and went out and had myself a so-called good time.

Live Aid was just another night out for me. And the real highlight, if highlights there had to be, was when the Zeppelin mob came prancing through the backstage area that evening on their way to the stage, surrounded by armed guards and big black fuckers yelling, 'Outta the way! Band comin' through here! Outta the way!'

Who the fuck cared? Everywhere you looked there were bands. Bands and film stars. Over there was Jack Nicholson and over there was Chevy Chase and over there was some other famous face from the fabulous world of showbiz . . . None of them seemed to require a ring of armed heavies to escort them to the stage. Why these boys?

Because they were Led Zeppelin, that's why. And that's the way

151

they did things on their planet. Heavy. Full-on. They might be here to feed the world but that didn't mean the world could intrude on their karma, could mingle and say hello. Sorry, wrong legend. No fucking touching allowed.

They looked absurd. They looked incredible. Jimmy Page looked completely out of it, of course, magnificently so, in fact, staggering towards the stage like an over-dressed crab. The living embodiment of the unsaveable '70s, good old Jimmy looked like he had never given less of a fuck in his entire life. He was here to do his gig, that was all. Plug his leads in, man, and he would go. The rest they could make up for themselves.

Robert Plant, following close behind, looked superb, too, but in a different way. Short, bouffant '80s hairdo, noticeably tight, flare-less trousers, gym-trim figure . . . If it hadn't been for the craggy old face, he could have been the singer in Def Leppard. Here was a guy who obviously took his time in front of the mirror, and if anyone really understood what this whole goody-two-shoes deal was all about, it was Bobby The Plant. You could, as they say, just see it in the way he walked, sucking in those cheeks and tightening those buns like a twinkling old tart as he tottered gleefully towards his destiny.

Ozzy and Geezer watched the procession with amusement. They had both known Robert since the days in the '60s when they were all part of the same underground Birmingham scene – Ozzy and Geezer in Earth, who later changed their name to Black Sabbath, and Robert in Listen, the band he played in with that other well-known Brummy rock god, Zeppelin drummer John Bonham.

'*Oi, Robert, ya big girl's blouse!*' Ozzy roared. '*Doncha say 'allo any more then!*'

The guards visibly stiffened but as soon as Plant saw Ozzy he broke ranks and came gambolling over. 'Ozzy!' he cried. 'And Geezer! Great to see you both! How have you been?'

There was a bit of banter back and forth, Ozzy deadpan, Robert smiling like a sun.

'Are you coming up to watch?' he asked.

'Yeah, all right,' Ozzy said nonchalantly, and we fell into step behind Robert and the rest of the Zeppelin cuttin' crew.

Now I could start to see it, what walking up to the stage surrounded by all those heavies did for you. It gave you an attitude, made you ready, showed you off a little bit before you went up there and did it to them good one more time. What must it feel like to be Jimmy Page at that moment, I wondered? To know that it's all about you. Everything. To have the whole world waiting. Not to be fed, but to be fucked with . . .

We stood at the side of the stage surrounded by armed guards and well-wishers – Eric, Ronnie, Phil, all the old lags. The stadium exploded as they walked out there, the noise hit you in the face like a hot wind. Then they ripped into 'Rock and Roll' and the place exploded again.

As a kid, for me the brutal prole-riffs of Sabbath had always had the edge over the more cultured and flowery-sounding Zeppelin. But as the years had passed, the reverse had become true. I still loved my old Sabbath albums like *Paranoid* and *Master of Reality* the way I would always love *The Man Who Sold the World* and the first New York Dolls album. But what I was actually listening to on my Walkman as I sat there on my exercise bike down the gym with all the other '80s airheads, was 'Kashmir', 'Dancing Days', 'In My Time Of Dying' and 'D'yer Maker' (pronounced 'Jamaica', for those Americans who still don't know).

Too old to dance and too young to die, I was mildly surprised to learn that I had become a Led Zep man. Maybe it was because it was the blues. Ziggy wasn't the blues, nor was Ozzy. Not any more. But Zeppelin had somehow retained it, enlarged on it, and the older you got the more sense it made. The good stuff, anyway. And wasn't that what the blues was? The same old story passed down through the ages?

And then there was Africa, where it had all began . . . Had they heard of the legend of Led Zeppelin down in Chad and Mozambique? Maybe they would know what it all meant. The rest of us would have to wait to read our newspapers the next day . . . Then Jimmy began churning out that riff to 'Whole Lotta Love' and you forgot all about it again. Truly, this was heavy. You could feel the stage trembling beneath your feet.

In America, Zeppelin had always wielded an awesome power

over their audience, and so it was at Live Aid. Despite some appalling mistakes by Phil Collins, who had flown in on Concorde to drum with the band after completing his own set in London, as they reached the ecstatically cliché-ridden crescendo of 'Stairway to Heaven', it finally dawned on me that, yes, perhaps this was a great day after all. I had been to literally hundreds of rock concerts in my time. I had seen and done and written about it all, I thought. But I had never seen anything at a rock concert quite like that moment at JFK in July '85 when Plant came to that final line, 'And she's buy-uy-ing . . . a stairway-ay' – and the whole place, front stage and back, the whole world, stopped whatever they were doing and finished it for him – 'to heaven.'

It sounds like wet cotton-wool now but if you were there, for a fleeting moment it felt as if there might actually be some meaning somewhere in the universe. That maybe something meant some-thing, after all. That this was in some way . . . *real*.

Then it was gone again and we were back to being pushed out of the way by the bodyguards as the band sauntered off the stage, as drained-looking and as triumphant as though they had just done a two-hour show.

'*Outta the way! Band comin' through here! Outta the way!*'

We let them pass.

'I suppose, in ten years' time, I can always say, "I was there. I did it,"' said Ozzy, as we drove back to the hotel that night. 'It's one of those things you can look back on, I suppose, as an old man, and think, "Well, that wasn't so bad, was it?"'

I suppose.

*

It was easier, in those days, not to have too many strong opinions. I felt like I'd gone to sleep in 1979 and not woken up again until 1985. But while I had been away in junkland, the world had changed; moved on in some new and meaningful way. It wasn't just me and Mandy that didn't give a fuck any more, it was everyone. We were all just in it for the money, hanging on by our fingertips to whatever we were hooked on.

Only the slick survived and my yuppie landscape had been formed by my involvement with *Kerrang!*. The work had flooded in and I no longer needed to fake film reviews to get by. I was a cover story writer now, the fattest fat frog in the murky green pond.

In the past, when it had come to writing magazine articles, I had either known the magazine well as a reader, or had scanned it long and hard, trying to figure out how I could match the way I wrote with the things they published. It was taking the safe, middle road and a lot of safe, middle-road writing resulted.

This time, I knew little and cared less. *Kerrang!* was always a job that was going to end tomorrow, and my contempt for my subject-matter had somehow liberated the writing. My ignorance had somehow given me an edge; my indifference had added depth. You soon lose your fear of clichés when everything is a cliché. And *Kerrang!*, being populated by heavy metal idealists still too young or too naïve to actually believe in hell, had lapped it up.

Now I was along for the ride, for however long it lasted. Next to the *NME* and *Melody Maker*, *Kerrang!* could never hope to be taken seriously. The trick it had learned, though, was not to care. Like an early prototype of *Loaded*, the whole ethos behind *Kerrang!* in the '80s was an almost entirely subversive one. We gloried in our unfashionability, we lived for free lunches and trips abroad. A good review was only ever a drink away. If you were in on the joke, it was a good one. If you weren't, you frowned into your beard and thought of *Kerrang!* as somehow beneath you.

But that's where we lived. Beneath everything. Given the choice, we would always take the limo. And the chicks and the drugs. Even the fucking rock 'n' roll. What there was of it. And until Guns N' Roses and Metallica came along, that meant not much at all. Not unless you liked Motley Crue. And even I wasn't far gone enough yet for that. Unless you wanted to fly me to LA and put me up at a nice hotel, of course . . .

Free trips were our chief pleasure. Free trips meant bingeing on booze and whatever else you could get your hands on that was free from the moment you arrived at the airport until the moment you arrived back again. Free trips meant getting wasted first and inter-viewing the band (there was always a band somewhere) second.

An early example of what eventually became almost an art-form involved a trip to Belgium to interview Frank Zappa, and see him play the opening two nights of his 1984 European tour. A classic of its kind, Ronan the PR had turned up so late at the airport that we – myself and Roy, the *Kerrang!* photographer, and a couple of tweeded-up older dudes from the *Daily Express* – missed the flight completely.

We got the next flight out but it meant we would be late for our interviews with Frank. Being an internationally renowned control freak, Zappa was said to have had flunkies flogged to within an inch of their miserable, worthless lives for being even a minute late for meetings. The fact that we would be arriving more than two hours late meant almost certain death for Ronan. Which perhaps explained why we had to stop the taxi from Brussels airport into town three times while Ronan dived out and threw up violently all over the pavement.

We arrived at Frank's hotel just in time to catch him leaving for the gig. Frank was pissed off. Big time. He didn't even speak to us. He just strode off towards his tour bus looking like a pissed-off Frank Zappa. Very bad vibes indeed. But we dutifully traipsed off in a taxi after him.

When we got to the gig, Frank was soundchecking. Frank liked to soundcheck for three or four hours at a time, the tour manager told us, a mean-spirited hunk of lard with a face like an ox.

'Fuck this,' I told Ronan. 'I'm going back to the hotel. If Frank decides he wants to talk, call me and I'll get a taxi back again. Otherwise, forget it . . .'

Ronan was cool, though. He knew whose fault it was. But I had only just got back to the hotel and opened up the mini-bar in my room before the phone rang.

It was Ronan. 'Listen, Frank's about to break for pizza. Do you wanna come back as quick as you can and talk to him while he's eating?'

'Sure,' I said, cursing my luck.

Frank fucking Zappa. What the fuck was I supposed to ask Frank fucking Zappa after all these years? Like, hi Frank, so what's new? Still hating the world? Or is it the other way around?

But I went down there and sure enough there he was, looking like a pissed-off Frank Zappa eating pizza.

Ronan introduced me and I sat down at his table backstage. Frank just ignored me. I set up the tape-recorder and shuffled my notes. Still he ignored me. I coughed. Loudly.

He looked at me at last.

'Well, Frank,' I said, 'I thought maybe we could start with –'

'You know,' he said, scrutinising me, 'I've got a son at home about your age.'

'Really?'

'Mmm . . . I think maybe you should talk to him.'

It was the way he said it. I felt like I'd just been trodden on.

That night, before the show, we decided to let Ronan have it. The *Express* boys did anyway. They were obviously well versed in how to treat PRs who screwed up.

First, they got him to pay for a lavish meal at the hotel. I hate it when meals are described as 'lavish' but that's what this was. One of the *Express* guys, Pike, had been to Cambridge and really knew how to work a menu.

He ordered some starters in French and then continued for our benefit in English: '. . . and for our main course we'll have the Châteaubriand and a couple of bottles of the Nuits-Saint-Georges,' he told the waiter, a smirking statue on wheels.

They were the most expensive items on the menu but Ronan took it all with good grace. He knew he was being made to pay, in the most literal sense, but he didn't mind. It would all go down as expenses and, besides, we had all got our interviews and photos done, despite the aggro. Job done. Now it was time to unwind and if that meant keeping the troops happy with a bit of a splash-out on a meal, then so be it.

One of the new breed of '80s PRs who could handle it all without blinking, Ronan even managed to keep a straight face when Pikey mentioned the hookers . . .

'They've got these handy little cards they put by your bed in your room,' he said. 'Have you seen them? You just call them up, tell them how many girls you want and they send them straight up to your room.'

It sounded good. Ronan wasn't so sure but by the time the bill arrived for the meal, we knew the Zappa show would already be well under way and so we persuaded him to let us forget about it for that night. We could all go to the second show the next day, we decided. Then we got him up to the rooms and sat him down on the bed while Pikey put in the call.

'*Avez-vous quatre femmes pour moi, Mademoiselle? Dans la chambre, oui . . .?*'

Thirty minutes later there was a knock on the door. It was the girls! They arrived just as the room-service waiter was delivering the champagne.

'*Voila!*' cried Pikey. 'Now that's what I call rock 'n' roll!'

I had never experienced the high-price call-girl thing before. It was fascinating. They began by asking us what we were 'looking for' and then worked out how much it would cost on a pocket calculator one of them produced from her handbag. We all just wanted a straight fuck and a bit of fun. They punched in the figures. The total came to about five hundred pounds.

When Ronan laughed and said he didn't carry that kind of cash, they surprised us by simply saying that that was all right, they took credit cards, too. Reluctantly, the full folly of his actions only just starting to dawn on him, Ronan threw his gold credit card down on the bed. One of the girls immediately scooped it up and got on the phone.

'What's she doing?' he asked.

'Just checking,' said the tallest, who seemed to be in charge.

They got the clearance they needed on his card and a third girl brought out one of those card-machines you get at shop counters. She took Ronan's card and ran it through. Handed him the bill. He signed it and she gave him a receipt.

We were in business. Pikey poured us all some champagne . . .

The really funny part was that we somehow managed to persuade Ronan to go through the whole thing again the next night. Only this time he absolutely put his foot down and insisted on not paying for any hookers. We still missed the gig, though, arriving as we had that first morning, just in time to see everybody leaving.

'*Fuck me!*' Ronan cried. For a moment the calm PR façade began to crumble and he became distraught, inconsolable.

'You cunts! Look what you've done! We've missed the whole thing!'

Then he gathered himself and, like the true pro he was, he immediately came up with a plan. 'Listen,' he said, 'we can't tell him we didn't see either of the fuckin' shows. We'll just have to go backstage and crack on we were here.'

'No problem,' said Pikey, loving every minute of it. This was even better than the real thing.

We marched backstage, a nicely manufactured air of elation about us. That Nuits-Saint-Georges was good stuff.

'Frank!' cried Pikey, holding out his hand. 'A-mazing show! A-fucking-mazing!'

'Gee, thanks,' said Frank.

I couldn't tell who was taking the piss more.

*

But the thing I liked most about writing for *Kerrang!* in the '80s was that the metal bands seemed to stick around forever, their careers far outlasting that of most pop bands. They were hard-working live performers who played attractive shows in enormous arenas all over the world, and life with a successful rock band was comfortable, streamlined, with the emphasis firmly on the fun and the money. I'd done my share of roughing-it-in-the-van jobs to Bradford and back with a lot of joyless, punk herberts in my *Sounds* days. Next to that, sharing a limo with David Lee Roth back to our hotel in LA at five in the morning was . . . well, just much more entertaining.

After a while, the wheel came around so many times, you interviewed them in so many similar backstage places, that you did, finally, get to know them. Or at least a more personable 'them' than the strangers-with-attitude you are constantly forced to deal with in the pop business. You got to know their roadies, their girlfriends, their friends. And everybody knew your face, too. You were 'all right', which, loosely translated, meant you wouldn't squeal, that you could be trusted. Up to a point.

It was plush, conservative and vaguely sane. Not too many of us displayed pretensions to much more than doing our jobs and getting wasted afterwards. It was the '80s and the rewards were there to be had, it seemed. We were all sucked in, whoever we said we voted for.

I got paid more, too, for doing rock bands. Twelve-hundred-word articles in *Sounds* on The Lurkers or The Meteors or whoever I used to write about did not interest anybody outside of the bands themselves and their (few) British fans. A two-thousand-word write-up on Def Leppard or Iron Maiden or Bon Jovi or whoever, on the other hand, would sell and sell around the world, and by 1985 I had agents in London, Paris, Tokyo and LA, all reselling the stuff I was churning out for *Kerrang!*.

It seemed the whole world had gone mad for heavy metal. And just like the bands themselves, the more trite and meaningless the stories I wrote, the better they sold. I started out doing 'zany' intros before getting to the 'meat' of the interview. Then I started cutting down on the meat and going purely for the zany. Then I just threw it all out the window and wrote whatever the hell I wanted to, sitting there drunk and stoned at night, wondering whatever happened to real rock 'n' roll. Did Lester Bangs ever have to put up with shit like this?

Of course not. Lester was too good. Lester was too uncompromising. Good old Lester. But Lester would have understood, I felt sure. Heavy metal was the perfect soundtrack of the '80s. Like Reagan and Thatcher and the new-wave fascism they proposed, everybody knew it was all surface sheen and two-dimensional, but they didn't care. MTV came along and they decided they liked it that way. They wanted the fake Hollywood ending . . . dying in bed, applauded by adoring minions . . . even I'd take some of that.

I'd take all I could get, fuck you very much.

*

It was around this time that I was approached by Garry Bushell to help him finish the 'official' biography of Ozzy he had been working on. Garry and I knew each other from *Sounds*, and he had recently done a well-selling official Iron Maiden biog. His next project had been Ozzy's book (*Diary of a Madman*, as it was to be called) but by then Garry was starting to do a lot of work for *The Mirror* and then *The Sun* and he just didn't have the time any more.

As we were to discover, Garry had other plans, and having read my Rio piece on Ozzy, he rang up and asked if I wanted to split the Ozzy book – he would do the first four chapters, I would do the last four. We met at his house in Essex one Sunday afternoon to discuss it.

It was a memorable lunch not least for the picture it afforded me of the future tabloid king in action. As a PR back in the old days, I'd pulled a few stunts of my own – getting a story I'd made up into the tabloids about Wild Horses parachuting into Reading Festival and the like – but I'd never seen anything like this.

The phone rang late in the afternoon. It was someone tipping off Garry that David Bowie was at that very moment eating at a certain restaurant in the West End. Garry swung straight into action. He picked up the phone and dialled a kiss-o-gram agency and ordered them to send 'a blonde bombshell' to the restaurant. She was to wait outside until the Thin White Duke appeared and then leap on him with a kiss. Then he called *The Mirror* (or maybe it was *The Sun*) and got them to send down a photographer to wait outside the restaurant with the bombshell, so that he could get shots of her with Bowie.

That done, he lifted his portable typewriter onto his lap, and as I stood there looking over his shoulder, he began to write: 'BOWIE AND HIS MYSTERY BLONDE . . .'

'You don't mind if I quickly do this, do you?' he asked

What was there to mind? I was getting a masterclass in real journalism. I was enthralled.

He quickly bashed out a 150-word caption, then rang it in. The kiss-o-gram hadn't even arrived yet. It was the kind of high-altitude approach to work, to life, that I could only stand back and admire. I was deeply impressed.

Garry had written about Ozzy in *Sounds* many times, but it was plain that committing himself to an entire book about him – even half an entire book – was no longer high on his agenda. For me, of course, it was still a big deal and I set about my four chapters with real enthusiasm. It was almost inevitable that when the two finished halves were put together, they wouldn't quite make a whole.

The publisher axed Garry's half of the book and asked me to rewrite it so that the whole book looked like the way I had done the second half. Garry, to his credit, took it all very coolly. What did he care anyway? He was working full time for *The Sun* by then and you knew he'd bounce back. Though no one could have guessed quite how far, eh, Gal?

Diary of a Madman: The Uncensored Memoirs of Rock's Greatest Rogue was published in February 1986 and was my first little success. The *Virgin Year Book* described it as the 'rock book of the year' and the reviews were great, too. I was amazed. All I saw in it when I looked were cringe-inducing mistakes and typos. The whole thing – over sixty thousand words – had been written in under three weeks on a diet of beer, dope and no sleep till Christmas. Some of the worst writing I ever did was in that book. Yet the good reviews kept coming. The *London Evening Standard* ran a page on it and their cartoon that day was about the book, too. Then *The Star* did a three-day serialisation and I finally caught on. They didn't care about the writing, they just loved the stories.

Ozzy biting the head off a dove: 'It tasted like a warm Ronald McDonald's!'

Ozzy getting thrown in jail in Texas for pissing on the Alamo while dressed as his wife: 'Sharon had stolen all me clothes to stop me going out drinking, so I put hers on and went out and got pissed anyway!'

Ozzy tripping on acid: 'I went into this field and started talking to this horse. That was all right. Then the horse started talking back to me and I knew I was in trouble!'

And on and on and on . . . They loved the stories so much I later found out they paid twenty thousand pounds for the privilege of serialising it for three days. Not that I saw a penny of that. But that's another story, the moral being: never sign contracts without showing them to a lawyer first. Never.

And always check the small print. If the '80s taught us anything, it was surely that . . .

8

Monsters of Rock

For me, the turning point of the '80s came when I was asked to present my own TV show on Sky. It was 1985 and I had never heard of Sky Channel. I didn't even know Britain had satellite TV back then. But, apparently, in places like Milton Keynes and certain parts of Scotland, Wales and Ireland, where the first experimental cables were laid, we did. If you lived anywhere else in the UK, it was the same as now: you needed a dish to receive it. Only then the dishes were huge, unwieldy things that went for a couple of grand a pop, and only the idle rich and the major record companies actually had one.

In Europe, though, where cable was more readily available, the station was broadcast to something like ten million people in twenty-three different countries. Or so they told you. Nobody who worked there could afford a dish of their own and so none of us really knew what was going on. It was like writing for a paper that nobody ever read. You just went on faith. Faith and bullshit.

It was the very early, no-money days of Sky and, without MTV to compete with yet, the channel mainly survived on a hastily thrown together mix of cheap, home-made music programmes and reruns of old American soaps and comedies. After the *Pepsi Chart Show*, the most popular programme on the channel was *Mister Ed The Talking Horse*.

Most of the presenters were either multi-purpose old hacks like Gary Davies, David Jensen and Tony Blackburn, or bland next-generation hopefuls like Philip Scofield, Anthea Turner, Pat Sharp and Amanda Reddington. With the exception of Tony Blackburn, who struck me as a much darker, more complex character than the 'Sensational!'-spouting moron of Radio 1 fame, the rest of them were about as entertaining as trained monkeys. Watching them up-close, from behind the cameras, you realised what you'd always suspected: that they really weren't acting when they did their safe, pissy little routines, that this really was them. It was a horrible discovery.

Then you saw yourself on camera and you realised just how bad you were, too. It was nauseating just how low you would stoop to make a link, laughing at jokes not even a clown would find funny, introducing videos you wouldn't shit on as though they were gold dust . . .

In amongst all the other junk, they had an hour-long weekly heavy metal show called *Monsters of Rock*. It had originally been presented by Amanda Reddington, a cheerful, pretty, insecure, blonde model-cum-actress-cum-TV-presenter-cum-whatever-you-say-boss, who cheerfully admitted she didn't know anything about rock music, but who played the brainless heavy metal chick to the hilt. So, of course, the show was a piece of shit. The kind of rubbish rock fans were used to having thrown at them. The logic being: they're only heavy metal fans – they like shit, don't they?

Stuck for a guest one week, in desperation they rang the *Kerrang!* office and asked if they could interview the editor, Geoff Barton. Geoff agreed and then, as the day approached, decided he couldn't be arsed and asked me if I'd stand in for him. The show-off in me said yes immediately.

Like so many sad cases who end up on a stage being funny, I had been one of those kids at school who had learned to survive in the playground by making other, bigger kids laugh. It was a useful skill to have and one that had both helped me in my days as a PR and been a much-used tool in my subsequent dealings with hard-nosed heroin dealers.

Going on TV and cracking wise with some bit of fluff in a leather mini-skirt should have been meat and drink to a well-known gobshite like me. And so it proved, that first time at least, as Amanda struggled to keep up with my razor-sharp wit and sparkling repartee. In fact, the producers liked it so much they asked me if I'd come on the show every week and 'do a couple of links'.

My job, initially, as I understood it, was to bring a bit of 'cred' to the show. I was the guy from *Kerrang!* who would come on and review a few albums, always making sure to finish the link with an album we had a video for. Amanda's job was to sit there in her heavy metal slut costume, looking interested and feeding me the questions I had already prepared for her.

Me: 'It's the new album from Iron Maiden and even though every band always say this, I can back them up this time, because it really is their best yet . . .'

Amanda: 'Yes, this is their fifth album now, isn't it?'

M: 'That's right.'

A: 'And what's it called?'

It was chronic. Two dummies flapping their wooden lips at each other. While the first video was playing, Amanda would turn to me and hiss: 'Quick, what's next? Saxon? God, what can I say about them?'

We were so embarrassingly bad together that I would leave the studio each week feeling like a complete wanker. It wasn't the cheap pantomime or the shoddy fabrications that got to me, it was the fact that I did them so badly. It was one thing to pump out stoned drivel on the typewriter and get slapped on the back for it, but to go on pan-European TV and make a complete arse of myself every week was too much of a blow for my still fragile, post-smack ego to take.

I thought it might get better when they suggested I got involved with the interviews, too. One of the first had been with Ozzy but even there, a completely unwarranted attack of nerves left me trembling like a slapped bitch every time the little red light on the camera went on and the floor-manager did his fancy hand signals. My head was shaking so badly I could hardly get the words out right. I just froze. Stiffed out.

Slowly, I faced up to it: I was crap. And not just any kind of crap. I was more crap than Gary Davies! I was more crap than Tony Blackburn! I was more crap than them all!

For someone who enjoyed sitting on his couch sneering at

joshing imbeciles like Terry Wogan, this was the most devastating discovery of all. It turned the whole world around.

A friend of mine who worked on the *Wogan* show in the '80s once told me that Terry had different wigs which he kept in his dressing-room: one to make it look like he'd had a haircut, one for 'normal', and one to make it look like he needed a haircut. When I heard that, I decided that any guy who does that is the same guy who diddles with himself six times a day in front of the mirror.

Now, in the aftermath of my own humiliating experiences before the cameras, I began to see the Big Fella in a new light. He was on the box live three evenings a week and I never missed him. The guests were mostly drab, but Wogan carried off the whole thing with an old-world aplomb I could only gaze in wonder at. Having sat that side of the cameras, I could tell when he was watching the floor-manager or reading questions from the cue-cards, or just stuck for something to say, *and* he handled it all brilliantly. Even when he appeared to be losing it, I could tell it was just part of the act. Super fucking cool, Terry really knew how to play along.

Even the wigs – you had to admit, it was sharp thinking. If you're committed to wearing the damn things, you may as well go the whole hog. Most people had to do far more degrading things than that just to earn a crust.

As a TV host, Wogan was a master with a lifetime's experience behind him, and I was an upstart not fit to lick his hand-made shoes. As soon as I realised this, I wrote out my resignation letter to the producer – Bart, or Black Bart, as the crew used to call him behind his back, an evil-tempered, red-faced bastard who never really knew why we were doing a 'poxy heavy metal show' anyway. I was sorry but this obviously wasn't for me. Thanks and every-thing, but . . . I would bring it with me to the very next show and give it to Bart personally. Then I'd be out that fucking door as fast as my much-taller-on-the-telly legs would carry me.

Then a funny thing happened on the way to the show . . .

*

The day after I wrote out my resignation letter, I got a phone call from the office telling me that Amanda had been 'poached' by Sky's main rival in those days, Music Box, and that the show was now mine to present full time, if I wanted.

Oh, fuck, no.

'That's great!' I cried. But my mind filled with horror.

They said there would be two shows for me to present, followed by a short break of three weeks before the next series began. I decided to hold off with the resignation letter until the break came up. They had been upset by Amanda's abrupt departure and I felt I owed it to them to help out with the final two shows. Two more, and that would be it.

For the first show I presented on my own, there was a new producer in charge, a woman, Gail. Nicer, kinder, but far more hyper than sleazy Bart, she made me sit with my back to the cameras for the opening link, wearing a blond wig. The idea was 'the kids' would think it was Amanda, until I spun round in my chair, whisked the wig off and gave them the big announcement about how I was now going to be presenting the show. It would be a hoot. She said.

It took me several attempts to get it right and when Gail finally said, 'Cut! That's a take!', I felt like I'd just gone three rounds with Mike Tyson. Oh sweet lord baby fucking Jesus, what kind of weak and depraved character trait had led me to believe I could pull off shit like this? What kind of cunt was I, really?

We staggered through the rest of the show, seven more links, all tortuously done and redone until there could be no doubt about it – I was the biggest cunt that had ever walked the earth. I knew it, Gail knew it, the crew it, even the cameras looked on with resigned expressions. The whole world knew it. I was slowly being flogged to death by my own greed and stupidity. I was '80s Oaf incarnate.

I would sign that resignation letter in blood if they wanted, I decided, but I would not be coming back for more, that much was certain.

But when, a week later, we came to record the second and 'final' show, for some reason we went to a different studio and they had put together a whole new set around me. It was still the same clichéd mixture of Styrofoam gravestones and dry-ice, but somehow it felt different. And, perhaps because I had already made up my mind that it would be my last show, I was far less nervous. The whole thing sped by, most of the links done in one or two takes. I even got a couple of laughs out of the crew, a stony-faced bunch who didn't crack easily, and I felt strangely encouraged. By the end of the show, I was even starting to enjoy myself a little bit.

As I sat in the dressing-room afterwards, wiping off the make-up, Gail came in and sat down next to me.

'You see,' she said, 'I knew you could do it.'

'Thanks,' I said, 'but I think it was probably a fluke.'

'Nonsense! You're a natural. You've just got to learn to relax and go with the flow. Do like you did today – if you make a mistake, don't worry about it, just keep going.'

I thought about it. I still believed I had fluked it somewhat but at least I could see what she was talking about now, and as I walked from the studio to the tube that day, I felt I was six inches taller. Life was somehow just a little bit more special than it had been when I'd arrived there a couple of hours before.

And that's when I remembered the resignation letter, still in my pocket . . .

*

After that, I got good at it. Really good at it. Making an arse of myself for the cameras just came naturally. It was a bit like writing: the less I tried, the better things just seemed to go.

Working for Sky in those days was like I imagined it must have been back in the days of the original '60s pirate radio stations – low-paid, chaotic, with everybody running round like they knew what they were doing when none of us really did.

My fee for presenting an hour-long weekly show that got repeated twice a week was a hundred pounds. A week. If I was ill or couldn't make it, I got nothing. If they had a break in the series, I got nothing. Repeat fees: nothing. I didn't even know the other presenters had contracts until the producers told me they would not be able to offer me one.

But I got into the 'performing' side – as depressing as doing a bad show could be, doing a good one was like no other feeling in the world, better even than heroin and, as I found out, just as addictive – and the show began to evolve into more of a comedy hour than purely a music-based programme. The ratings started to shoot up, too, and soon we were getting so many letters from viewers, some poor girl was employed in the office for three days a week simply to open the mail.

Mainly it was from young metal guys and they didn't just write letters, they sent parchments burned at the edges and written in ancient monk-like script. They sent photos of themselves and their friends doing stupid things with guitars and bottles of Jack Daniel's, they sent home-made coffin-shaped posters with carica-tures of me painted on them. They sent pictures of their girlfriends with their tits out, they sent dolls, fake gold records, little crosses, fake blood capsules . . . anything they thought might amuse me.

And it did. Suddenly, I had 'fans'. At first, they were just the same old heavy metal freaks who would have written to any bozo with an Iron Maiden video on their show. But as I got better at it, and my own much more fucked-up sense of humour started coiling itself like a snake around the show, the letters got wilder and wilder. The ones written in real blood were starting to arrive. Now I was getting through to my people.

Surprisingly, I used to get sackloads of mail from girl fans, too. They were less inventive with their letters and their photos than the boys, but they were always the first ones I used to try and read. I couldn't believe how many girls sent pictures of themselves semi-naked, usually with a pair of stockings and suspenders on and high-heels. They would nearly always be lying on a bed, doing their best to look like a *Playboy* centrefold. Real babes, most of them, too.

Sometimes, you'd get two of them pictured together – a team. They were my favourites. There were two gorgeous young girls in Vienna – Hilda and Heidi – who regularly used to send me shots of themselves, either posing naked on their own or together, eating each other out and doing other things, along with little letters inviting me to join them.

'You do not look like a normal Englishman to us,' was how one typical letter started. 'You look like there is something bad and dirty about you. And you are funny. This is very sexy. We hope you find our pictures very sexy also. Do you ever come to Vienna? Perhaps next time you will like to join us?'

I'd never been to Vienna and I began to think maybe I would like to go there. But I always used to wonder who was taking the photos and I realised I'd never have the balls to plan something like that. I kept the pictures, though.

There were some really young ones, too. I once got a letter and a photo from a fourteen-year-old in Munich – the usual stockings and suspenders routine – who wrote that her parents would be visiting London in a few weeks' time and asked whether I would like to meet up with her. She left the address of the hotel and the phone number. I looked at the photo again. She was beautiful: long, shiny black hair, white, white skin and red full lips. I thought about it and began to get a hard-on. Should I stay or should I go?

Then I opened some more letters, looked at some more pictures and started to forget about it. I simply wasn't a big sex man. I needed it like anyone, and loved it as much as the next ex-drug fiend, but it had never ruled my life the way it does some men. The female, in her prime, was an endlessly beautiful sunrise to behold, but it was a force of nature I always felt most comfortable viewing from a distance, preferably with a drink in my hand or, better still, a decent smoke.

I didn't even know what I was doing with Belinda. As far as I could see, we had nothing in common except a willingness to stick our heads in the sand of financially secure mid-'80s conformity. We just looked all right on each other's arms as we arrived at after-show parties. It was a marriage of convenience that was becoming less and less convenient for both of us all the time.

Predictably, Bee did not find the girls' letters and pictures as amusing as the rest of my friends. The first time I brought some home to show her, she tore them up in a fit of rage and stayed in a bad mood about it for days.

'They're only writing to you because you're on the telly and they see you talking to rock stars and they think that makes you famous, too!' she snapped, her eyes frantic with loathing.

'I know that,' I said.

'If they met you in real life they'd soon see the side of you I see.'

'Look, I said I know that. But can't you see the funny side? It is funny . . .'

'No! It's not! It's all just sexist rubbish!'

Yes, she was jealous and yes, I might have been a bit more sensitive. But Bee had a problem with sex in general. Our own sex life had never been much more than what you'd call functional and to me this was just another boring manifestation of an old problem between us. Bee only wanted sex with the lights out. She didn't even like to see me walking round the flat naked in the mornings, so she bought me a dressing-gown. She was so uptight she tore up my *Playboy*s as quickly as she did those letters. I tried to put myself in her shoes and shuddered.

The whole thing with the fan mail was freaky, though. It only seemed like yesterday that women ran from me in the street in horror. Now they were writing to me and sending photos of themselves naked with their legs apart. It was kind of like when the crappy *Diary of a Madman* book got such good reviews: it proved, finally, that no one knew anything. That as long as you kept the clichés coming with a nice steady beat, everybody paid up and went home happy. Neither punk nor Thatcherism had changed a damn thing. We were all still hooked on the same old fame-and-fortune bullshit as we ever were. All of us.

*

Because Sky was still then a relatively unknown station in Britain, unless I was at a gig, where there were always a few kids who had either seen the show or had picked up one of the pirate video copies I knew were doing the rounds, at first the fact that I was on TV three times a week hardly had any impact on my personal life at all. But in Holland, Germany, Sweden, Italy and almost anywhere else I went on the continent, by 1987 I couldn't walk the streets without drawing a crowd of mad, long-haired lunatics all making devil-signs at me.

The worst time had been in Dublin when I walked into the gents at a little venue called the Top Hat. I've never been to Dublin and not had a good time, but I didn't know then that everybody there got Sky free on the cable in those days, and that the show was as well known over there as *Top of the Pops*.

I was standing there taking a piss when I noticed the guy at the next urinal staring at me. I thought he might be a bender but when I looked all I saw was a nervous-looking young long-haired guy in a leather jacket and Motorhead T-shirt.

'Sure, it's yer man, is it?' he said, his eyes widening like screens. 'Da fella off da telly?'

I smiled, gave him a wink. I had a bit of experience of this sort of thing by now. I knew just to play it cool.

I shook and zipped up, then went over to the basin and turned on the taps. In the mirror on the wall, I could see the young guy rushing to the door. He was gone for a moment, then he was back again, only this time he had his mates with them. There must have been about seven of them.

'*Mick Wall!*' one them roared.

'All right, lads, how's it going?' I said as I turned around.

They ran at me, all at once. They were all very friendly, too fucking friendly, and without thinking about it, I suddenly found myself with my back pinned against the wall, trying to sign autographs and answer questions at the same time.

'Izzut really you?' one of them asked.

'I think so.'

Then more people started to arrive, all trying to get through the door at once.

'He's in here!' I heard someone cry.

'It's him allri'!' yelled another.

'*Mick Wall! Da fockin' Monster o' Rock!*'

In less than a minute, there must have been over a hundred people in there, and still more clamoured to get in, to get a piece of the action. Bodies at the back were beginning to climb or fall over bodies at the front, and still more poured through the door until the room was choked with crazy people all losing their fucking minds. They were all shouting my name and grabbing at me. There must have been some women in there too because some of them started screaming. I didn't know why, it was just happening. Everybody was shoving forward and I felt myself being pushed under as dozens of pairs of hands yanked at my hair, my clothes, my arms, my legs, my face . . .

Hundreds of voices, all shouting and screaming.

'*Mick Wall! Mick Wall! Mick Wall!*'

I felt the fear rising in me like vomit.

'Please!' I cried. 'Back a little bit, lads, please. I can't move . . .'

But more and more people kept arriving, trying to get in there to see what the commotion was. Then something caught the back of my knees with a kick and I crumpled to the floor. They began to tread on me, still shouting and hollering my name. A knee caught me in the face and I felt myself going under. I knew they didn't mean to hurt me but I couldn't breathe properly. It was dark and almost nice.

Then I heard another voice, deeper, more menacing than the others. '*Out of my fockin' way or oi'll kill da fockin' lottov yers!*'

I felt the weight being lifted off me, piece by piece like bomb wreckage, as more and more feet were dragged away still kicking. Then I felt the two big hands under my arms like cranes hoisting me up to my feet.

'*Come on!*' he shouted. '*We'll make a run for it!*'

It was one of the security guys. A big ape-like guy with a long scar down one side of his face. He had frightened the crowd off for just long enough to get me out of there, but he knew that like a pack of wolves it would not be long before they decided they outnumbered us and attacked again.

We took off at a sprint down the back of the hall, aiming for a side exit. Most of the crowd came after us.

'*Get away or oi'll fockin' lump yers!*' shouted my saviour, waving his fists like giant red hams at anyone who got too close.

Then we were through the door and out into a side alley. Still some of the crowd followed, maybe twenty or thirty people. Now we really started to run. But even as we did so, I couldn't help thinking: this is ridiculous. What are we running from? More to the point, what were the crowd running after? Me? Why? 'Cos I was on the telly? I'd watched as much TV as the next couch-potato but I could not think of anyone I would have run down the street after.

We made it to the security hut and the guard held the door open for me. I ran in and he closed and locked it behind me. Outside, I could hear him tearing into some of the kids.

'*Get away now, yer little bleeders, or oi'll set aboutcha.*'

But he couldn't handle them all and some of them began pounding on the tin walls of the hut. I thought of *Night of the Living Dead*. Fame, even a tiny measure of it, turned the rest of the world into zombies, all out to eat you.

I lit a cigarette. I noticed my hand was trembling. Jesus Christ, I thought, what must it be like when you're name is Jon Bon Jovi and this happens to you every day? No wonder The Beatles all went fucking loopy. Mark David Chapman obviously wasn't as abnormal as they made out. He was just another fan chasing a Beatle down the street. Only this fan caught up with John Lennon . . .

But at least pop stars got paid well for their gamble with fame. My hundred a week barely covered my minicab bills let alone a bodyguard. Fame was fucked without the money to protect you from it, I decided. Given a choice between the two – fame or money – I'd have been the most anonymous millionaire in the world. But I knew I'd never be that, so instead I had to settle for a very minor, though sometimes quite dangerous form of fame.

Everything, as usual, was exactly as it seemed . . .

*

The best part for me was the incidentals. I may not have been raking it in from my TV work, but at least I was doing different stuff. Once I got the hang of it, I became cocky, too, and felt I could blow away all the other presenters. To prove it, I started appearing in guests spots on some of the other, more mainstream Sky shows – quiz shows, chart shows, seasonal 'specials' – all the kind of gormless guff either Gary Davies or Pat Sharp would routinely present. They were all so '80s-straight, they made it easy for you to sit there and take the piss and come off like you knew something.

It wasn't me that had to read the script with a big smile on my face to keep the sponsors happy, and I took full advantage of that, acting like an anarchist while pocketing their pitiful little cheques and guzzling their warm green-room wine.

The only one I ever had trouble competing with was Tony Blackburn. Monstrous old ham that he is, Tony worked harder than anybody to really make the show swing, no matter what piece of shopping-channel drivel he happened to be appearing on. He would do anything to put a bit of zing into a link, no matter how ridiculous it made him look, and though his jokes were stale and tawdry, he was a master at stealing the show.

No matter how small his role, Tony treated it all as though it were *Top of the Pops* and his old breakfast show on Radio 1 combined. He was undefeatable. He didn't drink, didn't smoke, and plainly didn't give a fuck. But even though he was dead against 'drugs', he was definitely on something.

Tony had an eye for the ladies. 'Sensational!' he'd say in that voice whenever some strumpet in a miniskirt brought him his coffee in the morning. But that was only partly it. He had a dark side, too. He had never forgiven the BBC for sacking him from Radio 1. 'It's been going downhill ever since,' he'd tell you with a straight face. And I think it was the combo of the bile and the sex-drive, plus some strange twisted quirk of his own which fed his manic on-screen personality. Tony was King of the Weird, the original legend in his own lunchtime. And those of us who had grown up going to school and then work on his breakfast show would all go to our graves knowing his voice, even if we still could not bear to listen to what it had to say. *Sensational.*

It was to try and stop myself turning into Tony Blackburn that I began presenting a second show for Sky. *UK Despatch* was basically me and one camera going out and doing lengthy 'serious' interviews for hour-long specials with people like Elton John, Little Richard, Bob Geldof, Boy George, Phil Collins, Simple Minds, Madness . . . the real day-time TV crowd. I'd get seventy-five quid a pop for one of those. Shit money but easy work. I'd usually churn out one a week for them.

Mostly, it was tame, dreary stuff, though occasionally it could

veer off on an unpredictable tangent. I remember going to interview Elton John just a week or so after *The Sun* had run their
ridiculous front-page story about the rent-boys he was allegedly
supposed to have procured for various parties at his house. *The Sun*
later retracted the story and paid Elton a huge six-figure sum by
way of compensation, but at the time we met, he was still on the
defensive and mightily pissed-off about the whole thing. We were
warned by his promotions man beforehand that we mentioned it at
our peril during the interview.

Personally, I couldn't have cared less if Elton had hired a legion
of soldiers to prance through his bedroom in tutus and dildos with
little sacks of cocaine dangling from them. I mean, so what?
Imagine what sordid little fantasies you might be tempted to live
out if you had Elton's millions. We can't all be Cliff Richard and
pretend sex doesn't exist.

But, in the event, we did talk about it. Elton couldn't wait to get
it all off his chest, and under the heading of 'the media', he went
into a long, pedestrian rant about 'media intrusion' and 'selling lies'
and whatnot. I thought, he's right, you know. But on the other
hand, what was all that shit about getting married to a lesbian in
Australia? Hadn't he already turned himself into a public peepshow
by inviting the world's media to that bizarre little exhibition of self-
flagellation?

I didn't have the balls to actually say any of that to him, of
course. But when asked how he'd survived his time with Hitler,
Albert Speer once said something like: 'When you sup with the
Devil, you use a very long spoon.' It struck me that it was the same
with the modern media, only Elton was not the kind of guy who
had ever used a very long spoon for anything. He was more of a
champagne-from-the-slipper kind of guy, lapping up the celebrity
like a dog drinking from a muddy puddle.

Well, now something had stuck in his throat, something he
hadn't seen coming, and he was spluttering so much he could
barely hold his wig straight. Poor little queenie. No wonder all the
other rock stars laughed at him behind his back.

But all that crowd are pompous poor-me jerks. Being the centre
of so much grovelling attention just makes you that way. You think,

it couldn't happen to me. Then you wake up one morning and you've turned into Barry Manilow. The rule seemed to be: the bigger the stars, the more painful they were to interview.

Like Genesis – all three of them sat round a table at a hotel out at Heathrow, as welcoming and friendly as the sliver of a cold winter moon. Boy George – grumpy and snivelling, not even witty any more, just old and smack-bitten. Bryan Ferry – as tense and aloof as all his cuttings had promised he would be, but even more boring. The Human League – far more swank and knowing than the panda-eyed innocents I worked with at Virgin, none of them even remembered me. Peter Gabriel – speaking so softly (he's an artist) I had to sit with my knees touching his as I leaned in trying to hear whatever it was he had to say, which, from what I could pick up, wasn't much.

But then none of them had much to say for themselves. And whatever old bollocks they did manage to unload on you, it all boiled down to the same thing. They all wanted hit records, money, and more interviews to moan about. Life crawled on, even with a new album out and a tour about to kick off in the UK on . . .

*

Some of the people I interviewed on Sky, like George Benson, for example, were at least pleasant to deal with, however. George was the first grown-up musician I'd ever met and we talked like men instead of mincey little boys. Two guys in suits who'd been around the block, rapping about the old days when George used to jam with serious cats like Herbie Hancock, Quincy Jones and Miles Davis.

After the interview, George complimented me on my suit – an expensive Louis Feraud that Bee had made me buy one Christmas and which I'd never had a reason to wear before – and asked me where the best places were in London to go shopping for some decent 'threads'. Coming from an old swinger like George, now that was a compliment. (Of course, I didn't know any shops, but I told him my 'people' would call his 'people' with some suggestions later that day. I got Bee to do it.)

There were other occasional surprises, too. In 1987, to promote his *Glass Spider* album, David Bowie had agreed for us to fly out and interview him at a hotel in Amsterdam. I had read that Bowie had developed the knack of always making his interviewers feel somewhat 'special', delivering his lines in such a way as to make the journalist feel they were going away with a little bit more than what anyone else that day might have got, only to discover, when the various interviews were broadcast or published, that Bowie had given exactly the same treatment – along with almost identical quotes – to every other interviewer he'd spoken to that day.

So I was half-expecting a bit of gush on his part, but I wasn't prepared at all for what actually happened.

As I entered the room where the cameras and mikes had been set up, Bowie was already in there, standing with his back to me, gazing out of the window at the street several floors below. I immediately thought of the scene in *The Man Who Fell to Earth* when he's in the lawyer's office and he looks out on the Manhattan streets, watching them turn from night into day.

'David,' said his PR (not the notorious Corrine Schwabb, which was disappointing – I had been looking forward to seeing the legendary battle-axe in action – but another, more junior skirt and blouse). 'David, this is Mick . . .'

He spun on his heel.

'Mick Wall!' he cried. 'Lovely to meet you at last! I'm a great fan of your work!'

What?

'Joey and I never miss a show,' he said.

This was too much. David Bowie is 'a great fan' of my 'work'? Surely that should have been my line to him.

'Really?' I said, vibrating with shock and pleasure as I shook his outstretched hand.

'Yes, it's Joey's favourite thing on TV. And I love that title – "Monsters of Rock"! That's what we are, all right! Monsters!'

'Like, er . . . Scary Monsters,' I said like a dweeb, unable to think of anything else to say.

'Yes, that's right!' he laughed and I got a flash of his gold fillings.

What the fuck was going on? I felt dizzy, sick. I couldn't get my head round this at all. 'Kooks', the song Bowie wrote in 1971 for his and Angie's baby son, 'Zowie' – now known to his father and his friends as the less bothersome 'Joey' – had been one of my old favourites from the *Hunky Dory* album. Now here I was sixteen years later and Bowie is telling me that the show I present is Zowie's – sorry, Joey's – favourite thing on TV? Too goddamned much.

Then we sat down and began the interview and my stomach started to settle. What a great interview he gave, too – sharp, witty, full of fun, full of stories. The Phil Collinses and the Bob Geldofs of this world could learn a thing or two from Bowie about how to give interviews. He was just on it like a motherfucker. He was an interview killing-machine.

I was pretty hot, too. Pre-*Tin Machine*, I knew everything there was to know about the schizophrenic Mr Jones. After Ozzy, Ziggy had been my mainman. He was from the future and I grew up believing *Diamond Dogs* and *David Live* were the greatest, most underrated albums of the '70s. The reason I started smoking cigarettes was because of the cover of *Young Americans*. I went straight on to the Gitanes and stayed on them right through *Station to Station*. My first serious drug comedown – six months in 1977 spent recovering from the anorexic and psychotic after-effects of a year-long speed binge – coincided with the spiritually wounded *Low/Heroes* period.

Since then, despite only recording one more great album, *Scary Monsters*, in 1980, I'd always found it hard not to follow whatever the Thin White Duke had been up to. Even as he sold out completely with designer-label dreck like *Let's Dance* and *Tonight* – the drab titles tell you all you need to know about the contents – I couldn't help but wonder sometimes where he was at.

Bowie had been there in my mind for so long that there was almost nothing left I wanted to ask him, except maybe 'Why?' and I knew even he would never be able to answer that. So we just danced around and had some fun. I let it drop that I had seen him on stage in *The Elephant Man* back in 1980, told him it was his best ever acting performance, in any guise, and he just opened up like a flower and beamed at me.

'Oh, I agree! I'm so glad you thought so, too. It really was quite an amazing experience . . .'

We could have danced all night.

The best moment, though, as is often the case, came after the interview was over. We were both standing there smoking cigarettes and I asked him to tell me a little more about Joey, how old he was (sixteen) and who his favourites groups were (The Beastie Boys) so that I could play a video for him on the next *Monsters* show.

'And what about old Bowie albums?' I said for fun. 'Do you ever catch him listening to any of them?'

'Um . . . sometimes,' he smiled, unexpectedly bashful suddenly. 'We've listened to them together sometimes, you know.'

'What does he make of those pictures of you as Ziggy and Aladdin Sane?'

'It depends. It seems to change as he gets older. Like changing his name. But I thought that was sensible.'

He looked at me.

'I'll tell you a funny story, though. We were at home together one night wondering what to do, whether to go out or stay in. Then we noticed in the paper that the film of the Ziggy farewell concert was on at the local cinema, and so for laugh we decided we'd go. Joey ran off upstairs to get ready and I pottered around doing a few things first, then got ready, too. Meanwhile, Joey was nowhere to be seen. I remember standing at the bottom of the stairs calling him to hurry up or we were going to be late . . .'

He paused and took a puff on his ciggy, then exhaled and shook his head.

'The next thing was, here comes Joey down the stairs – and he's got the full Ziggy Stardust outfit on! He's been in the bathroom and dyed his hair carrot red and gelled it all up and back-combed it so that it's sticking up, he's got all the make-up on and all these clothes, I don't know where he got them from, whether they came from old wardrobes of mine or whether they were his, I don't know . . . but I'll never forget it. The first words out of my mouth were: "You're not going out dressed like that!"'

He burst into laughter.

'Can you imagine? He just looked at me and said, "But Dad, this is you!" And I had one of those really strange head things where everything just zaps back and forth, your whole life passes by in front of you, you know?' He put his fingers to his temples. 'And I thought, wait, what am I doing? He's right! How can I *of all people!* tell him *of all people!* he can't go out dressed like . . . well, like me!'

I left him there, still thinking it over . . .

*

But no matter how many episodes of *UK Despatch* we did, no matter how big the star, the show that really pulled in the viewers was always *Monsters of Rock*. It was the comedy element, it just drew people in, and by 1988 it was the most popular home-produced show on Sky. I was getting letters from mums and dads now, too. Mums and dads, little kids, grandmothers, policemen, teachers, nurses . . . the whole world in their Iron Maiden and Kiss T-shirts, all doing little V-signs and laughing their stupid heads off. It was fantastic.

Not knowing any better, I just took it all for granted. The only big difference I noticed in my own life was how being on TV made the bands themselves relate to you in a slightly different, sometimes even more reverential manner. Being on TV still didn't mean they would ever totally accept you on their level, but it did place you in their minds above the average rock journo, whose personal experience of 'performing' was limited only to their imagination.

Def Leppard, for instance, used to watch the show every week while they were recording their *Hysteria* album in Holland. Then when I went to see them play a warm-up gig at a small club in Utrecht, the band looked on bemused as a large crowd formed around me at the bar before the gig started.

'I've been here in Holland for months and I think I've signed about two autographs,' Leppard singer Joe Elliot joked in the dressing-room afterwards. 'But you've been here less than a day and you must have signed about fifty!'

Even some of the bands themselves began acting like fans. Steve Harris of Iron Maiden, who became a regular guest, told me it was his favourite show on any channel, and 'Arry was not known for going out of his way to polish anybody's halo.

Then Jimmy Page got his office to call and arrange for me to meet him at his studio in Windsor. They sent a car to pick me up and as I sat there watching the countryside flash by, I thought, what is this all about? When I got there and Jimmy introduced himself, smiling from ear to ear, I stepped off my cloud for a moment and asked him straight. 'Jimmy, this is all great, but I have to ask you, what am I doing here?'

He seemed taken aback. Didn't I know? 'I just wanted to play you my new album,' he said simply. 'And I wanted to meet you. I really like the show. I think it's fucking hilarious!'

Yes, it was a trip, sitting there puffing on a joint and knocking back the beers while Jimmy played me his new album, *Outrider*, but I still didn't quite get it. The fame thing, minor though it was, had come too late for me to know what to do with it. If I were Gary Davies or Pat Sharp I would have known exactly what to do next. But I wasn't. Didn't even want to be. But knowing what you didn't want was the easy part. It was knowing the opposite that was hard.

When I left that day, Jimmy gave me a present. It was a framed cartoon taken from a 1979 *LA Times* based on a gag about how 'big' Zeppelin were. On the back, he had written in pen: 'Mick, For One Monster Of Rock From Another, KEEP ROCKIN', Jimmy Page.'

It still hangs on my wall today. It means something like: I dig your trip, man; I can relate. Now it was my turn to be taken aback. And though Jimmy and I have seen each other only infrequently ever since, we have stayed in touch and he is one of the very few rock stars I've ever gotten to know that I would actually call any kind of friend.

I once asked him outright why he was always so nice to me.

'Everybody else comes away from meeting you saying what a complete bastard you are,' I said.

'I know,' he said with a smile. 'But that's the other side of the coin. It's like the electric guitar and the acoustic guitar. Some people bring the heaviest noise you can make out of you, while others bring the more gentle acoustic side out. You've only ever seen the acoustic side of me . . .'

*

One guitarist I definitely saw the heavier side of was Def Leppard's Steve Clark. The first night we met in Holland we both ended up back in my hotel room plastered on coke and brandy. Joe was with us too that time and all three of us sat around on the bed asking each other things like: 'Do you get a lot of groupies?' and 'How much money do you actually make then?'

Well, groupies came ten-a-penny, of course, but the band had been working on the *Hysteria* album for nearly three years at that point, Joe said, and they'd already spent over a million quid on it.

'A million quid!' I cried. 'How many will you have to sell to make that back and start earning a bob then?'

'We'll have to sell at least a million just to get us back to zero,' said Steve dolefully.

'Yeah,' said Joe, 'but then we make quarter of a million dollars a night on T-shirts alone on tour in America. So that's half a dozen gigs and there's your million quid right there! It's not a problem.'

I told them how much I got for the *Monsters* show and they sat there staring at me in disbelief.

'A hundred fuckin' quid!' laughed Joe. 'They're taking the fuckin' piss, aren't they?'

'You should go to MTV,' said Steve. 'You'd probably get ten times that amount there. Honestly, man, you should. You're good.'

Oh, I was good all right. Especially at four in the morning with a bottle of brandy and a gram or two of coke on hand.

Steve and I would become good friends over the course of what became Leppard's fourteen-month-long 'Hysteria' world tour. Still writing for *Kerrang!* and now several other similar magazines, I ended up joining the Leppard tour six or seven times that year and on each occasion Steve and I would always end up in either his room or mine at some ungodly hour, snorting coke and drinking vodka and cranberry juice.

Steve liked the cranberry because it was supposed to remove the smell of alcohol from your breath. I was so drunk myself I probably wouldn't have noticed if he hadn't volunteered the information, but Steve had a serious drinking problem. He confessed that the band had even paid for him to go into rehab to try and clean himself up before the tour had started, but that it hadn't worked.

'All they do is sit you in a circle with a load of people who haven't got the faintest idea of who you are or where you're coming from,' he shrugged, the pain still there in his eyes for all to see. 'I mean, I'm not trying to be big-headed or anything, but the fact is, listening to some fuckin' postman who used to take a little bottle of Scotch into work with him in the morning because his marriage broke up or something – it just didn't do anything for me, do you know what I mean?'

He shook his head and poured himself another tumbler of voddy.

'My experience was so outside of everybody else's. Even the doctors that were there, they hadn't any idea what it's like, either. I mean, it's not like they have to perform their operations with twenty thousand people screaming at them, is it? And I'd be like, well, yeah, mate, that's bad, but with me it's slightly different. See, I *like* getting fucked up. I *like* drinking and snorting coke and anything else I wanna do. It's just the other stuff I can't handle . . .'

I never really found out exactly what this 'other stuff' was. But, superficially at least, it was something to do with feeling increasingly left out of it since guitarist Phil Collen had joined the group. Leppard had always been a twin-guitar band, but Phil was so technically adept and the band's producer, 'Mutt' Lange, so demanding a perfectionist, that Steve felt his own brand of different-every-time rock guitar was taking more and more of a backseat in the recording process. It didn't help either that Phil, who had once been Steve's big drinking buddy, had cleaned up his act and gone straight. Phil hadn't touched a drop of the hard stuff for over a year. And while Steve slept off another binge, Phil would be in the gym, pumping iron.

Now Steve's self-esteem was so low, he had become terrified of almost everything to do with being a rock star. At the start of the 'Hysteria' tour, he was so freaked out at the prospect of going on stage again in front of thousands of people that he had tried breaking his own wrists by repeatedly banging them against the bathroom wall.

He'd lost it. Big time. And the band had been keeping a watchful eye on him ever since. He knew it and it just made it worse. 'Don't tell the others,' he would repeat like a mantra as he sat there chopping out four more fat white lines on the mirror for us.

But it wasn't just his increasingly lowly place in the Leppard scheme of things that was bringing Steve down. It was something else. Something that had been eating away at him long before Phil had joined the group. Something much harder to resolve than who played what on which song.

When, a couple of years later, a mutual friend called to tell me Steve had died, a combination of booze and downers finally doing for him one cold January night in 1991, I hugged the floor and cried. Everything was such a waste. I wanted to put my arms around the world and hold it while we all cried together. I wasn't supposed to care what happened to anybody, and I suppose the truth is I didn't. But losing Steve like that hurt in all sorts of unexpected ways. It broke through the hard, shit-encrusted shell I had erected around myself. Was I losing it? Maybe, but I could feel the floor already beginning to move beneath me and it was all I could do now to hold on . . .

*

But at least those guys were in the kind of bands the *Monsters* show was supposed to be about. There was some connection there you could see that went beyond a quick celebrity fix. What really surprised me were the overtures we were starting to get from all sorts of bands whom I wouldn't previously have imagined on the show in a million years.

Depeche Mode were a typical example. I got a call from the Sky office one day telling me the band had been booked for an interview slot on Gary Davies's show but that they had put in a special request to be interviewed instead on my show.

'I know it doesn't make sense,' said Gail, 'but they say they're big fans.'

'Bollocks,' I said. 'Someone's pulling your chain.'

'No, seriously. I've had someone on the phone from their office just now. They're serious. They say they watch the show where they live in Berlin.'

'Forget it,' I said. 'They're just taking the piss.'

'So you don't want them on then?'

'Naw. Tell them to go back to where they belong on the Saturday-morning kids shows . . .'

I was getting Big Time. Starting to throw my weight around. It was not a good sign. Then I was standing drunk in the backstage bar of the Hammersmith Odeon one night when two guys came up to me and started blathering on about what a great show it was. I didn't realise they were in a band until one of them said, 'Yeah, you know, we'd love to come on some time ourselves, if you're into it.'

'Yeah, that would really surprise the kids who watch it every week,' smiled the other.

'I'm sorry,' I said, 'but are you in a band?'

'Er, yes,' said the first one. 'Spandau Ballet. Have you heard of us?'

I had to laugh. Weren't those the guys who pronounced rock 'dead' in the good old *NME* back in their toga-wearing days? They didn't seem to mind my laughing, though. I think they just took me for a metal guy and therefore not someone who would necessarily recognise the Kemp brothers when he saw them. Especially when he was pissed.

'Sorry, fellas,' I said, finally. 'But you're just not heavy enough . . .'

Their heads drooped. I told them to go home and write a few more decent guitar solos and strode off. Big Time. I had the whole world up my arse.

Sometimes, when I was sober, I would wonder how long it was going to last. I was always expecting the bubble to burst. Then when it did, I was taken completely by surprise. The new affordable Sky dish was on its way and with it came the capacity to receive MTV. The days of Sky making their own tatty little pop shows were numbered.

I didn't mind. I'd been riding my luck for so long by then I just expected something else to pop right up and replace it. As chance would have it, the very last *Monsters of Rock* show was recorded on the morning of my thirtieth birthday. I took it as a sign. The closing of one chapter and the beginning of the next. I even began to look forward to the break. I'd been doing a weekly show on Sky for nearly four years. A change of scene would be good now, I thought.

I didn't really know how much I missed being on TV until years and years later, when I first saw Anthea Turner presenting the National Lottery on the BBC. 'The biggest job in television,' Dale Winton called it, and he was right. I remembered how Anthea would be wheeled in sometimes to stand in the background and watch me work in the old days on Sky, particularly if I had a guest on the show. Anthea was always useless at interviewing people and they hoped she would pick up a few tips from watching me.

Then sitting there on the floor of my unfurnished house, years later, alone at last, drug-free, job-free, woman-free and furniture-free, wondering if I would ever get out of debt again, I couldn't help but draw the inevitable conclusion as I watched Anthea do her jiggle-giggle stuff: it could have been me, mutha. Then I thought about it some more and realised that, no, I could never have been Anthea Turner. The Lottery producers had chosen wisely.

There would be the inevitable half-hearted encores, of course – a Saturday-night show on Capital Radio that lasted a year, followed by a similar deal on the BBC's Greater London Radio that lasted about the same. And the sound of the crowd calling my name as they tried to crush me would be a memory I would hold forever. But, for me, the show was over, baby.

There was only one place left to go. The place where all the old-stagers eventually fetch up: LA. Land of endless sun and other clichés.

People said it was sick but I liked the sound of it. If you had to dangle your sickness somewhere, where better than out by the pool surrounded by bimbos?

Living in Hollywood would be like being on TV all over again, only this time it would be for real . . .

9

Big in America

Ross and I rented a nice two-bedroomed apartment in West Hollywood for six hundred and fifty dollars a month. It was just down the road from the Rainbow on Sunset – the white, moneyed-up part of town – and between us it worked out at about sixty pounds a week each. Less than what I was paying for my place back in London.

It seemed too good to be true but there it was. We had a 'sun garden' patio, a TV with over two hundred channels on it and a swimming-pool which we shared with three other apartments. Twice a week, a friendly middle-aged Mexican woman brought us groceries and other necessities and cleaned the place up, and once a month a young dude on rollerblades came by and did the pool.

The '90s had arrived like a drunk stumbling down the road, but no one in LA seemed to notice. People kept talking about a recession but the conveyor belt of bands hadn't appeared to slow down yet and we didn't know what else to do except keep on keeping on. What else was there?

Down on Melrose, retro-'70s chic was already big in the stores. But that's all it was: retro. Whatever happened next, the '80s had left such a mark on the world, it was hard to imagine things ever going back to the way they were. You could wear flares and buy lava lamps again but you'd never turn the clock back on AIDS. Promiscuity may have been back on the agenda, along with cigarettes and heroin, but free love was gone for good. Now everybody had to pay.

The only place I saw anything happening at all, weirdly, was in music. Groups like Jane's Addiction, Red Hot Chilli Peppers and Metallica had demonstrated rock's ability to regenerate itself into newer and fresher hybrids. But even there it was more a case of rummaging through the detritus of the '60s and '70s to try and say something new than it was actually having something new to say.

So bland and demographically driven had the '80s music industry become that the arrival of a band like Guns N' Roses – clichéd bad-boy rockers swigging Jack Daniels and singing about bitches and motherfuckers like they knew something about it – took on huge historical importance. We'd heard it all before, of course, but that had been back in the pre-MTV era, when rock fans still used to expect something from the lyrics. The fact that Guns N' Roses had arrived just at that moment when Bon Jovi – corporate Reaganomic rock at its zenith – seemed to have taken over the world, was more than just coincidence, I felt. It was the natural order restoring itself. If ever we needed a bunch of arseholes to throw their weight around, it was right then; and, for me, the '90s began in earnest in late-'88, when *Appetite for Destruction*, the first Guns N' Roses album, went to No.1 in America. It was almost exciting.

Meanwhile, the onset of rap and acid house had made it abundantly clear to anyone who still gave a shit that there were still some original artists working out there, despite the cynicism and the cost. I thought the signs were good and though I never bought vinyl records any more, I began to amass a surprisingly large collection of CDs, going back and rediscovering old stuff I'd completely forgotten about, like Little Feat, Steely Dan and Dr John, as well as dipping into new pools of wisdom from the likes of The Digital Underground, Ice T, Nine Inch Nails and Dr Dre.

CDs were where it was at, dude. More tracks, less hassle. And you could programme the tracks to play in any order you wanted, even skip the ones you didn't like. Here, at last, was real democracy at work in music. It was funny how all the old farts had such a downer on them. Even DJs that liked to think of themselves as 'new wave', like John Peel, displayed a sickeningly old-wave attitude to vinyl, building up an utterly unwarranted mystique about it, as though even owning a CD required some form of mumbling apology.

Peel still does the best show on the radio, of course, but this affectation for vinyl reminded me of those anal little strips of humanity who accused Dylan of being a Judas for picking up an electric guitar. It was all so much better in the old days, they seemed to be saying. Yeah, right. Steam trains, white bread, flat caps and shelves and shelves of carefully alphabetised vinyl . . . all the things I hated about musty, more-tea-vicar England.

The '90s, I felt, could not help but be a better time for music. Maybe it would be a better time for everything. We would all be richer, saner, older, wiser. All we had to do was pray they didn't drop the bomb, or that the aliens didn't finally reveal themselves and spoil the game for everyone. As long as neither of those two things happened we would all live happily ever after . . . That's how it seemed to me, anyway, sitting out there by the pool some mornings with my CD Walkman on, squinting into the smog and thinking about Pamela Anderson's breast implants.

The Gulf War had been a pleasant enough diversion – with CNN as the new MTV – and now they were going to vote in the first sax-playing, dope-smoking, draft-dodging, ex-hippy president. The fun just never stopped. Of course, he had lied about not inhaling. But then what hadn't he lied about whenever his personal life came under the media microscope?

No, Clinton was the genuine article. He knew it wasn't his job to tell the truth. If he was to be any sort of president at all, he knew his job would be to placate and reassure the TV-watching audience; to reinforce the lie that at least someone somewhere knew what was going on, and to deceive as many people as possible into believing all the things they wanted to hear.

It was a highly specialised job and only the very best could pull it off. But looking at Clinton, seeing him turning on the naughty schoolboy smile, you knew he'd fit in with the rest of the bleary cast no problem at all. Bill had mendacity written all over him. You knew there wasn't anything that pretty boy wouldn't do when the time came. He was perfect. There hadn't been such a smooth operator gunning for the gig since Reagan made the part his ten years before. But even the Russians fell for Big Ron. Maggie, too. Everybody loves a cowboy. Well, now they had another one.

Cowboy Bill and his feisty little woman, Hopalong Hillary . . .

Watching them work together on TV, it was clear it wasn't even a question of 'if' any more, but simply of how long they would be able to keep it up once they got through the Whitehouse doors. If they had both been like Hillary, you felt they would have breezed the full eight-year double term, no problem at all. But there was something about Bill, a certain smarmy, Southern overconfidence, that made you suspect it might not be too long before he did something, or didn't do something, or just put his foot badly wrong somewhere, and the whole house of cards would come tumbling down around them both.

It would be quite a show though, while it lasted. The most fawning of the Democrats were already calling them 'the Jack and Jackie of the '90s'. Like that was supposed to reassure us . . .

*

Ross was the pictures and I was the words. Every morning, at about half-past seven, we would jog down to the Sports Connection on Santa Monica Boulevard, where Ross would make sure we both sweated our asses off for an hour or so. Sitting there on the bike-machine some mornings, gazing through the high glass walls at the long poisonous snakes of traffic wending their way slowly up and down the boulevard, it was impossible not to reflect sometimes on how much my surroundings had changed since the days when Mandy and I thought keeping fit meant always having a clean set of works at the ready. I may have been a no-life junkie back then but at least I still had something to believe in. Something that would still come through whatever colour the moon was.

Back then there were things I would do and things I definitely would not do. Now, as I sat on the bike-machine, blowing and sweating like death was not an option, I found it hard to remember what it was I was still doing any of this for. I found it difficult to articulate even to myself what it was that was actually going on now. People say that about LA – that it turns out your lights and sends you to sleep. But it wasn't LA that had done this to me. Just like any other American, I came from a world I no longer wished to know. I wasn't necessarily looking for something better. I was just hoping vaguely that I could delay the worst.

But in between times – in between the gym and the pool and the backstage passes – I knew the worst had already occurred. Thoughts of death and mutilation filled my head. I kept waiting for an ending, that gunshot in the dark that would bring a climax to this movie. Good or bad, I didn't care, just that there should be one. But no ending came. The sun shone down regardless and the rain was merely rain.

Some mornings I woke up crying. I was losing it, I knew that. Only now I was becoming pathetic, too. I didn't care. Too frightened and weary to kill myself, I opted instead to kill time. The days were there to be disposed of somehow, and the nights . . . well, the nights were for whatever was left after the day, and that meant not much. Then there I would be again the next morning, still pedalling away on my bike that went nowhere, gazing through the windows and wondering . . .

Santa Monica Boulevard was boys town and the Sports Connection was mainly gay, but women packed in there, too. Gyms had taken over from discos as the No.1 pick-up joints in America. It was easy to see why. You got to check out the meat up-close and from every possible angle before you'd even said hello. And they kept the music up so loud in the gym that a lot of people did just stand around dancing when they weren't lifting weights or riding the bikes. It was hot and horny and I left there every day with what we called 'donkey-dong' – a kind of semi-hard-on that just hung there in your shorts in a state of permanently agitated near-arousal.

Then, after a shower and twenty minutes on the sunbed, we would have an enormous breakfast out by the pool which we'd order in from the nearby deli – fresh fruit, eggs, bacon, sausage, chicken, toast, fries, coffee, mineral water, Diet Coke, half a dozen different vitamins and, in my case, to top it all off, a nice skinny joint.

Ross didn't smoke and he would look at me with distaste. 'Do you have to smoke that shit first thing in the morning?' he'd scowl.

'Yep,' I'd say, letting out an enormous plume of blue smoke.

'It's disgusting!'

'No one's asking you to smoke it.'

'I wouldn't fuckin' want to! It rots your brain, that shit does.'

Living together like that, we would bicker constantly like an old married couple. It didn't mean much, it was just something to fill in the blanks with. It didn't matter that we seemed to have the same conversation every day. We were quite happy that way. It was safe and bland and nothing could touch us. We didn't want to change a thing.

'You've really got a problem, do you know that?' he'd say, waving at the smoke with his hand.

'The only problem I've got is listening to you telling me what a problem I've got.'

'Yes, very funny. And what if you get busted? You get busted and they'll send you home and that will be the end of it, mate! They'll never fuckin' let you back in!'

I'd look around. Almost everybody else in the apartment complex went out to work for a living. Except for weekends, we nearly always had the pool to ourselves.

'For God's sake, Ross. Who's going to bust me?'

'You never know.'

'For God's sake . . .'

Ross was a worrier. He was the old Jew who never stopped minding the store, never happier than when he had something to complain about, which was most of the time. When he got bored picking at me, he'd get on the phone and start giving grief to people in record companies, shaking them up a bit just for the hell of it. Most PRs I knew in LA were terrified of him. They would agree to almost anything just to get him out of their hair.

You could hear his voice halfway down the street.

'*Three o'clock today . . . my studio . . . and tell them: don't be late!*' he'd rant. '*And don't forget to tell them as well: no booze and no drugs! You got that? I don't want them all fucked up when I'm trying to shoot them. Tell them they can do all that fucking rubbish when they do their interview with Mick afterwards . . . yeah . . . He likes all that shit, too, . . . yeah . . .*'

Without Ross calling the shots, though, I would never have left the apartment at all. Bee had dumped me for some other poor veggieburger-eating sap not long after my TV career had gone down the drain, and LA was now 'home'. Ross and I had special journalist visas in our passports with the words 'Multiple Indefinite' stamped in red. It meant that, technically, we were foreign correspondents and could stay and work as freelancers anywhere we liked in the US for up to six months at a time.

Twice a year – summer and Christmas – we would go back to London for a few weeks. Just long enough to be sure of new six-monthly permits when we returned to LA. And we could never wait to get back. London had become 'there' and LA was now 'here'. Even the jetlag began working in reverse, so completely was my body now running on southern Californian time, and I even began to think of myself as an American.

Maybe because I was born in London, I don't know, but when things got bad there, there just didn't seem to be much you could do about it. But in LA there was always something going on, always something new about to happen that would take your mind off things. Everybody walked around with their head in tomorrow. They would talk about what they'd done recently but what they really talked about was what they were *going* to do. One day. Soon. Meanwhile, they lived their lives like the lead characters in their own Friday-night sitcoms.

Every dreamer in America headed for Hollywood sooner or later. But some of the parts they played while they waited for their big break were weirder then others.

There was the chick down on Laraby who liked being tied up and hung upside-down while she was being fucked. Her name, wonderfully, was Peggy-Sue. By day, she worked at the Gap and looked like butter wouldn't melt in her crack. But at night she turned into Daughter of Vampira. I found out too late and it scared the hell out of me the first time I walked in and found her hanging there like a piece of recently killed meat. It was like a scene from a pornographic version of *Harold and Maude*. She was an artist, she said, and I believed her.

Then there was Fat Frank, the only coke dealer I'd ever met who was grossly overweight. A former daytime soap star from the '70s who now got by hustling krel to other out-of-work actors and musicians, he should have been whip-thin and crippled with paranoia. Instead, Frank ate like a pig and constantly cracked jokes. Especially about the TV. If you had the set on when he arrived, you were done for. You'd be stuck there for maybe two or three hours. Frank knew every single face in every programme, every commercial, every news bulletin, every sports field, every pop video . . . Frank knew them all and had a story about every one of them. The only face he never saw on TV that he knew well was his own.

But even if you had the set off, it was still a most discouraging sight, watching the repulsive fat fuck wolf down a couple of Jack-In-The-Box cheeseburgers while simultaneously demolishing line after line of krel. He wanted to start his own restaurant, he said. But I used to give him the benefit of the doubt and hope he was only joking.

And then there was the woman who lived in the apartment across from ours. I didn't know if she was either very innocent or just an everyday exhibitionist, but every morning as we were having breakfast, she used to stand at the window of her bedroom with the blinds up, completely naked, inspecting herself in front of the mirror. You couldn't see the mirror, you just knew it was there from the way she positioned herself in front of it, standing on tip-toe and peering over her shoulder at her bottom, or holding up her breasts to their reflection and wondering. There are far too many beautiful women in LA. You never quite got used to it, but after a while you did take it just a little bit more for granted. That is, you stopped staring like an ape. Then came a woman like this, a special one the gods had made as a joke to taunt poor idiots like me and Ross. A wild quivering madness of flesh and hair that not even the sky could stop looking at and shaking, its mouth slightly open, drooling like a half-wit . . .

Ross and I called her The Woman In The Window, and though we had never spoken, I got to know her body so well I began to feel as if I was almost getting to know her mind. I stopped masturbating and began just to watch her, the way you would a cat. I had never seen her outside her bedroom, I realised. I probably wouldn't even have recognised her with her clothes on. But what did it mean?

Who was the weird one? Me for watching, or her for being watched?

Then I was queuing up at the counter of Book Soup one afternoon when a sudden, jolting vibe alerted me to the fact that someone familiar had come within range of my psychic radar. I looked around and standing right behind me was The Woman In The Window. I looked into her eyes for barely a second, just long enough to know for sure: she didn't recognise me. I had the answer to my question . . .

When I got home that night, I sat down at the laptop and wrote a letter.

> 'Dear Residents,
>
> We have had unconfirmed reports of a peeping tom in the neighbourhood. We advise all our female residents to be on the alert. The police say we have nothing to fear but that we should be careful not to do anything to encourage this sort of behaviour. So, remember, ladies, for the good of us all: PLEASE KEEP THOSE BLINDS CLOSED!
>
> Have a nice day,
>
> Gertrude Stein, Chief Operating Officer of the West Hollywood Residents Safety Association

I put a stamp on it and mailed it off and, sure enough, two mornings later, the blinds stayed closed in the apartment opposite. I still didn't know if I had done the right thing but at least I was no longer haunted by having to make the choice first thing every day. I had come to LA to get away from all that. I didn't want to know. I just wanted to be left alone to watch the Comedy Channel and work on my tan.

*

By noon, Ross would have the whole day and night's schedule worked out for us, so that wherever we went, we were almost always earning money. LA was a great place not just to interview people, but to gossip about them, to mingle and mix and make it happen. Everybody was there. Anybody that wasn't didn't matter. Particularly by the start of the '90s, before the riots and the earthquakes changed everything, when LA was still 'the new New York' of the music biz – the new centre of things.

It wasn't unusual for Ross and me to squeeze in as many as eight or nine interviews and photo-sessions a week. We would farm them out to all sorts of places – *RIP*, *Faces*, *Billboard* and half a dozen smaller metal rags in America, plus *Kerrang!* back in the UK, as well as *The Sun*, *The Mail*, and whoever else was interested. And that was before we got to all the Japanese, Australian and European titles our various agents were selling our shit to.

It was sweet. We weren't rolling in it, but it was becoming harder and harder to remember what it was like to be really poor, and we honestly couldn't see how that might change. Ross earned far more than me, of course – words go out of date so quickly, you can't keep selling them on for years and years the way you can with certain pictures – but I still had more money than I knew what to do with.

We tried hard to piss it away, eating out every night, usually in Ross's favourite Japanese restaurant, the exorbitantly priced but ultra-fashionable Matsuhisa, on La Cienega. If we found ourselves with a day off, we would invariably go shopping on Melrose, buying dozens of T-shirts and whatnot from Gap, or cruising the Beverly Center, throwing money away on faxes, computers, watches, cameras, tape-recorders, mini TVs, wide-screen TVs, just more and more and more crap, as much as we could get our hands on. It was the American way.

I had never been a shopaholic before and I wasn't really much of one now – not compared to Ross, who really knew how to spend – but there wasn't much else to do. Whenever I looked, I always seemed to have thousands in my English and American bank accounts. Cheques seemed to arrive every other day and the way LA was then, you felt life would just go on like that forever.

Even when it rained, you still sat around in your shorts and your sunglasses, donkey-dong throbbing like a toothache between your legs. In LA, the sun never stopped shining, whatever the weather.

Sometimes friends from England would come and stay. But either they liked it too much and we could never get rid of them, or they couldn't get their heads round it at all and went away grumbling inanities about the place. Usually, the latter.

I didn't get it. The main objection seemed to be that the people in LA were 'false'. And they're not in dreary, class-ridden London? Was that it?

Well, fuck London, fuck England, fuck whatever the old world thinks about anything. Coming from dirt-poor Irish immigrants, I'd never had the hang-up about American dollars that so many little Englanders seemed to have. Seething with racist envy, they clung to the idea that LA was just *Baywatch*; that Americans really did have smaller brains and that, somehow, not being an American gave you some sort of edge.

It's an unpleasant and hypocritical attitude that persists to this day. The same old con trick the English have been pulling on the rest of the world for centuries. We're better than you. The intellectuals are the worst. They see *The Player* and they think they've seen it all. Lord Puttnam was too good to survive? Don't believe the hype. It wasn't Big Ben old Putters was dreaming of when he was living high in the Hollywood hills, it was Walt Disney.

No, the English flew in, sat around pale and confused for a few days, watched too much television, went on all the rides, made pricks of themselves in public and went home happy. They had seen all they wanted to see. The real fun was to be had afterwards, sitting around smug London dinner tables, imitating the accents and taking the piss with all their other went-there-once friends.

'And they say "Have a nice day" to everything!'

Yes, and we say 'I'm sorry' to everything.

I knew what I preferred to hear, and by the start of the '90s, I didn't care if I never saw England again. We'd sit there at night in Massa's, us and Bobby De Niro and Jerry Bruckheimer and the boys, and as I was sipping my miso I'd think to myself: I fucking love LA. As far as I was concerned, I was going to live there forever. Or until the Big One came and threw us all into the stinking sea . . .

*

Working out at the gym, answering the phone, interviewing rock stars and writing about it as though it meant something . . . This was as straight as I could get. No real interest left in anything. Not even sex. Donkey-dong or not, fucking anybody other than myself was just too much like trying. It was like going back to school. It required words I could no longer utter with a straight face; deeds I no longer felt capable of performing with any dignity.

There were dinner dates with divorcees and days spent out at Venice Beach with girls nearly half my age – they liked my accent, they liked my otherness, they liked that I was in the music business. But there were also nights when I could no longer get it up, either mentally or physically. Somewhere along the line, I'd lost a few steps. Not through the smack – you didn't have to be a junkie to grow weary of the chase. Too much sun and not enough time, that was my excuse.

But it was more than that. Or, rather, less. There comes a point as a junkie when no matter how much gear you shoot into your body, all it does is keep you straight. You just can't get high any more and all it does is keep you going till the next fix and the next. And that's when, if you have any brains left at all, you finally quit for good.

Now, somehow, I had reached that point again. Not through heroin this time but through an even more pervasive form of junk. I was high on life, man. And it was slowly killing me. I'd tried quitting so many times, I didn't even have the energy for that any more. I just took the money and took the money and waited for it to end. After a certain point, even money becomes worthless. I knew I would never be a millionaire and once you know that and the rent's paid, what else is there to think about? You didn't have to be a millionaire to work it out, you just needed to have known a few.

I remember going to interview Stevie Nicks at her house in LA one evening for the *Daily Mail*. I had never been a big Fleetwood Mac fan – not in the literal sense, anyway – but like most hetero-sexual guys my age who remembered her sashaying about to 'Rhiannon', I had often wondered what it would be like to get the sexy, hippy-chick singer into bed. With those big, soft, cow eyes, warm curves and long, naturally curly hair, she looked as cute and unblemished as a little china doll.

Only her long, grandmother shawls, her shin-length skirts, her hippy beads and her long witch's fingernails gave away any clue to the real personality behind the dazed I'm-only-dancing pout. Stevie was '70s Rock Chick incarnate. If she hadn't made it in Fleetwood Mac, she'd have been a wine-bar singer, sitting there on a stool somewhere in Sacramento, in an enclave of candles and joss-sticks, some whey-faced boyfriend strumming the guitar beside her.

But she had made it with the Mac. 'Dreams', the song she was best known for after 'Rhiannon', had been a US No.1 in 1977. *Rumours*, the album it came from, had not only been No.1 but had sold over 25 million copies, making it the biggest selling album of all time – a record it kept until Michael Jackson's *Thriller*.

From there, commercially at least, it had been steady all the way for both Stevie and the Mac. *Tusk*, the album that followed *Rumours* in 1979, was another No.1 and there had been a handful of further Top 10 Mac albums like *Mirage* in 1982 and *Tango in the Night* a few years later. But the '80s had seen Stevie breaking away from the group and indulging in solo albums that sold fewer and fewer copies and a personal life that seemed to totter from one 'emotional crisis' to another. At least, that's what the story I read in the *LA Times* said.

Sensibly, Stevie only went back to Fleetwood Mac now when she needed a hit. It was like one of those open marriages from the '70s, where both sides could fuck around as much as they liked as long as they promised to come home and pay the bills every once in a while.

Despite her millions, she was still a tortured artist, you see. Sitting up all night writing her poetry, the eternal student, keeping a journal of all her old affairs and filling it with dead flowers. She reminded me of Maria and about a thousand other angst-ridden hippy-chicks I had known. They were all cigarette smokers and they all drank too much and drugged too much and fucked too much and just did everything too much. I couldn't blame them. If I had been born a woman, I would have been the same. Fucking men. Why should they get all the laughs? A woman had an asshole, too, didn't she? Why shouldn't she use it to blow farts at the world?

Which reminds me . . . the story that used to do the rounds in the biz when I first started out was that Stevie was the original Ice Queen when it came to the old krel. Apparently, her favourite trick was to have the coke blown up her ass through a straw by a willing accomplice. But to me it always sounded like the typical male chauvinist fantasy that famous females everywhere have to endure, and I was never quite sure what to do with that information. There was, after all, only one way to really find out . . .

*

Stevie had just turned forty-three when I met her, in the summer of 1991, and although she still had the same cute baby-doll face, her body had filled out and she was considerably thicker round the hips and the waist than the slender hippy-waif I remembered from the '70s. And her voice sounded like old ashtrays being scraped clean, more of a croak than a whisper.

But she was still beautiful, dressed in a tight black mini-dress with a low plunging neckline. She was all cleavage and high-heels, lots of expensive jewellery, lots of make-up, her hair still tumbling down her shoulders in a waterfall of ringlets. Okay, she was show-ing some wear and tear, but I liked it that she wasn't one of those neurotic forty-year-olds in LA who pay a doctor to suck and cut them back into twentysomething shape. She was not young any more but she wasn't so old she couldn't be funky about it. I'd still have blown up a straw for her, if she'd asked.

'May I ask you a question?' she said within a few minutes of our meeting. 'What star sign are you?'

'Cancer,' I said. 'Near the cusp of Gemini.'

'Wow,' she said. 'I'm Gemini, near the cusp of Taurus! Do you know what that means?'

'No.'

'Neither do I, but I think it means we're gonna get along just fine,' she smiled.

I smiled back at her, trying to think of some witty rejoinder. None came.

Her house was out in Encino, a big white-walled castle-like structure with three floors and a watchtower. As you drove through the main gates it was like driving straight into the bowels of the house. There was some kind of courtyard with a central stairwell leading to the rest of the place, and a fountain with lights bouncing discreetly off it in the middle.

One of her girlfriends was waiting at the bottom of the stairs to meet me. She looked about Stevie's age and she also wore a tight black miniskirt, high-heels, and a tight black top with low plunging neckline. And she had a smile on her face like Romeo had just stuck his thumb up her ass.

'Hiya!' she called. 'Welcome! Welcome! Stevie's upstairs in the kitchen. She can't wait to meet you!'

Stevie wasn't one of those women you ever imagined in the kitchen, but when I got there that's where she was. In a kitchen surrounded by more girlfriends and big baskets of flowers and fruit. There didn't appear to be any men around. Everybody was laughing and in the background there was music playing. Lite rock.

She was standing there uncorking a bottle of red.

'Hiya!' she called as she saw us. 'Would you like some wine?'

'Hi!' I called back. 'And, yes, please . . .'

But she couldn't work the corkscrew.

'Here, let me,' I said.

I began pulling at the corkscrew but it wouldn't come. I pulled harder while trying not to appear to. 'Don't make me look a prick!' I screamed at it in my mind. And then – pop! – it came and Stevie gave a little whoop of pleasure.

'Ooh, you must be strong!' she cooed.

'Well, I . . .'

'Do you work out?' one of the women asked. She came over and started feeling my arm muscles.

'Uh, well, I . . .'

'Ooh, yeah, just feel that hardbody,' she giggled.

'Ooh,' said Stevie, 'can I have a feel, too?' Then she came and over and started squeezing my arms. 'Mmm, nice,' she said.

Then they were all there, all four of them, all touching my biceps and squeezing my shoulders and going, 'Oooh, ooh, ooh . . .'

I thought, easy, boy, they're giving you the treatment. Getting you on their side. Californian women were all very touchy-feely, that's what made them so special. They knew you liked it and that's why they did it, because you liked it. Touching kept you in line. Turned you into a good doggy.

Stevie went back to the table and poured everybody a glass of the red. Then she picked up the bottle and led the way into a large candle-lit lounge. We sat there next to each other on one of the couches for a moment, just nipping at the wine. It was delicious and smelled of chocolate. She asked me what kind of story I was trying to write and I explained that *The Mail* wanted something about her and something about the house. Ross would be coming by the next day to take some shots.

'Okay,' she said. 'Well, I'd better give you a tour.'

She filled our glasses again, then took me by the hand and led the way. First she took me back downstairs and showed me the waterfall and the stairwell and all the gold and platinum records on the walls. Then back up to the first floor where she had the kitchen and a couple of other big rooms full of paintings, rugs, chandeliers, expensive knick-knacks, all sorts of rich person's crap.

It looked like any other rock star mansion, although admittedly a little more feminine. Everywhere you looked, there were tiny lit candles. There were so many of them, at first I just assumed they were fake electric ones, like chains of party lights. But as I wandered through the house, I noticed it was the same in every room, hundreds and hundreds of tiny, flickering candles. They were enchanting and I wondered who she employed to light them all for her every night, and who put them out again later. If indeed she ever let anyone put them out.

Then we went upstairs and she showed me the bathrooms with their gold taps and fittings and the guest bedrooms with their TVs and phones and so on. And then, finally, she took me into her own bedroom. I knew it was her bedroom right away just from the smell. There's a certain smell a woman's bedroom gets when she's slept in it hundreds and hundreds of times that exists nowhere else in the house. A heady mixture of perfume and pussy that hovers over the bed like an extra blanket.

'Yeah, nice,' I said, looking at the bed and wondering vaguely how much action it had seen lately. I had expected a four-poster but it was just a normal-looking double bed with a nicely patterned quilt thrown over it and lots stuffed animals all sitting, panting, on top. All staring intently at the intruder.

'And then there's this,' she said, taking my hand again and leading me to another door.

Through the door there was a ladder, which went right to the top of the watchtower. She led the way.

'This is my secret space,' she said in a hoarse whisper.

As I climbed up the ladder behind her, her dress was so short I couldn't help but see up it. The skirt kind of flared out at the bottom and her big, marvellous ass bobbed like a mad thing in front of my eyes, the black tights stretched over it like a miracle. Here was a piece of old Hollywood up close, where the cameras rarely go. Now I was getting it. Beneath the tights I could see her knickers, which were dark, too, and skimpy. They looked good there, riding up the cheeks of her ass. I noticed her legs were still good, too. Plump, but I liked that. And those thighs! Lord, lord, what I'd have given for just one little feel . . .

'This is where I come when I want to be alone and think about things,' she said, when we got to the top. 'You can look out on the whole world from here.'

'Yeah,' I said, my mind elsewhere, 'it's an amazing view all right.'

*

As long as you didn't overstep the mark, LA was a good place to live out all sorts of tawdry little fantasies. But it was finding the mark. You would never know where it was until you had already crossed it.

The downfall for me was when, more out of boredom than anything else, I began to allow elements of the truth to enter my stories. I wasn't trying to blow the gaff, it was just that, at thirty-three, I simply couldn't keep churning out the laughs like I used to, and if there was anything left to write about, I'd forgotten what it was. I was sick of being backstage, knowing exactly what was going on but pretending I didn't. I woke up tired in the morning and went to bed at night like I'd been punched in the guts. I was starting to crack.

With someone like Ozzy, it wasn't so bad. It didn't matter what you wrote, it would never match the real story and you both knew it. He'd tell you everything. All you had to do was try and keep up.

The younger ones, though, like Poison, Motley Crue, Guns N' Roses, read every single word and took it all to heart, even the ones they didn't understand. And the temptation to try and shove a little reality under their noses was simply too great sometimes.

I remember interviewing Motley Crue's guitarist Mick Mars on the phone the day after they had cancelled some dates they were supposed to be doing at Wembley Arena, in London, in the winter of '88, because, according to their press office, they were afraid that too much snow on the roof of the building coupled with the weight of their own stage equipment hanging from it might make the ceiling collapse on them halfway through the show.

Ross and I pissed ourselves when we heard that one. Only a few days before, we had been told by friends who had worked on the tour that the band had gone completely over the top on a recent visit to Japan, waving guns in public and smashing up their dressing-room when no one could find them any drugs. Singer Vince Neil had badly gashed his arm when he stuck his hand in a giant-size jar of mustard then smashed it against a wall. He was pissed off because he didn't have his own individual mirror in the dressing-room like it stated in the rider.

It was also around this time that bassist and band leader Nikki Sixx ODed on heroin. At one point, his heart stopped for over a minute, they said. Nikki had made it but had given himself such a scare he'd since gone into rehab. The word was that the whole band planned to follow him in there. There was no way in the fucking world they would have been able to play those shows in London. They didn't need any snow – the roof had already fallen in on them.

So there I was a couple of days later listening to Mick Mars – the grizzled old Goth of the group, whose money it was that had kept them going in the early days – telling me all about the snow and the roof and dah-de-dah-de-dah and I just couldn't hold it in any more. It was making me ill.

'Listen,' I said, 'isn't it true that this stuff about the snow is just a cover-up for the fact that the band are in such bad shape right now you couldn't possibly have played those dates? Isn't that the real story?'

'Uh . . . excuse me?' he said.

'Look,' I said, 'Let's cut the shit, all right? We all know why the dates were cancelled. And it was nothing to do with any bloody snow, was it? Eh? So why don't you tell me the real story, Mick?'

The line went dead. He'd hung up on me. Shit, I thought, he must really be rattled. He'd gone away to check. I gave him ten minutes. Sure enough, a few minutes later, he called back.

'Uh, sorry, I think we got cut off,' he said. 'So what was it you wanted to know?'

I could have softened it up for him, then – at least he'd called back. But why should I? I thought of all those terrible Motley Crue records and all those tedious guitar solos. Here was one of '80s rock's least charismatic yet most successful figures. Purveyor of metal pap most *ordinaire*. He deserved to be treated like an adult for once.

I went through everything I'd heard point by point: the guns, the drugs, the ODs . . . It was all great copy and if he'd had half a mind Mick could have really turned it into something good. But he and his band had been schooled in the '80s way of doing things and back then you just didn't admit to stuff like that. You could do it, you just couldn't talk about it.

'Gee,' he said, 'I can't say I know anything about that, no . . .'

'So are you saying none of it happened or that it might have happened but you can't remember?'

'Hey, well, I guess I'd remember something like that. But . . . I don't know. I really don't know what you're talking about.'

I imagined him sitting there in his full Goth drag, white-powdered Dracula face and black-painted fingernails, just waiting to get off the phone and call up his manager and give him hell. Some poor fucker would pay for this, I knew, but it wouldn't be me. Not this time.

*

We had even more fun with Poison. Poison epitomised everything that was fucked about '80s rock. Their image came straight out of the bottle and their albums were so shallow you couldn't even go paddling in them. But what they lacked in musical talent they more than made up for by possessing the one thing all rock bands wanted most: they were big in America. Much bigger than David Lee Roth, who they were opening for on tour, and more popular than Motley Crue and Ratt put together. They were hot and that was enough, and so Ross and I had flown up to New York to catch them on the Roth tour. All that was required from us was another on-the-road story full of snappy one-liners and lots of backstage-with-the-boys shenanigans. The usual old bollocks, just different names.

Then, to our great fortune, the band did something insane: they fucked us off. I couldn't believe it. They just left us standing in an empty room next to their dressing-room for several hours while they got ready for the show. We were told we weren't allowed to leave the room until someone came with our passes, but no one came. There was a door linking the two rooms but a bodyguard came and pointedly locked it after about half an hour.

We were confused. We kept expecting someone to throw back the door and shout: 'Surprise! Come on in, boys, and have a beer! Betcha thought we were gonna leave you in there all night!' That would have been tedious but I wouldn't have minded. Not once I'd got that beer.

Instead, we were forced to wait in this empty room for hours. No tables, no chairs, not tea, no coffee, not even a toilet, nothing. Just us. And the smoke beginning to trail from our nostrils.

After a couple of hours, Ross and I were so pissed off we decided to leave.

'I've had enough,' I said. 'Let's fuck off.'

'What about the story?' said Ross.

'Fuck the story. What am I going to write? That we were locked in a room and left to die?'

'Yeah,' he said. 'Why not?'

I tried to think of an answer and couldn't. The question was so simple, so obvious, it had not even occurred to me.

'Wait,' I said. 'I've changed my mind. I want to stay.'

'What?'

'Let's hang on.'

'Why?'

'To see how it turns out!'

'What and then write about it?'

'Yeah.'

'You haven't got the bottle.'

'Oh yeah? It's not my fault they're a bunch of cunts, is it? If they wanna play games, we'll see how fucking funny they think it is when they read about it.'

'You haven't got the bottle.'

'Haven't I?'

We waited. Hours went by. It was starting to be funny. We could hear them in the next room, all laughing and cracking beers and getting ready to rock. Then we heard them going out the door and down the corridor towards the stage. Still no one came.

Twenty minutes after the band went on stage, their tour manager, an amiable subnormal, arrived to collect us and take us out 'to see the show'. I was lying on the floor, reading a magazine and smoking a cigarette.

'What show?' I said.

'Uh, the show. The show. The show.'

'Oh, that . . .'

I yawned theatrically. He looked down at me, and then across to Ross who was leaning against the wall.

'What, you don't wanna see the show?'

'Naw . . .' I said.

Ross said nothing, just glared at him.

'But the band . . .'

'Oh, the band,' I said. 'Why don't you go and watch them for me? You could do a little dance, take the night off.'

'Hey, you're funny.'

'Yeah? You're not.'

He couldn't tell if this was some kind of fag limey joke; then the vibes got to him and he knew. He wanted to get angry but he wanted to make sure it was all right first. I went back to my magazine. Began flicking through the pages. In the distance you could hear the band poncing about on stage, the thousands of other subnormals all screaming and cacking their pants. It was a subnormal, pant-cacking kind of world. The tour manager continued standing there for a while wondering what to do. Then he left. Off to tell the boss . . .

Well, Ross and I left the venue that night with our asses in the air but the story I eventually wrote about the whole encounter became one of my best known. Not because it was well written (it wasn't) but because it completely took the band apart, puffing up the saga of The Empty Room into a *tour de force* of ridicule and chicks-with-dicks snidery.

Poison, God bless 'em, had done me a huge favour. Given me an excuse to unload all my pent-up frustrations about the state of MTV-led rock in the '80s. The following week, of course, I was back to penning buddy-buddy stories on Bon Jovi, Def Leppard and the boys, but the Poison story had given me a taste for the kill and from this point on I started to take my magazine work more and more seriously. I began to take *myself* more and more seriously. It was a bad mistake to make so late in the game. It wasn't just the stupid groups that were getting to me now, I began to fall out with every-one. A few too many tequilas and my anger would become uncon-tainable. Soon everything I thought, everything I wrote, became laced with it. Which is partly how I came to fall out so spectacularly with Guns N' Roses that they decided to write a song about it. If I was looking for trouble, I'd come to the right place . . .

*

In some way that still makes me cringe to admit it, being accused by Axl Rose, in 'Get in the Ring', of, in essence, lying to 'the kids', represented the peak of my career in LA. Axl singing about wanting to kick my 'bitchy little ass' was the ultimate compliment. And yet whenever anybody asks now why my name ended up in that appallingly funny song, I still never know quite what to say. It's like being asked why you broke up with your girlfriend – like, how much time do you have?

On one level, 'Get in the Ring' was just a lot of LA puff about nothing; a big, teary, hair-pulling tantrum from an over-indulged child-star shouting and swearing because he can't get his own way. So Guns N' Roses had got some bad write-ups in the press. So what? Name one band anybody's ever heard of that hasn't. The accusation that certain members of the press had made things up was a more serious one, perhaps, but hardly new. Again, name one star that hasn't made that claim a zillion times over the years.

Did I make things up, though? What for? The Gunners were the Oasis of their day, and the whole beauty of writing about them then was that there was always so much going on around them – the drugs, the fights, the riots, the band break-ups and reunions, the models and brat-packers and all the other hangers-on – you certainly didn't have to make anything up. Controversy and headlines followed them around like dogs snapping at their cowboy-booted heels. You simply had to be there to write it all down.

Slash and Duff were always the most amenable, a great double-act when partying, and the most accepting of the idea of success. They had their moments of confusion and despair, like anybody who lived in a goldfish bowl would, but on some deeper level they both understood that it was no less than they had expected. They didn't get into bands not to be rock stars. This was what it was all about, dude! And we did a number of very entertaining interviews together between 1987 and 1990.

Axl I had seen around a fair bit, too, once I got to LA. He was a *Kerrang!* reader and, without discussing it directly, we both sort of knew we'd get around to doing something together one day. 'You don't need to talk to me yet, anyway,' he had once remarked. 'You're doing a pretty good job getting it all from Slash.'

I left it at that. Part of my act back then was never to hassle anybody. Just let them know I was around and leave the mental arithmetic to them. It usually worked, too, and, as I was to discover, in some respects at least, Axl was no different from any other rock star.

Fast-forward to January 1990, and a phone call just as I was getting ready to hit the sack late one night. It was Axl, wanting to know if I could come over to his place right away because he had something important he wanted to say. Something that just wouldn't wait until morning. Sure.

When I got to his apartment, he was raving. It was all about the Motley Crue singer, Vince Neil, who, he claimed, had jumped Gunners guitarist Izzy Stradlin from behind and roughed him up a couple of nights before. The argument was over Vince's wife, who'd claimed Izzy had come on to her, while Axl now insisted it was the other way around and that it was Vince's wife, a former mud-wrestler at The Tropicana, that had made a pass at Izzy . . .

Or something. It was a lot of nothing about nothing. But Axl was mad, he was pissed off! He was going to make Vince pay! He began ranting about how he wanted to 'kill that motherfucker'. He chundered on for a full ten minutes before he finally calmed down long enough for me to set up the tape-recorder. He was saying crazy things, fantasising about what he was going to do to Vince once he got hold of him, and before the interview began, I sat on the couch and scribbled down some of things he had said, so that I could throw them back at him in the interview, including some hilarious statements like 'guns or knives, anyway you wanna go, motherfucker' and a few other choice phrases.

Then we sat down and began taping. Once Axl had got his Vince spiel off his chest, though, not only did he end up giving me a two-hour interview for *Kerrang!*, but he also let me do a second more 'staged' interview for Capital Radio, where I was still presenting a Saturday-night show. We taped a sort of mini-*Desert Island Discs* together, where he got to pick some of the tracks that had affected him most as a child – I remember 'D'yer Maker' by Led Zeppelin and 'Bennie & The Jets' by Elton John were two he chose. It was a good interview and afterwards he was in such a good mood he even did a couple of station IDs for me. ('This is Axl Rose and you're listening to my mainman, Mick Wall, on Capital Radio.')

Later, though, when I came to write up the interview we had done for *Kerrang!*, I tried to give the full flavour of how whacked Axl had sounded during the early part of my visit, and included all the stuff he had said on tape plus one or two of the things I had written down that he had said when I first arrived and he was still on a roll.

But when I read it back I realised how heavy it all looked in black and white, and I decided that, to be on the safe side, I should contact him, just in case he had changed his mind, or wanted to lighten it up a little. We spoke on the phone and I explained my fears to him and asked if he wanted to retract any of the more inflammatory quotes. He just laughed at me. 'No, man,' he said. 'I still stand by every fuckin' word!'

But when the story ran on the cover of *Kerrang!* in April 1990, it immediately caused uproar in both the Motley Crue and Gunners camps, and suddenly it was nothing to do with Vince or Izzy any more. Coming from the same town, the two bands ran in many of the same circles – Nikki and Slash had once been big pals – and they shared many of the same friends and business acquaintances. By making such a confrontational public statement, Axl may have briefly got to Vince, but he had also started something no one else in either band would have wanted. He had started a war.

And my feeling is that it was at that very moment that Axl realised what he'd done, that he first began to turn against me in his mind. Nothing was ever his fault. If something had gone wrong, it must have been someone else's fuck-up. In this case, mine.

The first indication I had of the trouble brewing was when Axl got one of his flunkies to call and ask me to send them a copy of the interview tape so that the band could run it on their own special Guns N' Roses telephone line in America. My suspicions were immediately aroused. Why on earth would they want to run that interview on a phone line?

When I asked for the number of the phone line, there was a lot of spluttering and back-pedalling down the other end, and that's when I knew something was up. Axl didn't want the tape so he could run it on a phone line, he wanted it so he could listen to it, to see if he'd really said all the things I'd reported in *Kerrang!*.

When I refused to send the tape and confronted one of Axl's publicists with my fears, she admitted that there was a 'problem'. Axl, she said, 'just can't believe he said some of those things. He doesn't even think he would speak that way. He, er, thinks it's kinda funny . . .'

Kinda funny? *Kinda funny?* The more I thought about it, the more outraged I became. For years, I had always done my damned-est to play fair with Guns N' Roses. I never pretended to be a saint, but when Slash came to me for advice on how to get off smack, did I run to *The Sun* with the story? No, I did my best to talk to him and try and put him in touch with Dr Jewel. And when Duff talked to me at length about the break-up of his marriage, wiping away the tears as he poured his heart out to me, did I turn it into something I could have sold around the world three times over? No, it was the Christmas holidays and I offered to spend time with him, to try and help him get over it.

There were other things, too, stuff that had never come within a million miles of publication. As far as I was concerned, I had proved myself. I was not a stitch-up merchant; I was a friend. Now this: Axl with his knickers in a twist because his big mouth had got him into trouble again. But why the subterfuge? If he had wanted to hear a copy of the tape, why hadn't he just called and asked for one? Why did he have to get someone to call and invent some story? What did he have cooking?

Axl on an ill-tempered bender was a crazy man, capable of almost anything. I played the tape back to myself and checked my notes. It was all there. I thought about making a copy of everything and sending it to him. But then I began to get paranoid. Surely he wasn't that far out he didn't remember saying those things? But rock stars can convince themselves of almost anything if they want to; there are always enough people around who will tell them they're right, no matter what they say or do. And I wondered if he wanted a copy of the tape so that he could . . . well, doctor it in some way. I knew it was ridiculous, but there were a lot of ridiculous things and people surrounding Guns N' Roses in those days, and I believed anything might be possible.

There was also a part of me that simply resented the implication in being asked for a copy of the tape. My word was no longer good enough. Further proof was required. Well, Axl could go fuck himself, I decided. If he had a problem, let him call me himself and tell me about it. I relayed the message in no uncertain terms to one of his minions the very next day, but of course Axl never did call back and that's the way things stayed until we met up again nearly a year later at the Rock In Rio II festival, in Rio de Janeiro, in January 1991.

The Rio shows were the Gunners' first since they'd opened for The Rolling Stones at the giant outdoor LA Coliseum, in November 1989, and, understandably, they were the focus of attention everywhere they went throughout their week-long stay. But then they had been the centre of attention wherever they went for nearly three years. What was different now was the way they went about it.

The first time I saw Axl, he was walking into a club surrounded by about a dozen bodyguards. They were all huge and black and ominous and he looked like a little rag-doll being dragged to the playground by a pack of ravenous Dobermans. As I approached, Axl gave no sign of recognition and two of the Dobermans bared their teeth at me and growled. I retreated quickly.

Then later that same night I spied Slash across the room in the hotel bar. I waved hello but he just looked at me for a moment, before giving an almost imperceptible nod in my direction. Then he turned his back and began talking to someone else. This was not the Slash I used to know. But again, as I tried to approach, a ring of Dobermans formed around him. He saw what was happening but pretended not to. I took the hint and split.

Most embarrassing of all, though, was a few nights later when Duff and I ran into each other backstage at the Maracana Stadium, where the festival was being staged.

'Hi,' I said. 'How are you?'

'Uh, yeah, okay,' he mumbled, then swept past me down the hall as fast as his gangly legs could carry him. Were they all under instructions not to speak to me, I wondered?

Apparently so. By not submitting to the master's will and handing over the tape to Axl the moment he'd snapped his fingers, I had broken the unwritten code of the road: I had snubbed the singer. And in so doing I had crossed the boundary between 'trusted confidant' and 'bad news', and now found myself somewhere in 'asshole' country. Well, if I was gonna be treated like an asshole, I might as well start acting like one, I thought. I decided not to pull any punches in the feature I wrote about the event for *Kerrang!*. If

I couldn't introduce the readers to the band any more, at least I could let them meet the bodyguards.

Before the article appeared, however, I was at home in LA one evening when I received another unexpected phone call. It was Axl. 'We need to talk,' he said, and I agreed to meet him at a nearby bar. When I got there, he had three other people with him. They all looked very serious. A great cloud of thunder appeared to be hanging over them.

I sat down next to Axl and asked him what was up but he couldn't bring himself to look me in the eye. Instead, he spoke to me in profile. He began by issuing a warning.

'I've heard you're writing a book about the band and I just want to let you know that if you do, I will track you down,' he said. 'I will track you down and kill you.'

The other three all leaned in and did their best to look mean. One of them began a long, involved story about the time someone else crossed him and what they did to him. It was like something out of a movie. A very bad movie.

But even bad movies can have scary endings and I decided there and then that there would be no Guns N' Roses book from me. Axl was only half right, however. I hadn't actually been writing a book about Guns N' Roses, I had merely been planning to publish a compilation of all the various interviews I had done with them for *Kerrang!*, all together under one cover. I did try and explain this to him but it only seemed to make him more agitated. And that's when I began to suss what was really going on. It was more the thought of the Vince Neil quotes being reproduced again that Axl was worried about, rather than any larger general principle.

He repeated his threat: 'I don't care what kind of book it is, whether it says we're a great band or whatever; if it has our name on it, I will track you down, I will find you and I will kill you.'

I knew it was mostly just a show of bravado but, in truth, I was rattled. Then, when the *Kerrang!* Rock In Rio article appeared a few days later, the whole thing erupted again.

This time I got a phone call at about 2 a.m. It was him.

'Hey, Mick, this is Axe. I just wanna say, I'm sitting here reading the new *Kerrang!*, and I just wanted to say one thing: see you in court, buddy!' Then he hung up.

And that was when I'd decided I'd had enough. Had enough of being pushed around and threatened by someone I knew I could probably take out with one punch, if he only had the balls to lose the bodyguards and the publicists and all the other little munchkins he surrounded himself with and come and meet me man to man sometime. What was my crime, anyway? Writing things down as I saw them? Let's see, Axl could write a bigoted piece of shit like 'One in a Million' but I couldn't write about Guns N' Roses being surrounded by bodyguards and treating people with contempt?

The first thing I did was ring my publishers in England and tell them I'd changed my mind again and wanted to go through with the book after all, but that I wanted to re-do it, so that it wasn't just a collection of old interviews, but contained lots of new, previously unpublished stuff, too. They loved the idea and I hurriedly set about completing the work.

I wasn't so pissed off I was going to put anything in there that I'd previously promised Slash or anybody else I wouldn't. But I was going to do a book. I'd consulted some lawyer friends and some other music biz hard-cases whose opinions I trusted and they all assured me that what Axl was doing was not only morally suspect but possibly even illegal.

And the rest, as they say, is history. My Guns N' Roses book, *The Most Dangerous Band in the World*, came out at about the same time as both the *Use Your Illusion 1&2* albums were released, in the summer of 1991. When people heard 'Get in the Ring', they merely assumed the song was in reaction to the book. But the song – originally, before Axl hijacked it, a straight punk rocker written and sung by Duff called 'Why Do You Look At Me When You Hate Me?' – had been written and recorded long before the book appeared, and I still believe it all goes back to that ill-fated interview we did together in January 1990.

Looking back now, it all seems so tame by comparison to some of the antics bands like Nirvana and Marilyn Manson subsequently got up to. But it all seemed to mean so much at the time, to Axl and to me. And yet it was strange to find such a private dispute broadcast so publicly. I suppose I had written my story, now Axl was writing his.

But again, like the Poison story, being vilified so publicly actually brought unexpected rewards. I remember talking to Sharon Osbourne about it on the phone not long after the album had come out.

'What a jerk!' she laughed. 'If he hated you so much he should have just ignored you. By putting your name in his silly little song, he's made you the most famous rock journalist in America.'

Well, not quite. But I immediately had three different publishers wanting to put the book out in America, all because of the publicity generated by 'Get in the Ring'. It was ridiculous. Apart from the very last chapter, which discussed the disappointments of Rio, the book heaped nothing but praise on the band. It was as safe as sitting on grandmother's knee.

But then Axl had so many people surrounding him then, all with their own secret little agendas to push, all whispering in his ear at the same time, it's amazing he still even knew how to exhale back in 1991. The truth is, we were both famously prone to tantrums in those days, and if anything I'm just sorry we never got a chance to speak about it personally. To sort it out like grown men, not stupid boys. Ah, but those were different times, ma . . .

*

The only rock star I ever met that I could really relate to was Ozzy. Not just because he was funny, but because he was real. He was the only one I'd ever known who really felt his luck. The rest all fooled themselves into believing they had made it on their own somehow; that they were really something special.

'I know I'm just some bloke who won the Lottery,' I recall Ozzy telling me more than once. 'It could easily have gone the other way for me . . .'

Ozzy was the Great Confessor. And though we all still laugh along with him as he regales us on TV with another ludicrous anecdote from his incident-filled career, one of my fondest memories is of when I went to visit him when he was incarcerated at Huntercombe Manor, a posh people's rehab joint in Buckinghamshire, where he was sent by the courts after being arrested for the attempted murder of Sharon, in 1989.

Ozzy himself still swears he can't remember exactly what happened that night, but for Sharon it was an experience she is never likely to forget. The couple had recently returned from Russia, where Ozzy had been appearing on the bill with Bon Jovi and Motley Crue at the Moscow Music Peace Festival. Although the festival had been staged to raise funds for the Make A Difference Foundation – a charitable trust in the US set up to help people with drink and drug problems – behind the scenes, the organisers had presented Ozzy with a case of Russian vodka.

'It was amazing,' he told me. 'All these little miniatures of different flavoured vodkas. I couldn't wait to get my hands on it . . .'

Sharon described what happened next for me.

'It was supposed to be a quiet Saturday night at home. It was our daughter Aimee's birthday and we were all having dinner together to celebrate. But Ozzy started drinking all this blasted vodka that he'd brought back with him from Moscow and it sent him crazy,' she said. 'He really did go mad. It was terrifying. I mean, me and my old man have had fist fights before, we've broken up rooms and all that, you know. But never anything like this . . .'

At one point, she said, Ozzy had his hands round her throat and tried to strangle her. And that was when she raised the alarm and called the police. Ozzy had been bundled into a police car and kept in jail for the rest of the weekend while he sobered up. After appearing in court on the Monday morning, at Sharon's suggestion, the judge ruled that he should enter Huntercombe Manor before being brought back before the courts for further assessment a few weeks later.

The story made headlines around the world but Ozzy refused to talk to anyone. I was in London at the time and I read about it in the papers like everyone else. Then, a couple of nights later, the phone rang and it was Sharon, asking me if I would go out to the Manor and visit Ozzy. He was desperate to explain his side of things, she said, but he didn't trust anyone else.

When I got there the next day, I found a much more subdued

madman of rock than I had ever seen before. He was abject with grief. His kids – Aimee, Kelly and Jack – had all been to visit him earlier that day and the tears welled in his sad clown eyes as he tried to describe what it felt like having to explain why Daddy wouldn't be coming home with them that night.

'They kept asking me, "Why are you here, Daddy?" I didn't know what to tell 'em . . . It nearly broke my fuckin' heart waving goodbye to them as they all drove off . . .'

We sat in his room and talked for a few hours. Although we taped a lot of it, it wasn't really like I was doing an interview, it was more like being a good Samaritan. He was in a bad way and just needed somebody to talk to. After a while, I turned the tape off and slipped it back in my bag. He didn't want me to leave. Or, rather, he didn't want to be left alone.

'What would you do if you were me?' he asked.

'I don't know,' I replied. 'I don't even know what I would do if I were me, let alone you.'

We sat there thinking it over. I had a little lump of hash in my pocket. 'Can't you quit the booze and just have a little puff of dope now and then?' I asked, wondering if I had any skins.

'Not according to this lot in here,' he frowned. 'They don't even like it if I smoke a fag. They make me stand by the window.'

'Oh . . .'

I forgot about offering him a joint and poured myself another Diet Coke. God, it was boring being straight. How on earth was he going to cope? How on earth did any of us cope? By taking it straight? Like a man? Like an Ozzy?

No. I'll try anything, babe, you know me, but please, not that . . .

*

By 1991 we were both living in LA and Huntercombe Manor was just a distant memory. Ozzy was making what would become his *No More Tears* album and he was temporarily holed up in a small apartment a couple of streets down from mine. With the kids at school in England, and Sharon away so much of the time, he had gone back to his old ways and his prized possession at the time was a big, beautiful green bong he had purchased from some head shop down on Melrose.

'It's top of the range,' he'd say as he sat there stoking it up.

It was a lethal weapon and after three or four hits, even an old stoner like myself had a struggle to keep his eyes pointing in the same direction. The trick, Ozzy told me, was to take little sips of brandy in between.

'It helps cool down the lungs,' he explained.

Then out would come the coke. Always primo gear, and always plenty of it. Sometimes I'd bring a gram or two with me, or a little bag of weed or whatever, and even though I threw them on the table and tried to get him to share them with me, he would always pull a much bigger bag than mine out from behind a chair or a cupboard somewhere and insist we take all we needed from that. Ozzy was always very generous that way. But then he was also quite lonely. He had grown accustomed to paying for company.

'You know what they say,' he'd tell me. 'You're never alone with a bag of coke. I guarantee you, you could be on a fuckin' desert island, if you've got an ounce of coke at least twelve fuckin' people will knock on your door before the night's out.'

I arrived at his apartment one night and he was sitting there with some kid I didn't recognise. He had the finished tracks of some of the songs he was putting on the new album playing on the cassette deck and he was singing along to them at the top of his voice. The front door was open as I arrived and the music was playing so loudly they didn't even notice me enter the room.

The kid sat there intently, his eyes glazed. I thought it might be one of the musicians on the album. Ozzy was always picking up younger and younger musicians for his backing group. Then the song finished and Ozzy noticed me and turned the machine off.

''Allo, mate, 'ow's it going?'

The kid jumped up before I could answer and began spluttering his farewells. It was plain he was in a hurry to leave.

'Gee, Ozzy, man, thanks, man, that was awesome, man. And thanks for the autograph, too! But I gotta go, man. But, gee, you know, thanks so much! And nice meeting you too, sir,' he said, turning to me briefly. His face was white and he looked shaken, as though he'd just stepped off a rollercoaster.

'Yeah, awright, then, mate, cheers,' said Ozzy as the kid made his escape.

'Who was that?' I asked.

'I dunno. Some kid who was waiting outside for an autograph. He told me he'd been waiting there all afternoon, so I thought he might like to hear a bit of the album, you know? I think he liked it as well. Here, let me play you a bit . . .'

He sat there playing his tape and singing along while I joined in on the bong. I noticed he had some good songs on the tape. That made a change. Ozzy hadn't made a really good solo album since his first two with Randy. Maybe the '90s would be kinder to him, too. And if they weren't, what the hell, there was always the Black Sabbath reunion. Though he continued to deny it, my guess was that the closer we came to the Millennium, the more likely we were to see a full-on Ozzy and Sabbath reunion. Even if it was just for one tour and an album.

'No way,' said Ozzy. 'I'm not going near those cunts again!' But I'd have bet anything on it.

At about one in the morning we went for a drive down Sunset and bought a big chocolate cake from the Pink Dot which neither of us could eat when we got it back to the apartment. I told him I liked what he was wearing – loose-fitting abstract-patterned beach trousers popular in LA at the time called 'Crazy Pants'. He went to his bedroom and retrieved an unwrapped pair – he had bought ten or twelve pairs, he said – and gave them to me. I put them straight on and we loaded up the bong again.

'Here, I've just remembered,' he said. 'I've got something that'll make you piss yourself. It's a video Steve Vai gave me . . .'

He put the video on and there was a woman slowly doing a striptease while talking to the camera.

'You see, Steve, when I see you on stage, it just makes me want to act crazy . . .'

Then when she was completely naked she began doing odd things with her pussy. Rubbing it like she was trying to remove a stain and then putting things up there – lit candles and long brown fingers of candy and other crap.

'Are you watching Steve?' she sighed.

Ozzy could barely contain himself. 'No, but I am, darling!' he roared with laughter.

She began to breathe heavily. 'Oh, Steve, oh Steve . . . I can almost feel you inside me . . .'

She wasn't bad-looking but the whole thing was gross. Not the nudity, just the concept. At one point, she started making little farting noises with her pussy.

'Watch this, Steve,' she giggled, and she crouched over a lit candle, made a little pussy fart and blew the thing out. 'Am I a clever girl, Steve?'

'Ten out of ten, darling!' laughed Ozzy. 'You should fuckin' be on *Saturday Night Live* . . .'

I sat there laughing along with him. The tape kept playing but the longer you watched it the less funny it became.

The laughter petered out and we grew maudlin. Two old drunks, stoned out of their minds, not knowing what else to do, just staring at the TV and wondering. Outside, it was America.

I looked over at him. 'Man, I gotta go,' I said. 'I'm fried . . .'

'I'll call you a cab,' he said.

I left Ozzy's place and staggered down the corridor to the elevator. I pushed the 'down' button and waited for the damn thing to come. As the elevator doors opened, I could hear the demo tape begin to blare from his apartment again. How did the neighbours put up with it? Or was this just another night in hell for them?

I stepped into the elevator and rode it back down to the ground like someone going somewhere.

The doors opened again and I stepped out into the dimly lit lobby. It was warm and empty. I made it through the door and down the steps onto the street. I stood there for a moment watching people walk around.

Then, doing my best to look and sound straight, I climbed wearily into the back of the cab. There was a tough-looking young Chicano behind the wheel. I checked his mugshot in the photo on the back of his seat. It was legit.

I told him where to go but he'd never heard of it. I tried to keep my eyes open long enough to give him directions . . .